E/ESCWA/EDID/2015/3

Economic and Social Commission for Western Asia

Arab Development Outlook

Vision 2030

United Nations
Beirut

Preface

The Arab region is in crisis and it is easy to take a bleak view of the future. Shaken by conflicts and instability, the region has a long history of failed economic policies. Gaps in governance remain stubbornly wide. Increasing pressures on natural resources in an era of climate change could exacerbate the situation.

Arab citizens have realized to what extent partial and inequitable development, combined with the stifling of dissent, undermines human progress. They have called—and in some cases sacrificed their lives—for new ways of governing that are inclusive and accountable. Such principles are also at the heart of the 2030 Agenda for Sustainable Development.

The Arab uprisings were not just about settling past grievances, but about proclaiming resolve to pursue a brighter and prosperous future. This report takes its cue from those events and embraces possibility and hope. It envisages a day when all citizens can freely voice their opinions and practice their beliefs without fear; when the rule of law applies equally to rich and poor; when every household has the security of gainful employment, health insurance and old-age pensions; and where basic necessities for a decent life are affordable even for the lowest earners.

Such a vision requires choices to be made: whether to lay new foundations on which to build societies blessed by growth, prosperity and freedom, or slip into a spiral of deepening violence, instability and recession that will undercut development for generations to come; whether to mend internal fissures, transform the structures of Arab economies and political systems, and integrate first from within, or to continue on a trajectory leading to further political and economic dependence.

To implement the ambitious goals contained in this vision, the Arab region would require at least three consecutive five-year cycles. The report contains an analysis of the political landscape and current conflicts, which must be resolved before progress can be made in other areas. We look at challenges and potential in the region under two scenarios. The business as usual scenario extrapolates present socioeconomic conditions that weigh on the region and would continue to do so. The vision scenario explores trajectories that could lead to tangible improvements in human development returns. The ultimate aim of this report is to suggest the contours of policies and action needed to serve as a catalyst and beacon of hope.

The Arab region has immense resources, foremost of which are its people. Their call for change has echoed around the world. The region has an opportunity to make choices that will improve governance, advance social justice and human well-being, and transform economies, including by deepening regional cooperation and integration. The region can follow a new path, guided by a new vision and, ultimately, a development master plan. Such a plan should be informed by the difficult lessons of the present and chart a course to a peaceful, prosperous future. The citizens of the region deserve no less.

Mohamed Moctar El Hacene
*Director, Economic Development
and Integration Division*

Acknowledgements

This report is the result of more than four years of research based on consultations between the authors and a broad range of United Nations and independent experts and revisers. This final version, completed in the past two years, does not necessarily reflect the views of all those who contributed.

The core team of the report consists of Mr. Khalid Abu-Ismail (Economic Development and Integration Division, EDID), Mr. Tamim al-Barghouti (Office of the Executive Secretary), Mr. Aljaz Kuncic and Mr. Niranjan Sarangi, of EDID. Mr. Abu-Ismail and Mr. Al-Barghouti are the core team leaders.

The report was produced under the management of Mr. Abdallah al-Dardari, Director of EDID, and his successor, Mr. Mohamed Moctar El Hacene.

The lead authors wish to acknowledge and thank Mr. Mohamed Hedi-Bchir for his macroeconomic modelling and forecasting methodology, results and inputs, Mr. Vito Intini for his forecasting methodology, results and inputs to governance indicators, and Mr. Hisham Taha for providing a background paper on regional integration.

We are greatly indebted to this report's reviewers, Professors Ali Abdel-Gader and Galal Amin, for their constructive review of the first draft and for providing detailed comments and feedback, and to the readers of the report, Ms. Noha el-Mikkawy, Ms. Gretchen Luchsinger, Mr. Mohamed Mohieddin and Mr. Mohammad Pournik.

The report has benefited from research contributions from Mr. Salim Araji, Mr. Rabih Bashour, Mr. Rabie Fakri, Ms. Mona Fattah, Ms. Nathalie Grand, Mr. José Pedrosa-Garcia and Ms. Denise Sumpf. Valuable research assistance was provided by Ms. Zara Ali, Mr. Seth Caldwell, and Ms. Rhea Younes. We are also grateful to Mr. Fouad Ghorra for editorial and research support.

We would like to thank the University of London School of Oriental and African Studies (SOAS) for hosting an expert group meeting of the Economic and Social Commission for Western Asia (ESCWA) in August 2014 to discuss the report methodology. Mr. Abdelwahab el-Affendi, Mr. Hazem Kandil, Mr. Terry McKinley and Mr. Jan Vandemoortele attended.

The authors are also grateful to many of our colleagues at ESCWA for their technical advice and feedback on an earlier draft of this report: Ms. Naeem al-Mutawakel, Ms. Monia Braham, Mr. Youssef Chaitani, Ms. Carol Chouchani, Mr. Habib el-Andaloussi, Ms. Mehrinaz el-Awady,

Mr. Ayman el-Sherbiny, Ms. Naela Haddad,
Mr. Adib Nehme, Mr. Oussama Safa and
Ms. Johanna von Toggenburg.
Last but by no means least, we are greatly
thankful to Ms. Maral Tashjian for her diligent
administrative support.

This report would not have been possible
without significant contributions from this
multidisciplinary team. We have tried to the best
of our ability to incorporate all their comments
and suggestions.

Report core team leaders
Khalid Abu-Ismail and Tamim al-Barghouti

Contents

List of Boxes

1. A Vision for 2030

The Arab world is immersed in a crisis that touches every country. Not only is there widespread conflict and insecurity, but the legacies of failed economic policies and gaps in governance persist and add pressure on scarce natural resources, which could further exacerbate current challenges.

Yet, the region has a rich history. Its citizens have called for the principles of freedom, equality and accountability, and some have even sacrificed their lives in doing so. This report embraces hope and envisages that, by 2030, the region could enjoy a new era of long-lasting peace, stability and inclusive development if the appropriate policies are pursued.

Apart from thematic areas such as energy, water and education, little has been written on the future of the Arab region, a gap that this report aims to fill.[1] Any move forward, however, should start with acknowledging current shortfalls and establishing priorities for development policy. An early focus on governance is essential, given its shortcomings and instrumentality for progress in all other arenas, including peace and stability. The structure of Arab economies must be transformed in order to make growth more inclusive and sustainable. This will help to solve many problems, such as the provision of decent jobs and fiscal space for social policies. Regional integration can play a pivotal role by expanding employment, easing the flow of goods and services, and underpinning political stability.

The report advocates five critical areas for achieving its vision for 2030: political transformation, good governance, structural economic change, human development and regional integration. It does not rely on any single methodology or indicator to gauge development success or failure. Rather, it calls for a complete rethink of the development model in the Arab region and a nuanced conceptual framework that sets forth development constraints, levers and accelerators.

Development constraints vary in severity. Justice, peace and security are fundamental for development, and their absence in some countries is a powerful force for 'de-development'. Public policies are the main levers of development and vary widely. This report focuses on those over which Arab countries have some degree of control. Development accelerators increase the rate of progress towards desired goals. Structural change and regional integration are essential accelerators to the Vision 2030.

These issues are interconnected and best treated from an interdisciplinary approach. Development cannot take place without minimum levels of peace and security and effective public policies. Interdependent development goals and targets should be pursued in combination with each other rather than as isolated objectives. Generating decent jobs, for instance, is the surest and fastest way to reduce poverty, which, in turn, contributes to peace and security.

The question of which actions will have the greatest impact on multiple challenges is crucial achieving the Vision 2030. Finding the right answers will lead to a transformation of the present situation.

The report contains policy recommendations that hold particular promise as levers of change. They are put forward with the caveat that national situations differ greatly in a region with some of the world's richest and poorest countries, and with many States vulnerable to cross-border spillover and internal strife, or suffering from conflict. Each country faces its own development challenges and options for progress. The recommendations are offered to steer efforts towards reinitiating development. Ultimately, the aim is to combine national efforts into one regional project.

A. Development challenges

The human development performance in the Arab region has been far from dismal. There has been a steady rise in human capabilities, especially among young people and women, reflected in most national and regional Millennium Development Goal (MDG) indicators on health and education. The middle class was the dominant economic group in most Arab countries in 2010.

Nevertheless, the first Arab Human Development Report, published in 2002, highlighted, as did subsequent issues, deficits in freedom, gender equality and knowledge in the Arab region. A number of other United Nations-led reports, including the Arab Development Challenges Report,[2] have highlighted such problems as food insecurity, skewed income distribution, social exclusion, fragile and oil-led economic growth, high unemployment, weak trade and industrial performance, and slow progress on the MDGs in Arab least developed countries (LDCs).[3] They, and many others, suggest diverse reasons for why the region reached boiling point in late 2010.

First, the quality of social services in non-oil middle-income countries has deteriorated rapidly since liberalization began in earnest in the 1990s.[4] Secondly, governance indicators are embarrassingly poor. Some Arab States disbursed subsidies and rents in exchange for little or no public accountability. This democracy deficit is accompanied by a profound gender equality deficit, particularly in terms of power-sharing and employment.[5]

Thirdly, opportunities for decent employment in the Arab region are limited, despite the presence of an educated labour force and relatively high growth rates between 1990 and 2010. Over the same period, job creation occurred in informal, low value-added activities, mainly in the services sector. Consequently, productivity dropped, real wages froze and, in countries such as Egypt, poverty rates soared. Inequality deepened, but was not reflected in official statistics. Young Arab people with higher educational qualifications, in particular, became disenfranchised and increasingly sought to migrate. However, that option became unavailable to the vast majority after the countries of the Gulf Cooperation Council (GCC) changed immigration policies in favour of cheaper labour from Asian countries.[6]

The surge of the middle and poorer classes on to the streets of Egypt and Tunisia can be explained partially by the frustration of young Arabs, whose increased capacities have not been translated into decent jobs, higher incomes and broader political participation, and the significant decline of public-sector salaries and service delivery in many countries during the 2000s.[7] In Egypt, for instance, the average mean real expenditure per capita among professionals, comprising mainly salaried formal-sector employees, fell by 19 per cent between 2000 and 2011, compared to a negligible decline in that of the total population.[8] The erosion of the Arab middle class and growing frustration have played into the hands of violent non-State actors.[9]

The resulting situation is largely a product of poor governance and unfortunate economic policy choices. Proponents of economic orthodoxy maintain that, in order to stimulate economic growth and reduce poverty, countries must adopt liberal policies that typically involve fiscal restraints, monetary austerity, privatization of State-owned enterprises, and trade liberalization. Many Arab countries that adopted such policies, however, did not experience faster growth. In cases where faster growth did take place, it was mainly due to high international oil prices or the discovery of new oil fields. Indeed, those policies have adversely affected employment, income distribution and, above all, the social dimension of State functions, especially the quality of public education and health. Their most enduring legacy, however, was the systematic reduction of the State's role in development planning, and the crony capitalism that emerged as a result of distorted privatization and liberalization policies.

Against this backdrop, the uprisings represented an attempt by Arab citizens to regain sovereignty over economic, social and political matters, including fundamental issues of economic and social justice, human rights and citizenship. Five years on, the region is at a crossroads that could either lead to growth and prosperity, or to a new cycle of violence, instability and economic recession that could stifle the future of generations to come. Average economic growth after 2010 was barely above population growth in many Arab countries, which may cause unemployment rates to spike to more than 15 per cent for skilled and unskilled labour.

The region faces five major challenges: ending conflict and occupation; reforming public institutions and systems of governance; diversifying economic growth sources to generate widespread and decent employment without further harming the fragile environment; meeting social justice and human development demands in line with the ambitious Sustainable Development Goals (SDGs) on health and education; and ending the destruction of Arab cultural heritage and elevating the Arabic language to its rightful place.

External and internal conflicts pose the gravest threat to the region. Today, Iraq, Libya, Palestine, Somalia, the Sudan, the Syrian Arab

Republic and Yemen are all directly affected by conflict. Egypt, Jordan, Lebanon and Tunisia can suffer significantly from conflicts in neighbouring countries. A Saudi-led Arab coalition is conducting military operations in Yemen. The Comoros, Djibouti and Mauritania are struggling to maintain power-sharing formulas, avert military coups, deal with border frictions and survive extreme poverty.

The continued settlement by Israel of Palestinian territory, in violation of international law, has rendered a two-State solution almost impossible. Regional instability has been worsened by the war in the Syrian Arab Republic, fighting in Iraq, sectarian stand-offs and the growing abyss across the region between religious and secular approaches to the affairs of State. Vast areas of the Mashreq have been seized by radical armed militias.

The longer the conflicts in Iraq, Somalia, the Sudan, the Syrian Arab Republic and Yemen continue, the greater will be the devastation. Decades of development are being undone, adding greater misery to human insecurity.

The disastrous impact of conflict on a society is exemplified by the Syrian war, as discussed in a recent publication produced by the Economic and Social Commission for Western Asia (ESCWA).[10] The Government has lost control over large parts of the country; various States and external parties are backing contending factions; the cost of reconstruction is soaring; financial and human resources are scarce; the number of internally displaced persons (IDPs) and refugees has risen exponentially; public institutions have been shattered; fighting is preventing the delivery of humanitarian aid and medical services, causing the spread of diseases that could affect neighbouring countries; and terrorism and organized crime are thriving. In short: decades of development have been lost.

The success of armed militias in grabbing control of one third of Iraq, including the Euphrates valley and the city of Mosul, and half of the Syrian Arab Republic is the clearest example of the failure of the modern Arab State. Libya is struggling to maintain unity in the face of tribal, linguistic and ethnic divisions, which, in turn, threaten the security of Egypt and Tunisia. Separatist conflicts in Somalia and the Sudan are linked to racial and ethnic divisions.

With less than 5 per cent of the world's population, the Arab region hosts more than 53 per cent of all refugees and 37 per cent of displaced persons.[11]

The transformational growth scenario presented in this report rests on the pillar of peace and security. Although this is, to some extent, beyond the region's control, it is important to determine and act upon conflict-resolution and peace-building options that the region can influence. In this regard, a new formula for regional integration may be the key to a sustained "new deal".

An end to armed conflict and ensuing political stability would pave the way for a new, more inclusive development agenda championed by Arab developmental States. Governed by new, more legitimate and therefore stronger institutions, they would be well placed to prioritize social justice and seek broad consensus for difficult strategic trade-offs and policy choices.

Resource scarcity is another major issue. The region is not self-sufficient in food and water, and the situation will only worsen if current trends continue. Unless a pattern of economic growth is quickly adopted that relies on efficiently used, sufficient and accessible water resources, water scarcity may become another source of conflict. Primary energy consumption per capita is increasing faster than in any other region. As a result of this unsustainable situation, Saudi Arabia, the world's largest oil producer, could become a net energy importer by 2038 unless a shift in its domestic energy policies takes place long before then.[12]

The Arab region also faces a major cultural challenge. As noted in *Arab Integration: A 21st Century Development Imperative*, "the Arabic language has been affected by a dominant Western culture that claims to hold the keys to modernity and knowledge".[13] In an effort to reinforce allegiance to the nation-State, some countries have embarked on cultural policies directing attention away from pan-Arab landmarks and exaggerating the importance of local symbols.

Nevertheless, a reversal of this process of weakening the pan-Arab culture is possible through increased socioeconomic cooperation and development. Political economy of exclusion lends itself to cultural and social polarization, but an inclusive developmental region would be characterized by the absence of conflict between national and regional identity, or beliefs and affiliations (religious/secular, Arab/Kurdish, left-wing/right-wing), since an

open political space would allow diversity in the region to be seen as a strength.

In reality, however, the region is affected by physical destruction of its heritage. In 2003, during its occupation of Iraq, the coalition led by the United States of America (further referred to as United States or US) failed to protect Iraqi cultural heritage, and the ongoing conflicts in Iraq and the Syrian Arab Republic have led to large-scale destruction of heritage sites.

Israel continues to systemically destroy Arab and Islamic sites and cultural heritage, including historical monuments and mosques, in occupied Palestinian territory. In 2015, the United Nations Educational, Scientific and Cultural Organization (UNESCO) condemned the repression in East Jerusalem and the failure of Israel to cease the persistent excavations and works there, particularly in and around the Old City, and called for the prompt reconstruction of schools, universities, heritage sites, cultural institutions, media centres and places of worship destroyed or damaged by the Israelis in Gaza.

B. The state of play and why it cannot last

This report will examine the repercussions for the Arab region if the current situation remains unchanged – the business-as-usual scenario. It also provides an alternative vision of hope for the Arab world in 2030 – the vision scenario — and charts a course for achieving it. The 15-year time frame was influenced by the SDGs. Moreover, any period beyond that would have weakened the report's empirical projections.

In order to project the impact of stability versus conflict on development indicators, the report divides Arab countries into three groups. The first faces significant development problems as a result of widespread poverty, human deprivation and/or conflict and occupation. It includes the Comoros, Djibouti, Iraq, Libya, Mauritania, State of Palestine, Somalia, the Sudan, the Syrian Arab Republic and Yemen.[14]

Egypt, Jordan, Lebanon and Tunisia fall into a second group of low- and medium-resilience countries. They have limited fiscal space and are exposed to potential spillover from conflicts in neighbouring countries.

The third group of relatively high-resilience countries (GCC countries, Algeria and Morocco) is characterized by medium to high degrees of development, reduced exposure to spillover of conflict from other countries in the region and/or abundant fiscal space.

Other classifications are used in the course of the report, based, for example, on income levels, labour availability, economic diversification and geography, in order to illustrate particular points. When tackling issues related to employment, economic growth and structural transformation, the report highlights differences between countries based on their initial level of economic diversification and whether they are oil rich. It covers a broad spectrum of development goals, combining social, economic, governance and environmental aspects.

The report maintains that targets should be set at the country level and progress to the regional level. Where appropriate for projections, each country was compared to either "nearest neighbour" countries, or selected benchmark countries. The "nearest neighbour" countries are those that were at a similar levels of development in the past. Calculating the progress of the latter yields a realistic target value for the comparator country. National values can then be aggregated into a common 2030 regional target.[15] Using nationally tailored targets is more likely to increase domestic ownership and the legitimacy of any regional framework, and thus improve accountability.

Other 2030 forecasts made by international institutions have also been reviewed.[16]

1. A post-colonial view

The report's geopolitical narrative reflects the post-colonial school of thinking. In addition to Palestine, which still suffers from a case of classic colonial occupation, the rest of the region is still experiencing the repercussions of its colonial history.

It posits that colonialism foisted a manufactured identity on colonized populations, and that most local authorities were complicit in accomplishing colonial plans. Decolonizing thus involves throwing off such imposed cultural identities and political systems designed to subjugate the colonized peoples.[17]

It can be argued that modern Arab States were designed to provide raw materials, cheap labour and, most importantly, security to the colonial powers. A large security apparatus was built up in Arab countries, with some having more than 20 separate security organizations. At the same time, massive bureaucracies created job dependency on the State. Such States structured by colonial powers are not sustainable, and this report stresses the need for political restructuring and highlights the importance of regional culture. The following chapters are predicated on those ideas.

2. The failure of liberalization

This report adopts a heterodox stance on macroeconomic policies, reflected in its emphasis on social and economic justice. It also stresses that any assessment of causal relation between economic policy instruments and outcomes, such as growth or poverty reduction, is meaningless outside a country's historical and institutional context, especially its dynamics of distribution and structural change. This broader conceptualization of the growth process contradicts the narrow focus of mainstream economic growth theories on factors of production.

An understanding that economic structures and policy choices produce fundamentally different human and economic welfare outcomes informs the report's recommendations, explaining, for example, the emphasis on structural transformation as a basis for regional economic policy, rather than per capita gross domestic product (GDP) growth. Furthermore, this understanding underpins the observation that the dynamic effects of economic openness do not always necessarily materialize in all developing countries and that cooperation of the State with the market assisted countries to advance to higher levels of development in the past.[18] Without macroeconomic policies that create (or restore) the fiscal space to fund structural transformation of the economy, many

developing countries will simply not attain targets such as the SDGs.

Since the 1990s, Arab countries have significantly liberalized their economies to trade, investment and capital flows. In the realm of trade policy, tariffs have been significantly reduced and most non-tariff barriers eliminated. However, those reforms have not reflected positively on trade performance. The region's overall share in world trade remains insignificant and trade remains dominated by highly concentrated, low-value added exports in exchange for diversified imports. The dynamic effects from trade liberalization have therefore not materialized.[19]

3. Autocracy: a road to nowhere

The authoritarian model will be difficult to sustain in the Arab region until 2030. More than two thirds of Arabs prefer democracy, according to the most recent World Values Survey results.

The argument that socially tolerated authoritarian regimes achieved sustainable socioeconomic transitions in other regions in the past does not apply to the Arab region. Sustained economic growth in East Asia countries, for example, took place in the unique circumstances that followed the end of the Second World War. They were also more concerned with structural transformation and growth sustainability than short-term growth mainly directed to the elite, as is the case in much of the Arab region. Moreover, when countries such as the Republic of Korea launched their industrialization programmes, they already had sufficient human resources and a strong institutional foundation to implement ambitious structural transformations. This is not the case in most Arab countries today.

Authoritarian regimes can survive by disbursing significant rent. This may work for some, but not indefinitely. In more populated, low-rent countries, mediocre economic performance is bound to lead to growing domestic pressure as authoritarian regimes fail to deliver on promises of growth in exchange for limiting voice and accountability. As opposition calls for reform become louder, such regimes resort to more coercion to silence dissent, thereby fuelling greater polarization, conflict and ultimately the collapse of the authoritarian model.

This need not be the "business-as-usual" scenario. In a region where people have made clear demands for decent economic opportunities, dignity, freedom and social justice, a vision of their future cannot be based on trade-offs between these fundamental human rights.

C. Two basic issues

Two issues will frame the debate on the future of development in the Arab region.

1. Democracy and development

Evidence suggests that economic growth and social development can be sustained by a variety of political systems, including autocracies, although in high-income countries a liberal democratic model tends to be the norm.

This report argues that development depends on institutional and governance reform, and diverges from other analyses by focusing on indicators related to the rule of law and the legitimacy of institutions.

A major point in common between the report's proposals and the 2030 Agenda for Sustainable Development is the promotion of inclusive development as a policy package, in which achievements in one area can galvanize progress in others. While such synergies are beyond dispute, the exact degree of overlap is debated. Inclusive, accountable and effective governance and institutional capacity to oversee and make connections can significantly reduce the cost of achieving development goals, and improve capacities that feed back into more growth and prosperity.[20]

Effective, responsive and accountable institutions and more just and efficient State performance are not only ends in themselves, but are also needed to produce a range of positive spillovers on growth, justice, inequality and resource sustainability. Liberal democracies (countries with a high degree of freedom of speech and regular, honest elections) and autocratic systems can both spur economic growth, but democracies generally outperform autocracies. The common denominator is the presence of efficient, strong and stable institutions.

Sustained economic growth is not only an end in itself, but would foster better quality of life, improved health and education, and a cleaner environment for millions of Arabs. Strong institutions can improve the sustainability of natural resource consumption, encourage transformational economic growth and strengthen social justice.

2. A virtuous cycle

This report's development vision assumes peace and stability, based on stronger and better institutions, which lead to more inclusive and sustainable growth patterns (with structural transformation, employment generation and resource sustainability) and, in turn, increase opportunities for investing in human development. Human development leads to further improvements in governance, which reinforces another cycle of better growth and human development, and so on. This virtuous cycle naturally strengthens pre-existing peace and security.

Figure 1.1 Links between economic growth, employment and income

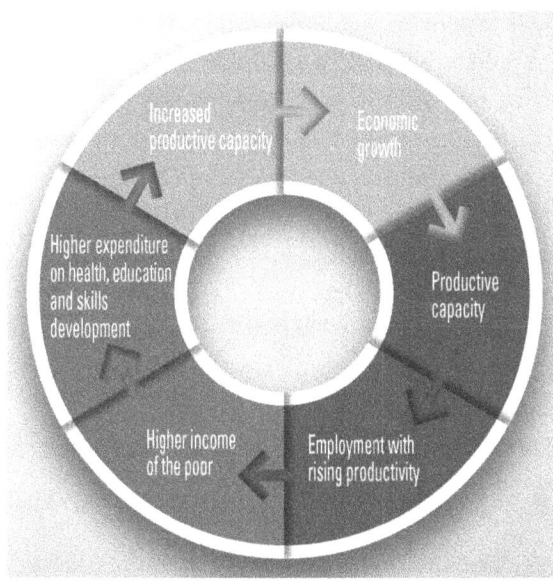

Source: Adapted from Islam, 2004.

There is evidence that economic growth, which increases productivity and generates decent work, can lead to rapid reductions in poverty (figure 1.1).[21] Real wage increases from higher productivity enhance workers' skills and boost their spending power, which, in turn, further increase productive capacity and contribute to economic growth.

The Arab region needs to focus on employment, as the lack of decent work is the main economic development problem in the region. A key issue is social policy on mass quality education. All assessments of the underlying success factors of the Asian economic transitions have highlighted the importance of human capital.

A fundamental feature of the five instrumental freedoms of the human development approach is that they are policy-related and that progress in one strengthens the others.[22] In this report's vision, regional integration, which is both a cause and an effect of economic and human development, plays an important part in speeding up the cycle. The economic incentives for regional integration are significant but its implementation is complex.

The development cycle is itself reversible. A vicious de-development cycle can ensue when poor governance and weak institutions, which slow down growth, strain natural resources and foster social and economic injustice, reinforce divisions that nourish conflict and hinder social and human development.

D. A new inclusive development model

This report assesses development achievements on the basis of "what it does to the lives of human beings", as Amartya Sen put it.[23] The enhancement of material living conditions is an integral part of our definition of development. At the heart of Vision 2030 is the idea of developmental States with "the vision, leadership and capacity to bring about a positive transformation of society within a condensed period of time".[24]

Arab countries have signed many agreements under the auspices of the League of Arab States and United Nations bodies, which could easily form the basis of a region-wide charter of rights and obligations, upon which individual countries could model themselves as developmental States.

A developmental State presupposes a governance system based on mutual accountability through social dialogue. By adopting an inclusive development model, it also enshrines within its system respect for the values of equality, equity, rights, participation,[25] and social and economic justice.[26] A developmental State cannot be characterized as socialist or free market; it joins private ownership with State guidance, and its Government acts as a "surrogate for a missing capital market",[27] and induces transformative investment decisions. It subscribes to the centrality of planning, but not necessarily to central planning.

An Arab developmental State must be characterized by a combination of "capacities, visions, norms and/or ideologies"[28] that lead to structural transformation and industrialization. By cooperating with the private sector to identify projects in which the profit motive dovetails with national developmental goals, it would become a "seamless web of political, bureaucratic and moneyed influences that structures economic life",[29] driven by committed leadership[30] pursuing development goals rather than personal enrichment or short-term political gain.

This report attempts to show how the region can recalibrate its trajectory. It envisages a day when all citizens can freely voice their opinions and practise their religious beliefs without fear; when the rule of law applies equally to the rich and poor; when quality services are accessible to all citizens; when all households have the security of gainful employment, health insurance and old-age pensions; and when the basic necessities for a decent life are affordable for all.

Under the vision scenario, the impact of colonialism will fade and autocracy will give way to democracies in which leaders are held accountable and justice and human rights are upheld. The region will be shaped by the aspirations of Arab citizens and their contributions to national policies. Transformative policies and deeper forms of economic integration will contribute to a new regional social contract. Supranational action will help to establish Arab economic citizenship[31] and a system of common values — a new Arab social contract.

Thus, by 2030, Arab countries are expected to have achieved or be on course to achieving the five strategic goals, or pillars, set forth below.

They each contain elements that affect one another and can lead to a virtuous cycle. Within the governance pillar, for instance, it can be argued that strong institutions require, first and foremost, equal access to justice and the rule of law. Where the rule of law prevails, the right to peaceful protest and freedom of belief and expression are more likely to be upheld. An environment where justice and intellectual liberty prevail will lend itself to greater accountability and less corruption.

1. Peace and security

Achieving peace and security is a prerequisite for realizing regional integration. Only then will the region be able to transform itself through a new Arab development model. All conflict and occupation in the region must therefore end. This report focuses on the Israeli occupation as an example of external conflict and the Syrian civil war as an example of internal conflict. However, the conclusions broadly apply to the many other conflicts plaguing the region. Whether under a two-State solution or a single democratic State within the pre-1948 borders, peace in Palestine can only be achieved by the full return of Palestinian refugees to their homes and the restoration of their right to self-detremination.

Under the vision scenario, the civil war in the Syrian Arab Republic would end well before 2030. In the wake of a regionally brokered and internationally sanctioned peace accord, antagonism between religious and secular forces would fade and regional players refrain from arming factions.

Equally, other crises in the region would also end. In Iraq, a degree of equilibrium could be reached by ensuring that all groups are involved in political processes, with prospects for sharing power and wealth. A national unity Government would include all of Iraq's communities and regions.

2. Governance

This report's vision rests on the assumption that Arab countries will achieve the following goals:

(a) By 2030, Arab countries will have a new governance model firmly in place. They will have abandoned the rent-based political economy and implanted political, social and administrative accountability mechanisms based on the separation of powers, an effective system of checks and balances, freedom of information and transparent policymaking;

(b) Successful democratic transitions will ensure that citizens can freely participate in setting policy, overseeing the implementation of development plans and holding leaders accountable for their actions. Civil society and local governments will become indispensable partners in the developmental State. The independence, integrity and efficiency of the judiciary will be safeguarded, not only for the sake of a just system, but also as a critical factor for long-term productive investment;

(c) Increased public participation in decision-making and transparent governance will act as an antidote to corruption in the public and private sectors. More effective anti-corruption legislation, reforms and policies should also help.[32] The spillover effects of economic growth and reduced unemployment will lessen the incentive to engage in corruption;

(d) Institutions, particularly those responsible for essential services such as social security, health and education, will be reinforced. They will ensure that all citizens, regardless of race, religion or socioeconomic class, have equal access to development opportunities;

(e) Countries affected by conflict and LDCs will have significantly closed governance gaps by 2030, and the Arab region as a whole will approach the global average on institutional quality indicators.

3. Structural transformation and resource sustainability

By 2030, macroeconomic policies will be geared towards supporting technically competitive sectors that promote growth and generate jobs, thereby countering the spread of informal work, which plays a major role in social exclusion and poverty. The focus on advanced sectors with high productivity and value added in Arab economies will benefit employees and nurture growth of the middle class. As growth rises above 6 per cent annually in the vision scenario, unemployment will fall to around 5 per cent. The gap in per capita GDP between the region and high-income countries will shrink.

The period 2015-2025 will be a preparatory phase, with little visible structural transformation as the regulatory and technical levers of economic growth are put into place. However, progress will become noticeable already in oil-producing countries, resulting in a 4.5 per cent decrease in the share of the oil

and gas sectors and a 3.6 per cent increase in the share of manufacturing. Between 2025 and 2030, progress in manufacturing and high value-added services will accelerate significantly in oil-producing and non-oil producing countries.

Regional economic integration and environmental sustainability will be fundamental to welfare and the survival of some Arab societies. By 2030, the region will have established an integrated economic policy model that will not be driven by the extraction of oil and natural gas. It will be based on sustainable production and consumption, taking into account energy and water issues.

To meet its energy requirements, the region will significantly improve and internalize appropriate technologies through local research and development. Solar technology, embarrassingly neglected in countries where it holds the highest promise of return, will become the leading sector for energy innovation and technological advances. Harnessing the region's energy requirements from the sun will bring additional benefits, even for water desalination and agricultural irrigation.

The region will achieve universal and equitable access to safe and affordable drinking water. It will substantially increase water-use efficiency, particularly in agriculture, through the use of modern irrigation systems, and by ensuring sustainable withdrawals and supply of freshwater. Renewable energy will account for 20 per cent of total energy consumption, made possible by phasing out all fuel subsidies by 2020 and improving energy efficiency.

4. Human development and social justice

By 2030, national and regional economic and development policies will be contributing to inclusive economic growth, poverty reduction, and social justice and human rights.[33]

All Arab countries will adopt the International Labour Organization (ILO) Social Protection Floors Recommendation, 2012 (No. 202). As a result, basic income security and social transfers will reach older persons and persons with disabilities, children, the unemployed and the working poor; and access to essential health, water and sanitation, education, food security, and housing services will become universal.

The region will address food insecurity by boosting food production, establishing an Arab food security partnership network and creating a strategic grain reserve in the form of a regional food bank.[34]

By 2030, the region will have eradicated extreme poverty and achieved significant reductions in income and wealth inequalities in line with the following goals:

- Eradicate hunger and poverty below $1.90 per day in 2011 purchasing power parity (PPP);[35]
- Reduce poverty rates by at least half, according to nationally defined poverty lines;
- Ensure regular monitoring and mandatory reporting on wealth and income and open access to data on household expenditure and living conditions;
- Develop fiscal policies aimed at reducing significant inequalities through more progressive taxation.

By 2030, health service quality will have improved greatly, resulting in far lower infant mortality (12 per 10,000 live births) and maternal mortality (50 per 100,000 births), largely as a result of ensuring quality health care, especially in reproductive health. Preventable infectious diseases, such as malaria and tuberculosis, will be eradicated; hepatitis C prevalence will decline; and the spread of HIV will halt with the commitment of Arab Governments to eradicate such diseases.

The pupil-teacher ratio will decrease to 11 pupils per teacher in 2030. This will significantly increase the ranking of Arab students in international education tests from low to above average. The region will have eradicated adult illiteracy.

Greater commitment at the national, local and individual levels to promote gender equality and women's empowerment will stimulate transformative changes, including freedom from violence for women and girls; prevention of early marriage; women's equal access to resources; and equal voice, leadership and participation. By 2030, female labour-force participation rates in the region will exceed 40 per cent, led by strong gains in LDCs and conflict-affected countries.

Transformative socioeconomic changes will be reflected in significant increases in Human Development Index rankings, which, by 2030, will rise to an average of approximately 0.76. Rates of progress will be significantly higher in the poorest countries and LDCs than in the richer and more developed ones, where the limits of many health, education and living conditions indicators have already been approached.

5. Regional integration

Given the security, social and economic challenges facing the region, there is a strong case for renewing efforts to promote regional integration. *Arab Integration: A 21st Century Development Imperative* has provided us with a wealth of ideas on how to do so.[36]

This report proposes an Arab Citizens Common Economic Security Space (ACCESS) that would include regional strategies and policies designed to strengthen the above-mentioned pillars and lead to the achievement of the following goals:

(a) Ensure the freedom and dignity of all people in the region by liberating it from occupation and foreign interference, and establishing good governance;
(b) Establish a strong and diversified Arab production structure by replacing the weak, inefficient and uncompetitive patterns of Arab production with diversified industrial structures and more flexible and knowledge-based enterprises that add more value;
(c) Revive Arab culture by drawing inspiration from the greatest achievements of Arab and other civilizations, enhance the Arabic language, protect diversity and boost knowledge acquisition.

ACCESS represents a new approach to regional integration, in terms of objectives, scope, modes, instruments and enforcement, based on developmental regionalism. It would provide single market conditions (in the areas of trade in goods, services, investments, labour, industrial development and technological innovation) and operate in tandem with the Arab Customs Union. For ACCESS to succeed, integration efforts with non-Arab countries pursued over the past two decades will need to be revised to serve Arab regional integration rather than undermine it.

By 2030, the economy of the Arab region will be highly regulated, allowing development and integration to be mutually reinforcing. As new trade patterns emerge, the region will consolidate economic and trade ties with its neighbours, the African continent and other advanced, developing and emerging economies. It will have consolidated its infrastructure and energy networks, with emphasis on renewable energy; developed new routes to enhance regional supply and production chain efficiencies; and become more accommodating to supranational governance that fosters the achievement of regional goals (box 1.1).

6. Vision 2030 and SDGs

Annex 1 sets out the SDGs, which are broadly consistent with the goals and targets in this report, although the latter are, in some cases, more ambitious. Sustainable development goals 1-5 and 10 are consistent with the report's targets on human and social development. Goals 6-9 and 11-12 resonate with the targets on structural transformation and resource sustainability. Goal 16 especially is in line with the report's stance on good governance, and goal 17 accords with its position on advancing developmental regionalism through deeper regional integration.

The SDGs provide a global framework for setting national development targets. However, this report's vision goes beyond merely quantifying targets by laying out a framework for the Arab region that combines political stability, governance and economic, social, environmental and regional integration in a systematic way, relying on a firm theoretical foundation and analysis of what has and has not worked for the region in the past.

Box 1.1 Ten regional integration goals expected to be achieved by 2030 on the basis of ACCESS

1. ACCESS will function as an Arab single market from an intraregional perspective and as an economic space for extraregional purposes.

2. Free movement of goods, services, capital and labour will be integral to the single market, thereby contributing to transnational socioeconomic justice.

3. All extraregional arrangements will be adapted to the common trade policy under the Arab Customs Union (ACU), putting an end to outlier effects.

4. A regional industrial space, creating a level playing field across the region in terms of standards, conformity assessment, subsidies, health and consumer protection to foster intra-industry trade and structural change innovation.

5. Free circulation of goods and cumulation of origin within the ACCESS area, thus facilitating trade, reducing costs and promoting clusters of small and medium enterprises; exports will bear a single mark of origin.

6. Liberalization of services in areas such as construction, infrastructure, banking, education, water, sanitation and health.

7. A basis for pursuing uniform policies to improve economic security and solve food, energy and water bottlenecks. Key elements include the construction of electrical grids, expanded transport infrastructure, improved digital networks and an integrated Euro-Arab power system, with Arab countries supplying Europe and meeting their own energy needs from solar and wind resources, thereby also contributing to the reduction of emissions.

8. Streamlined, region-wide operations of Islamic and Arab development and investment institutions to finance regional projects and provide trade financing, concessions and guarantees to the poorest Arab countries.

9. Macroeconomic policy convergence (fiscal, monetary and exchange rates), paving the way for a common currency.

10. Reform and enhancement of pan-Arab governing structures.

E. Conclusion

The daunting challenges weighing on the Arab region have fuelled a deep sense of pessimism about its future prospects. However, not to map out a path to a brighter future would mean failing to honour the aspirations of those who took to the streets, gave their lives and continue to yearn for dignity, freedom, equality, and social justice.

Certain constraints, first and foremost conflict, could derail the process of economic and human development and spark a descent into a vicious cycle of de-development. Sustainable development will only become possible when the wars plaguing the region end.

The machinery of development, namely institutions, economic activities, natural resources and human capital, can be used wisely to foster a virtuous development cycle. In the Arab region, however, those mechanisms have broken down. Poor governance is at the root of most internal conflicts and requires reform to produce stronger institutions that can foster economic growth, resource sustainability, social justice and human development.

Regional integration can play a central role in expanding markets, boosting employment and improving political and food security across the region.

The primary mandate of the developmental State is to maximize synergies in order to launch a virtuous development cycle on the basis of the five strategic pillars of peace and security, good governance, structural transformation and resource sustainability, human development and social justice, and regional integration.

The report illustrates how Vision 2030 can work, with chapters on each of the five pillars.

2. Peace and Security

A. Introduction

The future of development in the Arab region cannot be studied in isolation from broader strategic, military and geopolitical considerations. The region is undergoing radical changes akin to those that followed the First World War, with potentially redrawn borders and the rise of new forms of political organization.

Shifts in the global balance of power, the transfer of wealth from West to East, and demographic changes in Arab and neighbouring countries present the Arab region with new challenges and opportunities. Those global trends are not controlled by forces in the Arab region but have an undeniable impact on it. Arab State and non-State actors play a direct role in conflicts between Arab countries and external forces, inter-Arab conflicts, and transformations towards democracy. How Arab States approach those issues will largely shape their future development.

This chapter takes a broad look at the dynamics of conflicts involving actors external to Arab countries, civil wars and communal tensions, and transition scenarios. It does so by concentrating on key cases of each category: the Israeli occupation of Palestinian territory, which is the most enduring and incendiary issue in the Arab region; the civil war in the Syrian Arab Republic; and uprisings that did not lead to civil war. In the latter case, the focus is on Tunisia, where transition has thus far been the most successful, and on Egypt, where the outcome is crystallizing and could have a major impact on the rest of the region.

We look at future scenarios, whether business as usual, which could mean status quo or even a worsening of the current situation, or possible ways forward if Arab Governments grasp historic opportunities thrown up by political, economic and demographic transformations around the world.

B. External dynamics

Since the Second World War, the Arab region has witnessed at least one major war every decade, with at least one external actor.[37] They represent the most direct form of external intervention. Other forms include proxy wars and conflicting strategic alliances. Therefore, relations between different external actors must be considered in any analysis of the region's future.

In the early 1990s, a new unipolar world order, marked by a dominant United States, emerged after the collapse of the Soviet bloc. This brought about the two US-led wars on Iraq, in 1991 and 2003. The Madrid Conference of 1991, aimed at reviving a peace process that would lead to pan-Arab recognition of Israel in return for the lands occupied in 1967, was held in that context. The United States consolidated its influence in the area by expanding its network of military bases in the region, especially in the Persian Gulf.

As a new multipolar world order takes shape, the Arab region is undergoing major transformations, the results of which will be dictated by the international balance of power and regional dynamics.

Even if the United States remains the most influential external player in the region, the two wars on Iraq, other military interventions since the end of the Cold War and the failure to achieve justice in the Arab-Israeli conflict have weakened its ability to shape the political agenda in the area.[38]

Furthermore, by invading Iraq and by continuing to shield Israel from accounting for its actions and meeting its obligations under international and humanitarian law,[39] the United States continues to be viewed unfavourably by the majority of Arabs (table 2.1). The occupation of Iraq by the United States also fuelled the rise of other external actors, such as Iran and Turkey, and contributed to a renewed role in the region for the Russian Federation.

Table 2.1 Perception by Arab citizens of selected countries (percentage)

	Palestine		Morocco		Egypt		Jordan		Lebanon		Saudi Arabia		United Arab Emirates (Emirati nationals only)	
	Fav	Unfav	Fav	Unfav	Fav	Unfav	Fav	Unfav	Fav	Unfav	Fav	Unfav	Fav	Unfav
Russia	58	35	22	77	24	72	25	73	53	46	11	80	37	62
Turkey	72	24	40	52	60	38	64	33	29	72	59	38	54	45
Saudi Arabia	75	23	59	41	77	23	92	7	22	78	-	-	79	19
Iran	50	44	23	76	11	86	10	86	81	16	1	94	19	79
United States	27	70	21	77	30	67	18	75	14	86	22	74	44	54
China	55	37	31	68	60	36	63	34	69	31	50	46	49	47

Source: Zogby Research Services, 2014.

Note: Percentages may not add up to 100 per cent because of rounding and/or because responses of «not sure» are not included.

Economic factors are also contributing to the shift in the world balance of power. The largest transfer in history of real capital from West to East is likely to continue over the next 15 years. The economies of such countries as China and India are growing faster than those of the European Union (EU) and the United States.[40] China will continue to close the gap with the United States in terms of economic size[41] and military expenditure.[42] The growth of the two Asian giants will drive rising demand for energy, especially oil and gas. This should benefit the Arab region in the long term and will be of strategic importance for its development.[43]

Demographic changes in neighbouring countries offer additional opportunities. The young populations of neighbouring countries such as Iran and Turkey are maturing,[44] leading to a rise in productivity and the potential value of commercial cooperation between them and Arab countries.[45] Properly managed, economic ties between Iran and Iraq, for example, could strengthen the latter as the economy of the former grows. The same could apply to Turkey and the Syrian Arab Republic.[46]

The Arab region could equally benefit from demographic changes in China and the Russian Federation. The population of the Russian Federation is expected to decrease from 144 million to 113 million by 2050.[47] Its Muslim minority, however, is expected to grow, as it is one of the few population groups in that country with a fertility rate of more than 2.1 children per woman, the rate required to maintain population size. It is estimated that Muslims will make up nearly one quarter of the population by 2050. That could influence Russian policy in two ways: Moscow will oppose violent Islamist movements in order to discourage separatist tendencies among its Muslim populations, especially in regions like Chechnya and Dagestan; but it will probably adopt an impartial or critical position with regard to Israeli violations of the rights of Arabs, in order not to alienate its Muslim population and to reduce the threat of non-State actors within and beyond its borders.[48]

An exporter of oil and gas, the Russian Federation strives to guarantee maritime trade routes. The majority of those routes in the west, including the Baltic and North Seas, and the Bosphorus, are controlled by member States of the North Atlantic Treaty Organization (NATO). Russian gas pipelines from the Caucasus to the Black Sea and Ukraine are vulnerable to possible unrest in Chechnya and Dagestan, and competition from pipelines passing through Azerbaijan, Georgia and Turkey. The military presence and influence of the United States in Afghanistan, Pakistan and Central Asia complicates Russian access to the Indian Ocean. Those factors have prompted Moscow to seek closer ties with Iran, Iraq, Lebanon and the Syrian Arab Republic, in order to facilitate its access to the Indian Ocean, the Persian Gulf and the Mediterranean Sea.

Rising energy consumption in China will result in greater demand for oil from Arab countries, Iran and Central Asia. China will also have national security concerns regarding any separatist tendencies among the considerable Muslim minority it its western provinces. The position of China is therefore likely to resemble that of the Russian Federation with regard to the spread of Islamic radicalism and the Israeli occupation of Arab land. The convergence of interests between China, Iran and the Russian Federation will help to counterbalance the influence of the United States in the Arab region, offering alternatives to Arab countries that hitherto have been closely bound to the United States in strategic, military and economic terms.

C. Internal dynamics

Arab countries can significantly influence the outcome of external conflicts, such as the Arab-Israeli conflict, internal wars, such as the Syrian civil war, and the process of political transformation that began largely with the uprisings of 2011.

1. The Arab-Israeli conflict

The Israeli occupation of Palestinian territory and the discriminatory regime established by Israel remain a burning issue. Since its creation, Israel has been directly involved in 7 out of 11 of the major external wars waged in the Arab region, not counting the campaigns in Gaza in 2008, 2012 and 2014. Those wars, continued occupation, the military imbalance of power, the possession by Israel of weapons of mass destruction and their delivery systems,[49] and precedents for Israeli raids on Arab countries such as Iraq, Lebanon, the Sudan, the Syrian Arab Republic, and Tunisia, all contribute to a widely held belief that Israel represents an existential threat to the whole region.

The inability to liberate Arab occupied territories, arms proliferation and the dissemination of ideologies through new and traditional media mean that frustration among the Arab peoples has worrying implications for all Governments in the region. According to a 2014 opinion poll in Arab countries, 77 per cent of respondents view the Palestine issue as "a cause for all Arabs and not the Palestinian people alone". Most Arabs oppose peace treaties signed by Arab States and Israel (including the Wadi Araba Treaty between Israel and Jordan; the Egyptian-Israeli Camp David Accords; and the Oslo Accords signed by the Palestine Liberation Organization), and 87 per cent oppose recognition of Israel by their Governments.[50]

In recent years, Israeli officials have repeatedly made recognition of Israel as the "Jewish State" a precondition for moving forward on peace negotiations with Palestinians. The concept of the "Jewish State", as set forth in the 1947 United Nations Partition Plan for Palestine,[51] respected the principle of non-discrimination. It was not intended to provide more privileges for Jewish citizens over others, nor did it state that the demographic majority of one ethnic/religious group needed to be maintained. It stipulated that the constitutions of the Arab and Jewish States should include provisions "guaranteeing to all persons equal and non-discriminatory rights in civil, political, economic and religious matters and the enjoyment of human rights and fundamental freedoms, including freedom of religion, language, speech and publication, education, assembly and association (part I, section B, para. 10 (d))". It also stated that "no discrimination of any kind shall be made between the inhabitants on the ground of race, religion, language or sex (part I, section C, chapter 2, para. 2)".

The Israeli concept of the "Jewish State", however, focuses on retaining a clear Jewish majority. In 2003, the then Israeli Minister of Finance, Benjamin Netanyahu, said that if Israel's Arabs became well integrated and reached 35-40 per cent of the population, there would no longer be a Jewish State.[52] In May 2014, he proposed amending the Basic Law to define Israel as "the nation-State of one people only – the Jewish people – and of no other people".[53]

Since 1948, Israel has de facto established a regime that discriminates primarily according to religion with the aim of retaining a clear ethno-religious demographic composition, in which one group dominates all others. This entails violations of international law, namely regarding equality and non-discrimination.[54]

Israel governs everyone who resides between the River Jordan and the Mediterranean Sea, but it does not apply its laws uniformly. The population is divided into four broad categories:[55] Jewish Israeli citizens; Palestinians with Israeli citizenship; residents of East Jerusalem; and residents of the West Bank and the Gaza Strip. Another category, which overlaps with the latter and makes up the majority of the Palestinian people, is made up of refugees. They may number 8 million or more,[56] but 5.4 million are registered with the United Nations Relief and Works Agency for Palestine Refugees in the Near East (UNRWA).[57]

In practice, a five-tier system operates at the institutional, legislative and policy levels, affording different rights and legal protection for different population categories.[58] Jewish Israelis enjoy full citizenship and civil rights, and their co-religionists around the world have the right of return or *aliyah*. Palestinian refugees are denied that right on account of them not being Jewish. Muslim, Christian, Baha'i and Druze Arabs, among others, are divided into several groups. Those living behind the Green Line and who have never sought refuge elsewhere are citizens of Israel, albeit with fewer rights than their Jewish counterparts.[59]

Palestinian non-Jewish citizens of Israel face institutional and societal discrimination. In 2012, the United Nations Committee on the Elimination of Racial Discrimination expressed concern that "Israeli society maintains Jewish and non-Jewish sectors, which raises issues under article 3 of the [International] Convention [on the Elimination of All Forms of Racial Discrimination]", on racial segregation and apartheid.[60] Institutional discrimination against non-Jewish Israeli citizens is embodied in more than 50 laws.[61]

Palestinians in the West Bank and Gaza Strip live under Israeli military rule, enjoy only the rights arbitrarily granted by Israel's occupying forces and must obey laws and military decrees on which they have no say. These laws, decrees and other measures affect all aspects of Palestinian life, from freedom of movement to building homes or running businesses, as well as severe restrictions on the use of their natural resources.[62]

Palestinians with residence in East Jerusalem have more rights than those in the West Bank and Gaza but, unlike Arab citizens of Israel, they may not vote and their residence status is uncertain. Israel openly pursues what it labels a "demographic balance" policy in East

Jerusalem, under which laws effectively lead to the forced displacement of Palestinians.[63]

The Committee has also censured Israel for its policies in the territories occupied since 1967 under article 3, on racial segregation and apartheid, of the Convention.[64] Two United Nations special rapporteurs on the human rights situation in the occupied Palestinian territory have examined the question of apartheid. Mr. John Dugard recommended in 2007 that the question of whether "elements of the [Israeli] occupation constitute forms of colonialism and apartheid" be referred to the International Court of Justice for an advisory opinion.[65] Mr. Richard Falk later noted that the recommendation had not been acted upon and concluded in 2014 that Israeli policies and practices "constitute racial segregation and apartheid".[66]

Palestinians in the West Bank may elect a legislative council and executive body, jointly known as the Palestinian Authority, but its remit does not cover water, electricity, freedom of movement, or self-defence.[67]

Distinctions are also made between Palestinians in the West Bank and Gaza. Since 2007, those in Gaza have been collectively punished through a near-total blockade; they have been denied their rights to food, medicine, electricity, water and free movement, in addition to suffering from recurrent military offensives. Palestinians in the West Bank suffer from the excessive use of force by Israeli soldiers, settler attacks, settlement expansion, movement restrictions, land seizures and detention by the Israeli occupying forces, all of which the Palestinian authorities and police are powerless to oppose.[68]

(a) Business as usual: continued occupation

The Arab-Israeli conflict will continue as long as the Israeli occupation does, or even if a partially sovereign, economically dependent and militarily vulnerable Palestinian State is established, alongside an Israel that continues to refuse the right of Palestinians to return to their towns and villages, while encouraging Jewish people from all over the world to migrate to Israel. For a two-State solution to bring peace, the Palestinian State must be independent, which would entail granting Palestinians the rights set out in the Charter of the United Nations, including the right to individual or collective self-defence. The rights of return of all Palestinian refugees should be implemented and all laws that discriminate against non-Jewish citizens should be abolished.[69]

Israel does not accept the right of return and is unwilling to amend laws that discriminate against non-Jewish citizens. It justifies that stance by the policy of maintaining the Jewish demographic majority, thereby effectively annulling the possibility of just and durable peace.[70]

Current policies and practices indicate that Israel has no intention of allowing the creation of a viable and contiguous Palestinian State on lands occupied since 1967. Those policies and practices can be categorized as: (i) "land grab", including settlement activity, land confiscation and the building of the separation wall; (ii) population displacement, manifested in restrictions on construction and development activities, deportations, demolition of structures and homes, and transfer of communities; and

(iii) systematic oppression, which includes collective punishment, arbitrary detention, and excessive use of force aimed mainly at suppressing any form of resistance.[71]

The presence and expansion of Israeli settlements in the West Bank is not only illegal, but also reflects the strategy of consecutive Israeli Governments with respect to the future of the occupied territories. Between 1993 and 2000, a period marked by negotiations, interim agreements and other diplomatic initiatives, settlement activity continued unabated. During that time, which preceded the eruption of the second Intifada in September 2000, the settlement housing stock grew by 52.49 per cent and construction of 17,190 housing units in the settlements was approved and begun.[72] Moreover, between 1996 and 1999, Israeli settlers established more than 42 "outposts",[73] of which fewer than 10 were subsequently dismantled.[74] By 2000, there were 145 official settlements and around 200 "outposts" in occupied Palestinian territory. By 2012, the Israeli settler population on Palestinian land had more than doubled since the signing of the 1993 Declaration of Principles on Interim Self-Government Arrangements, better known as the Oslo I Accord.

As a result, approximately 40 per cent of the West Bank falls under the jurisdiction of Israeli local or regional settlement councils. The Israeli authorities have consistently refused to allocate such land for Palestinian use. In addition, more than 35 per cent of the land in the Israeli-defined municipal area of East Jerusalem has been confiscated since 1967 for settlement use, and only 13 per cent of the East Jerusalem area is available for Palestinian construction.[75]

In July 2014, Israeli Prime Minister Netanyahu said that "there cannot be a situation, under any agreement, in which we relinquish security control of the territory west of the River Jordan".[76] He reiterated his position during the 2015 elections.[77]

The implications are that any Palestinian State that may emerge would have partial sovereignty, at best in non-contiguous parts of the West Bank. The right of return would not be fulfilled, and non-Jewish citizens of Israel would continue to face discrimination based on their religion. A partially sovereign Palestinian State would be economically dependent on Israel and on the generosity of donor countries. A certain class of Palestinians, whose interests are bound up with those of Israel, would depend on marketing Israeli goods in Palestine and Arab countries or act as intermediaries, providing Israel with cheap Palestinian labour.[78] Many poorer Palestinians would have to seek employment in Israel. A Palestinian administration with limited powers would be unable to build a diversified and viable economy providing decent employment opportunities and ensuring the well-being of all.

Such a Palestinian State would also be militarily vulnerable to Israel and unable to guarantee the security of its own citizens. This has been the prevailing logic of the peace process, under which guaranteeing the security of Israel is seen as a precondition for establishing any kind of Palestinian State.

The circumstances under which the present Palestinian Government is forced to operate, largely deprived of real power by Israel, provide a foretaste of what such a Palestinian State might look like. Despite its lack of control over economic matters and inability to protect its citizens from incursions by Israel, the Palestinian Authority was asked to establish a large police force to help to protect Israelis from Palestinian individuals or organizations, but cannot defend Palestinians against the Israeli army or Israeli settlers.[79] The Palestinian security forces number 110,000. It is estimated that there is one member of the Palestinian security forces for every 25 Palestinian civilians in the West Bank,[80] akin to the teacher-pupil ratio in an elementary school.

Such a State, unable to defend its citizens against invasion and yet with ample force to establish domestic authoritarian rule, would be unable to fulfil the aspirations of the Palestinian people. That would inevitably lead to social tension and increase the chances of dissent or rebellion.

The situation would be exacerbated by the fact that one third of West Bank and two thirds of Gaza residents are refugees uprooted from their cities and villages when the State of Israel was created, and represent the poorest segments of the population. The elimination of the right to return, added to their economic hardships, would only inflate the number of opponents to that kind of a two-State solution. In any democracy established under such conditions, it is likely that parties opposed to such a solution would be elected, creating a threat to the political arrangements underpinning the new State's existence. In a 2010 opinion poll, 84 per cent of Palestinians said they would not support a peace agreement that includes "a Palestinian State … [that] had to make compromises on key issues (such as the right of return, Jerusalem, borders and settlements)".[81] It is thus unlikely that such a Palestinian State would be democratic. The absence of democratic institutions would have political and economic consequences: repression and corruption. Palestinians would find themselves deprived of political dignity and economic well-being. The Palestinian struggle, and consequently instability, would continue on two fronts: against Israel, on the one hand, and against a Palestinian government dependent on, and collaborating with, Israel, on the other.

(b) Vision scenario

Two solutions have been mooted to end the current impasse in Palestine: a two-State solution in which both States enjoy full rights and independence, or a single State in which all citizens are treated equally and without discrimination.

Under a genuine two-State solution, Palestine must be truly independent and fully sovereign. The rights and equality of all citizens in both States must be guaranteed. Creation of a Palestinian State would need to be accompanied by political reform in Israel to eliminate discrimination between Jewish and non-Jewish citizens, especially with regard to the right of return. Palestinian refugees should be allowed to return to the land from which they were forced to leave in 1948 and thereafter, and be granted full citizenship rights regardless of their religion. As highlighted above, this scenario is unlikely to come to pass without unprecedented international and regional pressure on Israel.

An alternative might be the "simple democratic solution"[82] of a single State within the pre-May 1948 borders, with equality and freedom from discrimination for all citizens. This would be more in line with the United Nations principles of equality, democracy and non-discrimination, while the two-State option on the table essentially treats people between the Mediterranean Sea and the Jordan River according to their religious affiliations. In practical terms, it would be less complex in many respects, including management of natural resources and security. The interests of the whole population would for once be aligned, regardless of religious or ethnic identity, as in any society that enjoys ethno-religious diversity, and would have to be managed accordingly.

This option also requires international pressure, and the Arab countries can play an important role in mobilizing it. The increasing likelihood that Israel will officially be labelled an apartheid regime, not only in the territories occupied since 1967, but also within Israel, could provide momentum. Eventually, the discriminatory notion of the "Jewish State", as a State for Jewish people alone, will have to change.

Discarding that notion will eliminate such concepts as demographic balance, demographic threats and the conflict over land and resources. The question of the return of Palestinian refugees could be more easily resolved, given that the basis of Israel's refusal to contemplate the return of refugees is essentially the demographic balance.

The new State would be accepted in the region as one of diversity that can forge normal political and economic ties, especially under "clean slate" conditions as provided for by the Vienna Convention on Succession of States in respect of treaties.

A one-State approach may prove inevitable. The Arab population in Israel and the occupied territories is growing at a faster rate than the Jewish population. By 2025, their number will exceed that of Jewish Israelis by nearly 1.75 million.[83] The Palestinian population is younger and has lower per capita income. It is keen to change the prevailing political system in Israel and has little to lose by trying to do so. Those factors, coupled with Israel's consistent ruling out of a genuine two-State solution, and the fact that settlement-building in occupied Palestinian territory continues, could make a one-State arrangement the only viable option.

2. Internal conflicts

According to the Office of the United Nations High Commissioner for Refugees (UNHCR), Afghanistan, Somalia and the Syrian Arab Republic together accounted for 53 per cent of the world's refugee population in 2014; Palestine and the Syrian Arab Republic alone account for more than 9 million of the world's 19 million refugees.[84] By September 2015, refugees from the Syrian Arab Republic numbered 4,086,760 men, women and children, while Palestinian refugees registered with UNRWA numbered 5,149,742; almost five years of civil war in the Syrian Arab Republic have generated almost as many refugees as half a century of the Arab-Israeli conflict. Arabs represent less than 5 per cent of the world population but account for more than half of the world's refugees.

More than one third of Arab countries have experienced at least one episode of conflict in the past decade.[85] Political and, in some cases, social order in the region is breaking down.[86]

(a) A new paradigm

Regular armies engaged in fighting in the region today are either defeated by militias or spared defeat with their help. Centralized, hierarchical organizations based on coercion and conscription, be they armies, police forces or entire States, are giving way to non-hierarchical, decentralized networks based on conviction, be they peaceful demonstrations or armed movements. These new networks use the unprecedented technological advances in communications and benefit from the wave of rapidly increasing population to challenge the old order. Narrative is replacing structure, networks are replacing hierarchies, improvization from the periphery is replacing central planning, volunteer militias are defeating conscript armies, demonstrators without orders are outmanoeuvering and overwhelming police forces. It is as though old forms of political organization can no longer contain their peoples.

The nation-State system in the Arab world was created with a set of structural contradictions. On the one hand, States were created by the colonial powers as guarantors of colonial interests, and they were expected by their own peoples to achieve independence and progress on the other.

It is costly for an invading power to directly manage a densely populated country. That involves turning the conquering army into a police force, the efficiency of which depends on

a considerable degree of social acceptance. The colonial power thus relies on local elites to provide security in return for the partial delegation of authority to them. They run the bureaucracy and security apparatuses, and invent a nationalism to legitimize the existence of both. The colonial powers entrust them with running the colonized State because of their relative legitimacy in the eyes of the people, but the more they collaborate with their colonial masters, the more that legitimacy is eroded.

Arab nation-States needed to cooperate with unpopular colonial powers to gain international recognition, and at the same time resist those very powers to gain local legitimacy. To complicate matters further, such States needed the legitimacy of resisting colonialism for their cooperation to be of any value. Their nominal resistance was the precondition for cooperation, and their dependence was the precondition for their nominal independence.[87]

After the defeat of the Ottoman Empire in the First World War and the subsequent abolition of the caliphate (in theory, a State for all Muslims), a series of secular nationalist entities arose, one of which was destined, and indeed designed, to become a Jewish State (in theory, a State for all Jews). That situation stirred religious forces that would put the secular Arab nation-States under considerable strain.

A century of reverses, starting with the French and British mandates and culminating in the US-led war in Iraq in 2003, as well as a string of defeats in wars with Israel, has seriously eroded confidence in the colonially created nation-State as a viable form of government in the Arab world. The current turbulence has seen States challenged or even replaced by other non-State entities, the role of which has come to include conducting war and managing peace. Those entities, whether religious or tribal, frequently transcend borders and are more often than not narrative-based networks. They reject not only the Governments of their respective countries, but even the idea of the country as a source of identity and focus of loyalty.

Unlike opposition parties and national liberation movements of the past, whose agenda involved taking over the State, these movements transcend the State rather than attempt to control it. They conduct war, peace and international relations and deliver their own version of justice, as if the formal State did not exist. For better or for worse, such conviction-based networks are supplanting the hierarchical centralized State and performing its functions, thereby rendering it obsolete.

By mobilizing popular consensus, such movements are able to neutralize the coercive power of the State. Unarmed mass demonstrations can effect real change, as in Tunisia in 2011, and in Egypt between 2011 and 2013. However, when the autocracies are able to exacerbate sectarian, tribal and other social divisions that are sufficient to prevent such a consensus, juxtaposing one narrative/identity against another, armed conflict becomes a threat, with one form of armed coercion challenging another.

Colonial powers drew up the present borders of countries in the region so as to perpetuate their economic dependence and military vulnerability. They governed through local elites and drove a wedge between different components of Arab societies, favouring some over others and leading to enduring feuds and latent tensions. The regimes that succeeded the colonial powers employed similar tactics to compensate for their legitimacy deficit. Diversity, usually a source of strength for society, was manipulated to trigger conflict. By keeping societies under the threat of social breakdown or civil war, authoritarian regimes could present themselves as the lesser of two evils.

The failure of Arab States since 2011 to respond positively to demands made in peaceful demonstrations, allowing the situation to deteriorate to the point where independent, heavily armed entities were established within them, underscores the structural problems of the Arab nation-State and the regional political order. Shortcomings in terms of legitimacy, governance, justice and independence are no longer just a hindrance to development; they have become a threat to the State's existence.

(b) Civil conflicts and the collapse of the State

The US-led invasion of Iraq in 2003 was preceded by 12 years of crippling sanctions, the 1991 Gulf War and Iraq's eight-year war with Iran. Defeated in 2003, its State institutions were dissolved. The ensuing period was marked by a sharp rise in sectarianism and violence, reinforced by the interference of rival international and regional powers, which resulted in marginalization and consequent frustration among a large portion of the Iraqi population, thereby fueling sectarian tensions that set the stage for the rise of extremist elements.

Yemen went through a relatively peaceful popular uprising in 2011 and slipped into violence in 2014. Events culminated in a regional military intervention by a Saudi-led coalition the following year. Even prior to 2011, the fragile Government exercised limited control through various tribes.[88] The question of southern Yemen had remained unresolved, with growing apprehension among the southern population due to perceived marginalization by the Government.[89] The failure to reconcile key internal players, and the regional contest for influence in the country, led to the most destructive conflict Yemen has experienced in decades.

In Libya, the collapse of the regime of Muammar Qaddafi in 2012 left the country with virtually no centralized State institutions. During the revolt, each region and town formed its own militia and de facto governing bodies along regional and tribal lines.[90] Various armed political and ideological groups emerged, each with a combination of regional or international sponsors. They failed to fill the vacuum left by the fall of Mr. Qaddafi, allowing religiously a variety of armed militias to gain a foothold. The inability of rival militant groups, split along regional (eastern versus western Libya), ideological (Islamist versus secular) and tribal lines to resolve their differences and resuscitate State institutions has led to a protracted, multipolar conflict.

Somalia has also been torn apart by civil war, fuelled by tribal divisions and the weakness of the State. Its strategic location on the Horn of Africa has attracted direct and indirect external intervention, further deepening divisions and encouraging the emergence of radical ideologies.

Other internal conflicts of varying intensity, such as in Lebanon, the Sudan and the Syrian Arab Republic, reveal similar characteristics: structural flaws in the State and social contracts and tribal, ethnic or sectarian divisions linked to external actors with competing economic and/or geopolitical interests.

(c) The case of the Syrian Arab Republic

At least 250,000 people have died in the civil war that has raged in the country since 2011, making it by far the deadliest and costliest of all current regional conflicts, and the most detrimental to the region's future.

The conflict that erupted in the Syrian Arab Republic in 2011 goes on unabated, as each party, with reinforcements from internal and external allies, attempts to end it by force. Foreign support of warring factions links the conflict to factors beyond the country's borders and the people's control. Many civil wars around the world in the past 50 years have led to foreign military intervention. In the Arab region, in fact, it has been the other way around, with foreign intervention arguably being the catalyst for civil war and further undermining regional security.

The underlying causes of the Syrian war are complex but at the heart of the matter have been the Government's insistence on using armed force on a large scale to repress protests and the decision by regional and international powers to arm the opposition. As more territory fell to non-State actors, and the ability of the Government to convince or coerce waned, people fell back on their myriad religious and ethnic loyalties as protective identities, sources of moral guidance and social refuge in the face of death. The fighting has reached such a degree of intensity that it will be one of the most important determinants of the future of the Arab region for years to come.

China, the Russian Federation and the local arms industry supply the Government with weaponry, while Qatar, Saudi Arabia, the United States and their allies arm the opposition via Jordan, Lebanon and Turkey. Unless the Government secures every kilometer of its borders, arms will continue to reach the opposition. And unless the opposition controls all ports and airports, the Government will likewise continue to be rearmed and resupplied. Without a political agreement, the two international alliances will continue to supply weapons to their partners and the conflict will carry on. With so many protagonists involved, the war is unlikely to end with a clear victory for any one side. In any event, victories in the field can be fleeting, as all sides have trouble persuading the people in areas under their control, whose loyalities may be divided between the State and one or more of the various opposition groups, of the legitimacy of their authority. Moreover, the interests of the warring parties are inextricably intertwined with those of their national, regional and international allies. The longer the conflict goes on, the more inflamed sectarian tensions in the region will become and the greater the risk is of violence spreading.

Any solution will hence require a regional agreement with international backing. Even if the Government reached an agreement through national dialogue with one or other of the opposition groups, it is unlikely that it would be acceptable to all the warring parties. Equally complex would be the process of disarming them. Should the regime fall, it would be equally difficult for any opposition group coming to power to disarm loyalist militias, the remnants of the defeated regular army and rival opposition groups.

The reliance of various Governments involved in the Syrian conflict on opposition networks and sectarian militias shows that they have accepted that non-State entities can be more efficient than the State itself in perfoming its functions, including war. The political order in the region is thus contributing to its own unravelling, nurturing ideas, discourses, networks and organizations that can, and in some cases already do, replace it. The confidence of decision makers in the capacity of the authoritarian Arab State to manipulate ethnic, religious, sectarian and tribal networks to their own ends has proven misplaced.

The contagion of fragmentation could spread from the Syrian Arab Republic and Iraq to neighbouring Mashreq countries. Old borders may be replaced by fluid boundaries shifting in accordance with volatile regional alliances.

(i) Business as usual: stagnation or invasion

The situation in the Syrian Arab Republic has allowed potent non-State actors to emerge and gain control of vast territories. This, predictably, paved the way for foreign intervention: an international coalition led by the United States launched air strikes against Islamic State positions on Syrian territory and in neighbouring Iraq. More recently, the Russian Federation intervened on behalf of the Syrian Government by conducting its own air strikes. The strikes, it was claimed, were carried out in defence of the territorial integrity of the Syrian Arab Republic and Iraq. However, inviting foreign forces to conduct military operations on a State's territory tends only to weaken the State. In light of recent history, intervention by the United States is an especially sensitive issue. Conflict could continue in one of the following three ways:

- An all-out ground invasion by external forces, the political and human ramifications of which could prove dire within and beyond the region;
- Continued air strikes that fail to dislodge the targeted non-State actors, further increasing their appeal to young recruits and their ability to wage a prolonged guerrilla war;
- Protracted and inconclusive air campaigns with sporadic ground clashes along shifting front lines with various States joining in or leaving according to their individual agendas. Such a situation would deepen devastation in the country, help to perpetuate sectarian strife, and deplete resources in the region, keeping it on a path to self-destruction and leaving it open to further foreign intervention.

A sudden collapse of the regime in Damascus, on the other hand, might be followed by a sectarian revenge campaign, with violence on a scale comparable to the 1994 Rwandan genocide. That could also lead to foreign invasion and, in reaction, heightened sectarian violence justified by resistance to the invader.

Israel stands to benefit most from any of the above scenarios, as a result of which its neighbours would be left weakened and its own military and strategic superiority in the region enhanced.

(ii) Vision scenario: end of the conflict and nation-building

The path to peace will require a broad, regionally negotiated solution. Ideally, an end to the war in the Syrian Arab Republic would be followed by reconstruction, the building of a democratic society in which human rights are upheld, the liberation of Syrian territories from Israeli occupation, and guarantees of the country's independence and territorial integrity.

Most of the country's neighbours, whether or not they support the Syrian Government, have a vested interest in ending hostilities. Turkey would not allow the fragmentation of the Syrian Arab Republic to result in the establishment of a de facto Kurdish State.[91] Iran also has an interest in ending the war, as it is fuelling sectarian strife in the Mashreq and threatening its position of influence in Iraq and, especially, Lebanon, from which it is able to retaliate for any moves by Israel against Tehran.[92] Cooperation between the two regional powers is thus conceivable, especially if Iran receives guarantees that a new Syrian State would not be hostile to it.

Although it does not face the same issues as Turkey or Iran, Saudi Arabia is concerned about the rise of radical non-State actors to its north, the war in Yemen to the south and the pressure on the country's alliance with the United States.

Iraq has lost control of part of its territory as a consequence of the Syrian war, and the national security in both Jordan and Lebanon is under threat. To be successful, a resolution of the Syrian war should:

- Preserve and maintain Syrian territorial integrity;
- End the fighting and protect civilians;
- Prevent partition and the displacement of citizens within the Syrian Arab Republic and into adjacent countries;
- Establish a just and democratic system of government that upholds human rights;
- Prevent foreign military invasion;
- End sectarian strife in Iraq and the Syrian Arab Republic and prevent its spread to Lebanon and the Arabian Peninsula.

Insistence on a final military victory by any of the warring parties or a foreign invasion would hamper the achievement of at least some of those goals. A temporary regional peacekeeping force, agreed upon and formed by neighbouring Arab countries, Iran and Turkey, should be deployed in coordination with all parties to the conflict.

The peacekeeping force would monitor multicandidate presidential elections, disarmament, border security and the release of political detainees. Regional and international powers supporting the peace process would be bound to accept election results, build good relations with the country and assist with reconstruction.

The regional force would need to protect the civilian population from possible revenge campaigns in areas previously held by any of the warring factions. It should therefore include members from countries with ties to the various

opposition groups, on the one hand, and the regime and its allies, on the other. Deployment should take into account local loyalties and affiliations: its components should be based in areas where the chances of hostilities between them and the local population are lowest.

3. The Arab uprisings and democratic transition

The 2011 Arab uprisings were the result of long suppressed political and economic tension. They offered a new model of political organization, whereby ideas and convictions replace centrally controlled structures in affecting people's political behaviour. An essential part of the political culture of a generation can be said to have been transformed by the uprisings. People saw how consensus among the unarmed on a common narrative can generate enough power in the streets to challenge the State through sheer numbers. In Egypt and Tunisia, people organized themselves without the guidance of an elected body. During their demonstrations, they established a form of independence from State institutions. Ideas were transmitted without any central communication structure, and accepted on the basis of their merits rather than for the identity or position of their source. Majority turned into consensus, and consensus into action. The sheer scale of the protest movements and the fact that they took place almost simultaneously was unprecedented in the Arab region.

Unlike in revolutions of the past, protestors did not attempt to occupy Government buildings; the formal State was a trap to be avoided rather than a prize to be won. The uprisings represented an attempt by Arab societies to conduct politics outside the existing State structures, bringing pressure to bear on the State from the streets and hampering its activities with demonstrations when it failed to respond to their demands. The streets, full of protesters standing up to armoured police vehicles, became the new seat of sovereignty. This was a temporary state of affairs, but its occurrence proved its feasibility, and that strengthened the political self-confidence of the people involved. In unprecedented numbers and with a hitherto unknown ability to communicate thanks to modern technology, ordinary people only needed that self-confidence in order to take a leap of faith into revolution. They could no longer be contained; if met with force, their numbers would overwhelm the police; if fragmented in a classic divide-and-rule scenario, the numbers of their armed fragments would still render the country ungovernable and the State obsolete.

Such popular movements are driven by demands and ideas rather than specific leaders. However, that absence of leadership becomes dangerous if consensus is lost and rival narratives and ideas fragment the multitude; factions can emerge with irreconcilable identities and ideas, giving regimes a new, albeit temporary, lease on life.

In some countries, the uprisings, while they did not end in violence, were stifled by a return to autocracy. However, in some cases, substantial steps were taken on the road towards democracy, the peaceful rotation of power and respect for human rights.

In Tunisia, the people ousted an authoritarian ruler and elected a constituent assembly and interim president. A new Constitution was adopted and presidential elections were held thereafter.[93] Reforms in Morocco also led to a new Constitution and more representative Government.

In Egypt, in 2011, people committed themselves to an unwritten social contract and common goals that guided their movements as if they were members of a mass organization. The people in the streets defeated the formal State in spite of its power. Although their achievements were later rolled back, Egypt still has the potential to present a new, revolutionary form of political organization. With relative demographic homogeneity, and a history with little internal strife and civil war in the past two centuries, building consensus on common narratives leading to mass mobilization remains possible. State coercion can be rendered powerless if faced by the overwhelming numbers of aggrieved citizens taking to the streets. Democracy in Egypt would benefit that country and the region as a whole, given the decisive role it can play in resolving the Arab-Israeli conflict, the Syrian civil war, and the crises in Libya and Yemen.

(a) Business as usual: tension and violence

The continued repression of demands for justice could place many Arab nation-States in jeopardy.

Equally, authoritarian Governments against which people once demonstrated could return to power with a vengeful agenda. Aware of the risk of new uprisings, they would probably adopt repressive measures in violation of human rights in order to cut them short, which in turn could unleash still more violent popular reactions. Rulers would not be defending a network of interests, but would rather be fighting for personal survival, making the struggle still more violent and costly.

Civil wars in some Arab countries have led to the proliferation of weapons throughout the region. Returning authoritarian Governments would face people filled with the same levels of self-confidence and dissatisfaction as in 2011, with the difference that many of them would now be armed. Moreover, the violence might not be contained within the borders of the countries concerned.

(b) Vision scenario: political renaissance

The lesson learned from the events of 2011 is that a return to oppression can end only in catastrophe. People are confident of their ability to rebel because they have already done so, and the availability of weapons can render oppression ineffective. Crackdowns in such circumstances would enrage rather than deter, with major political repercussions. To maintain peace and stability, it behoves Arab Governments to grant more political freedoms, establish democratic practices, respect human rights, dismantle and replace oppressive security institutions, and hold human rights violators accountable.

It is crucial that Governments adopt a foreign policy that protects national dignity, precluding cooperation with such forces of foreign domination or occupation as Israel. Peace treaties and strategic alliances with such forces should be submitted to referendums. Collaboration with foreign occupiers combined with oppression against domestic opposition is a recipe for disaster.

Democratization would allow the Arab uprisings to bear fruit. People with shared convictions are stronger and more effective than hierarchical, national bureaucracies. Under a new democratic model, in which public opinion wields the largest share of power, citizens would come to realize that building national coalitions through mutual compromise can render societies immune to external and internal divide-and-rule policies.

A social contract based on shared values and consensus-building would underpin the capacity of the people to influence the decisions of the State, and permit them to enjoy fully their political, civil, social and economic rights, whatever their differences. It would also free Arab countries from foreign interference and allow them to fight for more liberties at home and abroad. The building of democracy in each Arab country would contribute to greater regional independence. The inevitable restructuring of the colonially created State system in the region can thus take place non-violently, with the region moving towards integration and unity rather than sectarian and tribal fragmentation.

People who bring about a change in government and greater democracy in their own country can also demand change in other countries in the region where there is discrimination, as in the case of Israel, against certain citizens on the basis of their religion or ethnicity. Colonially supported despotism, foreign domination, occupation and apartheid-like regimes share the same fate in the region: if one falls, the others will probably follow. People who reached consensus on demanding their rights to freedom and independence while preserving cultural and spiritual diversity will be in a position to challenge occupation and hegemony without succumbing to sectarian divisiveness.

D. Conclusion

In this chapter, some key security and military challenges facing the Arab region, from external threats through to internal tensions and even civil conflict, have been examined. Various potential outcomes, positive and negative, have been considered. We have seen that the Arab-Israeli conflict could continue or escalate, or that circumstances could lead to a one-State solution. Unless the concept of a State whose citizenship is granted based on a certain religious affiliation is abandoned across the region, including in Israel, the region could slip into large-scale religious war. Civil wars could attract more foreign interference or be resolved by regional agreement. Internal political tensions can lead to violent revolution and civil war if regimes insist on stifling liberties, violating human rights and seeking the protection of foreign powers. In such struggles, conviction-based networks, be they masses of unarmed protesters or scattered groups of armed volunteers, are likely to overcome coercion-based hierarchies. The future of the political and social order in the region will depend on the outcome of such struggles.

The projections in the "business as usual" scenario of this chapter serve as a warning. The old order in the region is collapsing. If it remains unreformed, the collapse will be more violent, and it will give way to sectarian and tribal conflicts. If it is reformed, the region will go through relatively peaceful transformation. Since this report is partially directed to decision makers, the following chapters will provide policy recommendations to that end.

3. Governance

A. Introduction

In order to discuss governance challenges facing the Arab region, it might be useful to break the concept of governance down into core components, such as transparency, accountability, effective institutions, and the rule of law. Each can be addressed separately with policy reforms, on the understanding that they are interdependent.

Governance has four main pillars: structure, process, mechanism, and strategy.[94] As a structure, it refers to institutions. Process refers to the complex dynamics of policymaking. As a mechanism, it encompasses control and compliance procedures. Strategy stands for the decisions taken by stakeholders on how to design the remaining components.[95] State capacity is central to the concept.[96]

One month into the Arab uprisings in 2011, commentators already were referring to the failure of governance as one of the main triggers bringing students, workers, trade unionists, lawyers, and human rights activists on to the streets of Egypt and Tunisia.[97] The failure was linked to problems such as chronic unemployment, endemic poverty and income inequalities, rising food prices, insufficient public investment, violations of human rights, widespread corruption, and an oppressed civil society. Self-perpetuating authoritarian regimes, with flawed electoral systems and control by the elite, made it difficult to hold Governments accountable for achieving more inclusive, balanced development.[98]

Much has changed in the political, economic and social landscape since 2011, although not necessarily for the better. National dialogues on democratic governance such as in Bahrain, Egypt, Jordan and Tunisia are important. A combination of policy change and radical institutional reform is needed in order for the region to set off down a path of inclusive and sustainable development in response to the demands raised in the uprisings.[99]

This chapter outlines a vision for improved governance. It eschews traditional geographic or economic country groupings, and uses the country classifications according to conflict, level of development and fiscal space, as described in chapter 1, namely conflict-affected countries and LDCs, low- and medium-resilience countries, and higher resilience countries.

Each Arab country faces its own challenges but some, including human rights, democracy, constitutional and legislative matters, and security, are common to many.

If the right choices are made, governance in Arab countries in 2030 could look as follows:

New, more legitimate State institutions: With strong institutions, governance in countries throughout the region could rise from its current ranking, which is among the worst in the world, to come close to or even exceed the global average. Conflict-affected countries and LDCs, if they achieve peace and base reform of institutions on respect for the rights of all and the rule of law, could achieve close to average world institutional quality. Low- and medium-resilience countries will outperform averages on all measures of governance. Higher-resilience countries will make large strides in an area that today is especially problematic – voice and accountability.

Corruption in all Arab countries will be significantly reduced by 2030. First, measures will be taken to strengthen public and private institutions, and increase the stability, transparency and predictability of law enforcement. Secondly, formal justice frameworks will be strengthened, and anti-corruption principles based on national legislation, preferably constitutions, will be better enforced. Reliable and objective enforcement institutions will monitor implementation. Thirdly, inclusive policies will address economic determinants of corruption, such as unemployment and limited growth. Finally, strong and independent anti-corruption bodies will work to curtail high-level corruption and crony capitalism.

Development-friendly political systems: Arab countries will develop political systems with checks and balances and public accountability standards, which will help them to use all required resources for poverty reduction and development. They will use best practices and introduce tools such as the open budget initiative, and assure transparency.[100]

Participatory politics: Citizens will be able to participate in political processes, decision-making and peaceful demonstrations, and have the right to express their opinions freely and without fear. This will reinforce public accountability.

Human rights: Full respect for the Charter of the United Nations and the Universal Declaration of Human Rights will be enshrined in constitutions. Security apparatuses with records of repression and human rights violations must be replaced and officials responsible for such violations should be brought to justice.

This vision is ambitious but achievable. It requires urgent action to tackle legal, political and economic challenges. This chapter presents general policy recommendations for achieving good governance. They should be adopted at a national level, tailored to the different needs of each country. Sound governance is not an afterthought, but fundamental to inclusive, stable and sustainable development.

B. Governance challenges

This chapter examines the quality of governance in the Arab region and in specific countries, and addresses two main political challenges: systems and participation. It concludes by looking at issues of particular relevance to the region, such as human rights.

Governance indicator sets can differ from one another in terms of coverage or basic premises. Apart from the Arab Democracy Index, more regional governance indicators are needed. For the purposes of this report, we rely heavily on global indicators, such as the World Bank's Worldwide Governance Indicators (WGI) and Polity IV Project scores.

1. State institutions and overall quality of governance

Governance affects the economy, how a State functions and society at large, and is linked to differences in income and growth across countries.[101]

It is possible to gauge the quality of governance in the Arab region, relative and in comparison to the world, by looking at average values of 30 internationally comparable proxies of legal, political and economic institutional quality for the two decades after 1990,[102] and clustering countries accordingly. Clustering combines countries that are similar in terms of institutional characteristics and forms groups that are relatively homogenous within, and heterogeneous between each other. The majority of Arab countries for which data are available are placed in a medium-quality institutions cluster. They do well in some institutional variables and development indicators, and poorly in others. The countries grouped together on this basis are Bahrain, Jordan, Kuwait, Morocco, Oman, Qatar, Saudi Arabia, Tunisia and the United Arab Emirates. Although Jordan, Morocco and Tunisia are comparatively more participatory and have better governance than Gulf countries, they still have more governance similarities with other Arab countries listed than with any other grouping at the world level.

In comparison with all other countries in the world, this group of countries does relatively well in terms of the quality of courts and protection of property rights, but relatively poorly on freedom of the press and civil liberties. In terms of political institutions, they do relatively poorly on a measure of autocracy versus democracy, checks and balances, and democratic accountability, but relatively well on the perception of corruption in the public sector.[103] They also do reasonably well on the quality of economic institutions. Paired with a comparison of longevity, literacy rates and per capita GDP, those findings indicate that the countries in that group, although reasonably well off, do not provide all civil liberties equally to all citizens, and lack democratic accountability and free media.[104]

Under the WGI, arguably the best known of such indicators, governance is defined as the "set of traditions and institutions by which authority in a country is exercised. This includes (1) the process by which Governments are selected, monitored and replaced, (2) the capacity of the Government to effectively formulate and implement sound policies, and (3) the respect of citizens and the State for the institutions that govern economic and social interactions among them".[105]

The WGI proxies measure six dimensions of governance, whereby two indicators reflect each of the above three processes: voice and accountability, and political stability (for the first process); government effectiveness, and regularity quality (the second process); rule of law, and control of corruption (the third process).[106] To a certain degree, all of the indicators are interrelated.

Figure 3.1 displays a comparison of governance quality in the Arab countries with that of the rest of the world using the WGI. Scores, which range between -2.5 (poor) and +2.5 (excellent), suggest that Arab Governments have failed to promote good governance or governance for growth over the period covered (1996-2014). The region barely reaches the 33rd percentile of the world's overall ranking. It often falls below the global average of middle-income countries, and its ranking has deteriorated over time.

Individual indicators show that the ranking for voice and accountability has fallen in almost all Arab countries, with scores lower than in all other country groupings. Even high-income Arab countries score below the world's low middle-income countries. Interestingly, Arab

Resource-rich countries, in general, do well on regulatory quality, corruption, political stability, government effectiveness and the rule of law. Weak performance on voice and accountability may stem from a tendency to avoid reform and suppress debate on the use or distribution of returns from resources.

Between 1996 and 2014, the quality of voice and accountability in Arab countries in transition was more volatile than in other countries in the region, and dropped dramatically between 2000 and 2005. The variation was almost three times that of non-transition countries. Quality increased temporarily in Egypt in 2012 but dropped back to pre-2012 levels thereafter. After a rise in the same year in Libya, it also declined, albeit to a lesser extent. Voice and accountability has improved significantly since the 2011 uprising in Tunisia, and exceeded the world average in 2014.

Figure 3.1 Governance indicators in Arab countries and other country groupings, 1996-2014

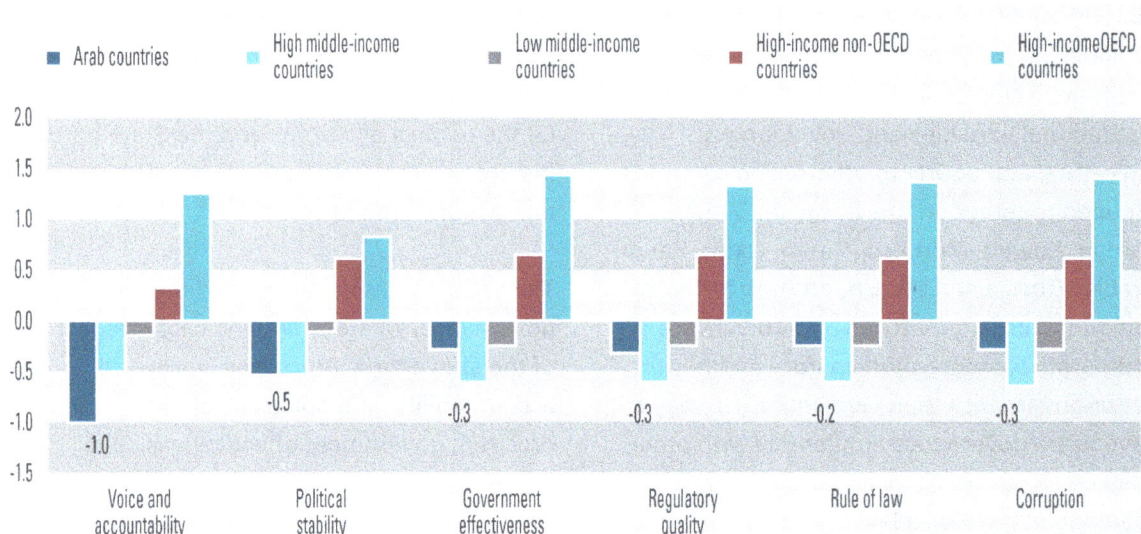

Source: Based on data from World Bank, 2015e.

In terms of political stability, Arab countries perform below the average of low middle-income countries, and far below that of high-middle income and high-income countries. In recent years, Bahrain, Egypt, Iraq, Lebanon, Libya, Palestine (under Israeli occupation), the Sudan, the Syrian Arab Republic, Tunisia and Yemen have all struggled with political instability, armed conflict, violent demonstrations, social unrest, and economic uncertainty. This has exacerbated the risk of national fragmentation, especially in Iraq, Libya, the Syrian Arab Republic and Yemen. By 2014, according to the indicator of political stability, those countries were performing, on average, at more than 50 per cent below their 1996 levels. Even the higher-resilience GCC countries suffer from greater instability than other high-income countries that are not members of the Organisation for Economic Co-operation and Development (OECD).

The region's score on government effectiveness is below the world average, although some countries, such as Qatar and the United Arab Emirates, have improved. Many have been below the fiftieth percentile of all countries over the past decade. Beyond the GCC countries, bureaucracies are ineffective and public financial management is weak. In transition countries, government effectiveness is below that of the region's non-transition countries and the world's successful transition countries. In countries where uprisings took place, government effectiveness has declined significantly, and the prospects for improvement are unclear.

The indicator on regulatory quality assesses measures to enhance private sector performance, and overall growth and development. Many Arab countries have undertaken reform in past decades, but most still suffer from low industrialization. State control of major production persists, along with capital controls, elite favouritism and a lack of competition.

Excluding Bahrain, Oman, Qatar, Tunisia, Saudi Arabia and the United Arab Emirates, ease of doing business in the Arab region ranks below that of Latin America. Arab countries performed better than Latin American countries on competitiveness, but lower than high-income countries. In trade liberalization, Arab countries performed below the average of middle- and high-income countries.

Across all Arab countries, regulatory quality has improved over time, but significant setbacks in transition countries have caused serious problems, especially with regard to regulating competition, investment (including foreign direct investment (FDI)), subsidies, environmental issues and trade.

Regulatory quality and government effectiveness are crucial to attempts by Governments to deal with high population growth, poverty and inequality. Rapid population growth combined with weak economic performance is considered a factor aggravating political instability in the Arab region, and underlines the need to deal with issues such as the youth bulge, rural flight to the cities and migration.[107]

Population growth and fertility rates are beginning to slow, but the failure to tackle demographic challenges continues to translate into low labour participation; limited empowerment of women; strains on the environment, resulting in food and water shortages; and infrastructure problems, including housing shortages and inadequate basic services.

Population trends vary greatly between countries and country groupings. Egypt and Tunisia have relatively stable population growth rates that will not change dramatically in the run-up to 2030, but low and - medium-resilience countries, particularly Jordan and Lebanon, will see a recognizable drop in population growth. Gulf countries, especially Oman and the United Arab Emirates, will also experience a sharp decline in population change rates by 2030.

Good governance is essential to reducing poverty and inequalities, including through accessible and high-quality public services. The positive impact of governance on poverty reduction is weak at present, for reasons ranging from ill-conceived subsidies that are meant to be pro-poor but benefit the wealthy, to a lack of trust in the ability of Governments to provide services without corruption.[108]

Public accountability is crucial, but little data is available for Arab countries. In 2015, the World Bank[109] analysed elements of public accountability in Jordan, Mauritania and Morocco. It found that all three have laws on financial disclosure. They also have laws on the restrictions of conflict of interest that, except in Morocco, are anchored in their constitutions and reiterated in codes of conduct for most public officials.[110] Freedom of information[111] is governed in Jordan and Morocco by specific legislation that allows public access to budgets, annual reports, legal instruments and

expenditure information. Finally, formal immunity provisions[112] to protect officials in performing their mandated duties appear to have no set duration, which can be problematic.

The indicator on the rule of law shows less variation than the others. Most Arab countries perform at a mediocre level higher than the average of all high middle-income countries. Some, such as Iraq, Libya, the Syrian Arab Republic and Yemen, perform poorly.

In Tunisia, the 2011 uprising led to a political transition and adoption of a new Constitution enshrining human rights in a process that was deemed participatory. Egypt also adopted a new Constitution that, for the first time in that country, refers to gender equality. However, article 204 allows for the trial of civilians by military courts. In both countries, doubts remain about the independence of the judiciary due to its close ties with the executive.[113]

Corruption persists through the practices of public officials, including embezzlement, non-transparent tax collection and bribery. Combating it is central to advancing economic and social justice, enhancing trust in political systems and actors, and thereby deepening political participation. Beside Kuwait, Oman, Qatar and the United Arab Emirates, Arab countries on average rank low with regard to the control of corruption. Based on the regional average between 1996 and 2014, the Arab region is far behind high-income countries.

Recent political turbulence has only worsened the situation, especially in conflict-affected countries and those in transition. In Iraq, corruption, mainly in national defence, nearly delegitimized the State and has been linked directly to recurrent political crises. In Lebanon, Libya and the Syrian Arab Republic, corruption is so widespread that it has become accepted practice in public and private transactions. In Yemen, it led to a dramatic reversal in the country's development prospects (box 3.1). Usually, such acceptance shifts people's focus towards guaranteeing individual interests and away from the problems of unethical and illegal behaviour, and from the collective good. The inclusion of anti-corruption principles in new constitutions in Egypt and Tunisia[114] could be a major step towards strengthening institutions and empowering the judiciary.

Quantitative analysis of the impact of corruption on the Arab region is limited. Results of the Corruption Perception Index[115] produced by Transparency International show that Middle Eastern and North African countries score on average 38/100, compared to a global average of 43/100. Qatar and the United Arab Emirates are seen as having the lowest public-sector corruption, which can be seen as a consequence of different perceptions of corruption (giving gifts, for instance, is not seen as corrupt) and of higher salaries and strict punishment for offences. The Arab countries with the worst scores are Iraq and the Sudan.

Box 3.1 Where would Yemen be if $60 billion had been invested in human development?

Yemen was one of the eight poor countries chosen by the Millennium Project for a pilot study to assess the investment and external assistance needed to attain the MDGs in 2004. The needs and implications of halving the rate of income poverty by 2015 were also the subject of a study led by the United Nations Development Programme (UNDP) in 2005. It was found that Yemen required $25-30 billion from 2005 to 2015 in order to achieve the MDGs, including the halving of poverty.

That investment boost would have led to greater public expenditure and created powerful second-round effects on the incomes of suppliers of goods and services to the Government. Those dynamic effects, combined with institutional and governance reforms, would have made achievement of the development goals possible and minimized the anticipated "absorptive capacity constraints" and macroeconomic imbalances. Effective implementation of such an ambitious development programme would have required a significant strengthening of institutional capacity. As much as an extra $10 billion might have been needed to build the State's capacity to oversee implementation.

So what actually happened after 2005? The international donor conference held in 2006 resulted in pledges of $5.7 billion, of which Yemen received little in actual aid. The per capita share of assistance and concessional loans remained far below what was required and only one third of the average received by LDCs. The Yemeni people were not only let down by the international community, but also by their own then president, Ali Abdallah Saleh. According to an expert panel commissioned by the Security Council, he amassed a fortune estimated at anywhere between $32 billion and $60 billion during his 33 years in power.*

Taking into account that the estimated costs were based on a lower average international oil price than actually witnessed between 2005 and 2015, the macroeconomic imbalances and the need for additional official development assistance would have been minimal had there been no corruption.

It is fair to conclude that, if those billions had been invested in the Yemeni people, their institutions and improving governance, the country's position and future prospects would have been dramatically different. It might, like neighbouring Oman, have become a development success story.

Sources: UNMP, 2005; Kakwani and others, 2005; and UNDP, 2010c.
*S/2015/125.

Figure 3.2 People's perceptions regarding corruption

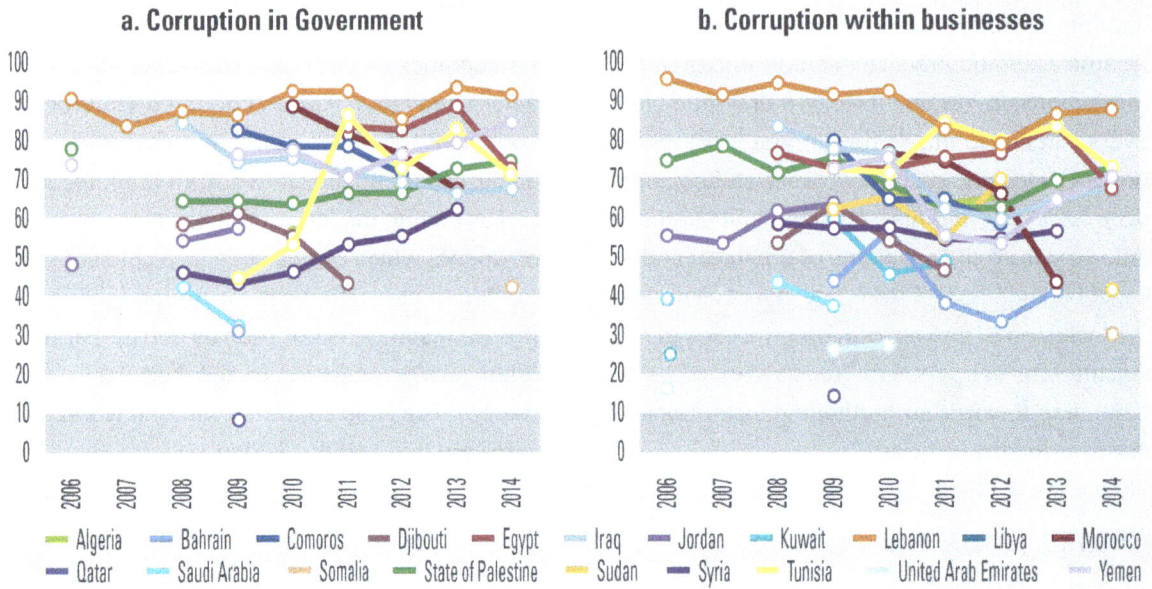

a. Corruption in Government

b. Corruption within businesses

Legend: Algeria, Bahrain, Comoros, Djibouti, Egypt, Iraq, Jordan, Kuwait, Lebanon, Libya, Morocco, Qatar, Saudi Arabia, Somalia, State of Palestine, Sudan, Syria, Tunisia, United Arab Emirates, Yemen

Source: Compiled by ESCWA, based on data from Gallup opinion polls. Available from www.gallup.com (accessed 30 November 2014).

Figure 3.3 Ease of doing business: Arab region

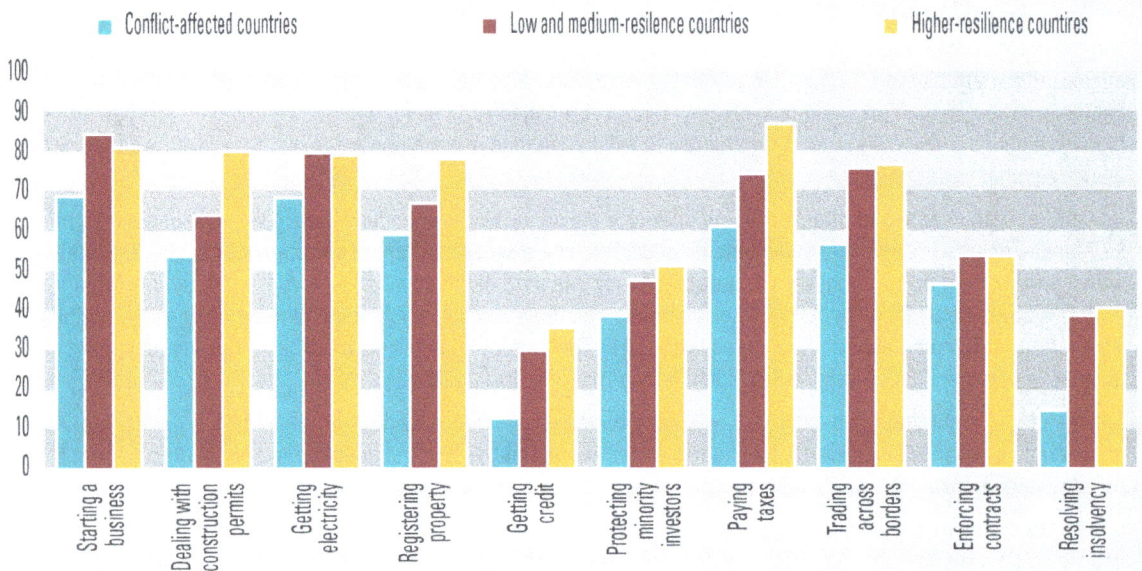

Legend: Conflict-affected countries; Low and medium-resilence countries; Higher-resilience countires

Categories: Starting a business, Dealing with construction permits, Getting electricity, Registering property, Getting credit, Protecting minority investors, Paying taxes, Trading across borders, Enforcing contracts, Resolving insolvency

Source: World Bank, n.d.a.

Overall, 84 per cent of the countries in the region score below 50, consistent with Gallup opinion polls showing relatively high perceptions of corruption in government and business (figure 3.2). The degree to which corruption in the Government is perceived to be a problem in the Syrian Arab Republic is growing, which may simply mean that respondents are expressing their views more feely now than in the past.

Transparency helps a great deal in the fight against corruption. Of countries in the Arab region, only Jordan, with 57, scores above 50 on a ranking scale from 0-100 in the Open Budget Index. Most score less than 15: Qatar scores 0, Saudi Arabia 1, Iraq 4, Tunisia 11, Egypt 13, Lebanon 33 and Morocco 37. It is the transparency and economic factors that affect the level of corruption first and foremost, in addition to non-economic determinants.[116]

Figure 3.4 Ease of doing business: regions of the world

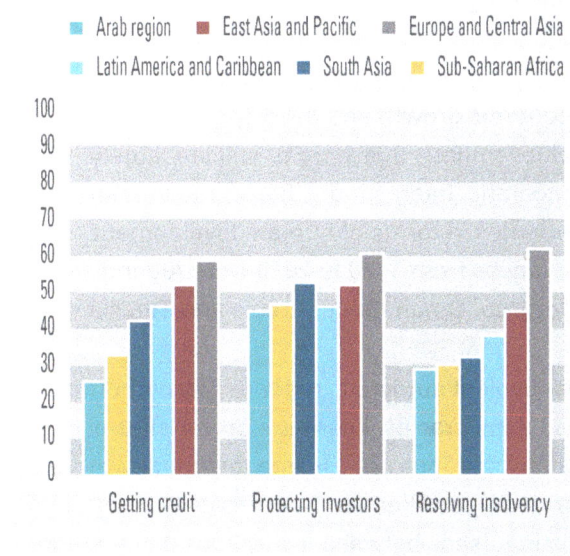

Source: World Bank, n.d.a.

Insight into the quality of governance in the Arab region, particularly in economic terms, can be found in the Ease of Doing Business (EDB) indicators. EDB ranks countries on private-sector governance and gives overall scores and rankings using frontier estimation on a range of data. For example, scores on the ease of starting a business are based on four criteria: the number of procedures required to register a firm, time required to register a firm, cost of registration (measured as a percentage of income per capita), and the minimum paid-in capital required (measured as a percentage of income per capita).[117]

In the Arab region, performance on EDB indicators matches up well with the country groupings as set forth in this report's methodology (figure 3.3). Conflict-affected Arab countries and LDCs score lowest in all categories, while low- and medium- resilience countries outperform higher-resilience countries only on two indicators. The Arab region performs particularly poorly in three categories: "getting credit", "protecting minority investors" and "resolving insolvency".

Ranked against other regions, the Arab countries score the lowest in all those categories (figure 3.4). In such circumstances, it is difficult to encourage private sector growth.

2. Political systems and development beyond rents and crony capitalism

Institutions and governance as a whole have many facets that do not need to develop at the same pace. In this section, we examine political institutions, especially of political systems and their relationship to development and social uprisings.

The Arab region has had and continues to have more than its share of autocratic Governments (table 3.1), and they have tended to be long-lasting.[118] The root causes are complex and include natural resource wealth, the Israeli occupation of Palestinian and other Arab territories, and poor policy choices.[119]

Poor governance contributes to the frequency and prevalence of conflict, whether caused by internal factors such as non-inclusive government or external interference.[120] Confessional systems in the region are also prone to conflict.

Each Arab political system allows for varying degrees of participation, and has system-specific barriers to participation (tables 3.1 and 3.2). Polity IV scoring of political systems on a democratic-versus-autocratic scale, where elections, competitiveness, the nature of political participation, and checks and balances are evaluated, is presented in table 3.1. In the first decade of the new millennium, the Gulf countries, Libya, the Syrian Arab Republic and Iraq all scored very low (although data are missing between the early 2000s and 2010). Some countries have, since 2010, made strides forward, which may be a result of pressure applied to Governments by popular uprisings. Nonetheless, half of the Arab States are still on the negative end of this scale today.

The causal relationship between the degree of democracy or autocracy and economic and social development is unclear.[121] Countries might be on different long-term trajectories determined by a range of variables, which, in turn, affect the mix of development and democracy the country gets.[122] Additionally, due to omitted variables in empirical work and feedback effects, it is unclear in which way the causality runs. In any given list of economic miracles and failures, almost all the economic tigers and economic disasters are autocracies. In general, democracies yield more predictable long-term growth rates, handle adverse shocks (such as terms-of-trade declines or sudden stops in capital inflows) on the economy better and produce greater stability in economic performance. Moreover, they result in higher wages, leading to more equitable societies and greater investment in human capital through health and education.[123]

Nevertheless, "the potential dividends from democracy are neither large nor automatic or easily obtained. The dividends from democracy seem to depend on the new political institutions taking place within a context of good governance, such as strong rule of law, or delivering better economic governance institutions".[124] There are clear examples of countries, such as China, with excellent economic growth and development achievements, that were or still are largely autocratic. Interestingly, five of the top ten countries in terms of human development advances from 1970 to 2010 were Algeria, Morocco, Oman, Saudi Arabia and Tunisia.[125]

Benevolent autocratic regimes can outperform bad democracies. Literature on varieties of capitalism does not assume that market or strategic coordination is intrinsically better, but distinguishes between institutions that support one or the other, and looks for combinations that produce the best results. "The key notion here is institutional complementarity: put simply, institutions across different areas must be consistent with one another in order to support economic development".[126]

Resource riches and social fractures are key factors to consider when looking at the impact of political systems on growth and economic development in the Arab region. The interplay between them contributes to whether a particular political system produces good economic and development results.

Collier and Hoeffler conclude that, in the absence of resource rents, democracies outperform autocracies.[127] However, they also find that the combination of high natural resource rents and democracy reduces growth in developing countries. This could be remedied by intensifying checks and balances, but they are largely absent in oil-rich Arab countries. Natural resource rents tend to encourage corruption where political institutions are poor and have a negative effect on contract enforcement, which, in turn, hinders financial development and ultimately results in lower growth.

Table 3.1 State of democracy

Higher-resilience countries			Conflict-affected countries			Low- and medium-resilience countries		
	2000-2010	2011-2013		2000-2010	2011-2013		2000-2010	2011-2013
Algeria	0.2	2.0	Comoros	5.8	9.0	Egypt	-4.4	-3.0
Bahrain	-7.1	-9.3	Djibouti	2.0	2.7	Jordan	-2.4	-3.0
Kuwait	-7.0	-7.0	Iraq	-6.0	3.0	Lebanon	6.0	6.0
Morocco	-6.0	-4.0	Libya	-7.0		Tunisia	-3.8	
Oman	-8.2	-8.0	Mauritania	-3.9	-2.0			
Qatar	-10.0	-10.0	Sudan	-4.9	-2.0			
Saudi Arabia	-10.0	-10.0	Syrian Arab Republic	-7.0	-8.3			
United Arab Emirates	-8.0	-8.0	Yemen	-2.0	1.3			

Source: Centre for Systemic Peace, n.d.

Note: The score is computed by subtracting the AUTOC score from the DEMOC score; the resulting unified polity scale ranges from +10 (strongly democratic) to -10 (strongly autocratic).

This so-called natural resource curse occurs only in countries with poor political institutions. There is no such problem, for instance, in the oil-producing economy of Norway, which uses the proceeds from natural resources to diversify the economy and save for future generations. Democracy alone is insufficient. Only inclusive societies with effective checks and balances are able to use resource riches to enhance growth.[128] Table 3.2 shows that Arab countries lacking in inclusiveness (political democracy) and with inadequate checks and balances are experiencing a form of resource curse.

The Arab region is one of the most homogenous in the world in terms of ethnicity and religion, but most countries individually are ethnically and religiously diverse. That, when State institutions are poor and the policies of those in Government are aimed primarily at consolidating their hold on power, can lead to social polarization. It gives rise to Governments that draw their support from one group or another and run the State on the basis of their religious, ethnic or other particular interests. The phenomenon has typically been accompanied by crony capitalism, where national wealth is appropriated by those in power, their families, friends and backers. Two examples are the former president of Yemen (see box 3.1), and the former president of Tunisia, Zine el-Abidine Ben Ali, under whose regime industrial policy was used to benefit the 220 firms allegedly owned by his family.[129]

Corruption takes many forms: land appropriation at below-market prices; barriers to entry in highly regulated markets; concessional borrowing from State banks; privileged access to subsidies; preferential treatment in public procurement; ad hoc bail-out guarantees; illicit funding of political campaigns; and a widespread practice of bending rules in favour of the elites. The situation has been fuelled by a poorly conducted process of liberalization over the past quarter of a century in a context of autocracy and weak State institutions.

The combination of autocratic government with fading legitimacy, favouritism and a lack of inclusiveness produced varying results when Governments were faced with the Arab uprisings.

Table 3.2 The two facets of a political system

Political system	High inclusiveness (political democracy)	Low inclusiveness (political democracy)
High commitment (checks and balances)	Use resource rents to diversify and grow (Australia, New Zealand)	May use rents to grow but political transition remains a challenge (China, Malaysia)
Low commitment (checks and balances)	May experience curse (Greece, Latin American countries)	Experience curse (populous, oil-producing Arab countries, resource-dependent sub-Saharan African countries)

Source: Adapted from Elbadawi and Soto, 2012.

The strategy employed by an incumbent trying to prevent revolt may depend on the extent of resource rents.[130] With high resource rents per capita, rulers tend to attempt to "buy their way out", investing in public goods, expanding public sector employment and extending social transfers to the people. That is what has happened in several Gulf countries in recent years.

Where resource rents are not high enough, political repression may ensue, which can lead to a spiral of violence between the Government and opposition. This is especially true when the ruler, who wants to prevent democratization in a fractured society, has strong links to or the backing of certain section(s) of society. The availability of resource rents hinders democratic transition at lower values of GDP per capita, but possibly not at higher levels or when the country is surrounded by other democracies. Conflict in the country or in neighbouring countries also hinders democratic transition. The immense problems facing the Arab region in terms of political systems and development are the result of a combination of lack of democracy, social fragmentation, resource riches, the domino effect of conflict and external influences.

3. Political participation

Most Arab countries have had some form of election in the past decade but the results have rarely increased trust in State institutions. Prior to the Arab uprisings, studies showed that citizens were motivated to participate in elections mainly because of the expectation of gaining access to State resources via *wasta* (connections) or benefits conferred by the elected candidates; there was little identification with policy issues.[131] In 2002, the first Arab Human Development Report spoke of an Arab "freedom and democracy deficit".

The Arab uprisings re-opened formal and informal avenues to engage in political activity. The political participation of women, as exemplified by the voting turnout and their presence as candidates in a wide range of electoral contests, was unprecedented. In Egypt, for example, women's participation as voters and candidates was higher than ever.

One study on electoral participation in Algeria, Jordan, Lebanon, Morocco, the State of Palestine and Yemen used public opinion surveys to investigate individuals' choices and contextual factors influencing electoral participation, given that elections in the region have been mostly designed to confirm or give token legitimization to authoritarian rulers. It found that the preferred means of political participation was voting: 65 per cent of the sample population chose only to vote, and not to protest or rally. However, 24 per cent of the population chose not to vote but to protest instead.[132] In addition, the protesting population appears less involved in multiple forms of political participation and to have a different logic of participation overall. The question remains as to what constitutes or triggers such a different logic: short-term incentive, degree of grievances, degree of ability to organize critical mass, or other factors.

Political participation also entails citizen involvement across economic, societal and political systems to shape policy and guarantee accountability for the implementation of commitments and the fair use of resources. Participation can, for instance, help to ensure that the benefits of improved economic and social policies reach all the population, including its most vulnerable and marginalized members.

Despite the transformative events of the Arab uprisings, questions remain as to how citizens can best function as agents of their own development. The region's history is characterized by an "authoritarian bargain", whereby citizens, especially the middle class, traded voice and participation for economic favours that turned out to be limited and short-lived. The pattern undercut democratic participation,[133] which over time resulted in frustration, especially among a younger generation intent on achieving economic development and a voice in governing their lives. Further complexity stems from deep-seated identity politics, which in many instances surpasses national identify, if it even exists.[134] The Polity IV scores for institutionalized democracy across the country groupings (tables 3.1 and 3.2) speak volumes about the prevalence of autocracy in Arab countries, leaving a lot to be desired in terms of inclusiveness of political systems.

A demand for a new social contract between the public and the State unleashed the Arab uprisings. People took to the streets to express their discontent with notions such as the administrator as ruler versus the people as subject, or the administrator as expert versus the people as client.[135] They took personal risks to demand more interactive, participatory relationships, in which administrators are held accountable for acting on public priorities.

There was, however, a gap between the high expectations for democratic governance and political reality on the ground, especially in Egypt, Libya, Morocco and Tunisia, as measured at different time points in the period 2010-2014.[136] Initial excitement and momentum, especially in Egypt and Libya, might have given way to a realization that change can take time, during which all stakeholders need to learn new ways of thinking and acting. That is even more the case in hierarchical or authoritarian societies, in countries without pre-existing social, civic and institutional frameworks to support political participation, and/or in countries in which the relationship between authorities and the people is dominated by fear and distrust.

The Arab uprisings showed that the middle class can play a significant role in triggering social and political transformation, but cannot achieve it alone.[137] They also demonstrated the key role played by women in bringing about change, regardless of their class or educational background.

As the "protest demographic" made clear, the middle class is not homogenous. Lip service is paid to the role of democracy but, when asked in surveys to rank concepts in order of importance, people who see themselves as middle class still value stability and low inflation twice as much as participating in decision-making processes and protecting freedom of speech. They also increasingly express a preference for a strong leader.[138] Such are the choices that will determine the future of Arab democracy.

Political activity is often seen as linked to education, income and better occupations.[139] One might assume that having these would spur more people to engage in political activity, but in the Arab region such a development has been hampered by the "authoritarian bargain". Voice and accountability, therefore, do not improve with income (figure 3.5).[140] Over time, especially in GCC countries, the relationship between income and voice and accountability has even been negative (figure 3.6). Beyond the undemocratic nature of Governments, that can be explained by factors such as the deficit in civic skills, which are not encouraged through education or social norms.

Members of the middle class with higher education[141] and steady jobs may have less time for political activity. There may also be generational[142] and gender dimensions at play. Arab youth are better educated than decades ago, but their unemployment rate (25 per cent for men and 48 per cent for women)[143] is high, leaving time for political activity. Frustration with non-inclusive political institutions grows with increased education and lack of employment. The skills learned in school and university may not meet the needs of the Arab labour market, but they may correspond to "civic skills" that encourage political activity.[144]

The Arab uprisings "blurred the lines between formal and informal political spheres", but the post-revolutionary Arab region is undergoing a transition process that may not necessarily lead to democratic consolidation.[145] Political participation depends on the existence of functioning political institutions that enable/provide a direct and observable relationship with the process of national policymaking and access to decision makers.

Specific barriers also block political participation by women: the prevalent patriarchal relations that define the social roles of men and women; institutional barriers such as lack of funding for elections; and the view among some that political activity by women is a foreign agenda imposed on Arabs.[146]

The lack of broad-based political participation or inclusive leadership in the region, the "authoritarian bargain", and the able use by some Arab leaders of the West's focus on preventing terrorism, energy dependence and the Palestine stalemate to deflect pressure for reform, have led to the "striking underperformance of most Arab Governments in political, economic and social terms".[147] In 2009, the Arab Knowledge Report stated:

"Stringent legislative and institutional restrictions in numerous Arab countries prevent the expansion of the public sphere and the consolidation of opportunities for the political participation of the citizenry in choosing their representatives ... on a sound democratic basis. The restrictions imposed on public freedoms, alongside a rise in levels of poverty and poor income distribution, in some Arab countries, have led to an increase in marginalization of the poor and further distanced them from obtaining their basic rights to housing, education and employment, contributing to the further decline of social freedoms."[148]

Figure 3.5 Links between voice and accountability on a world and regional scale

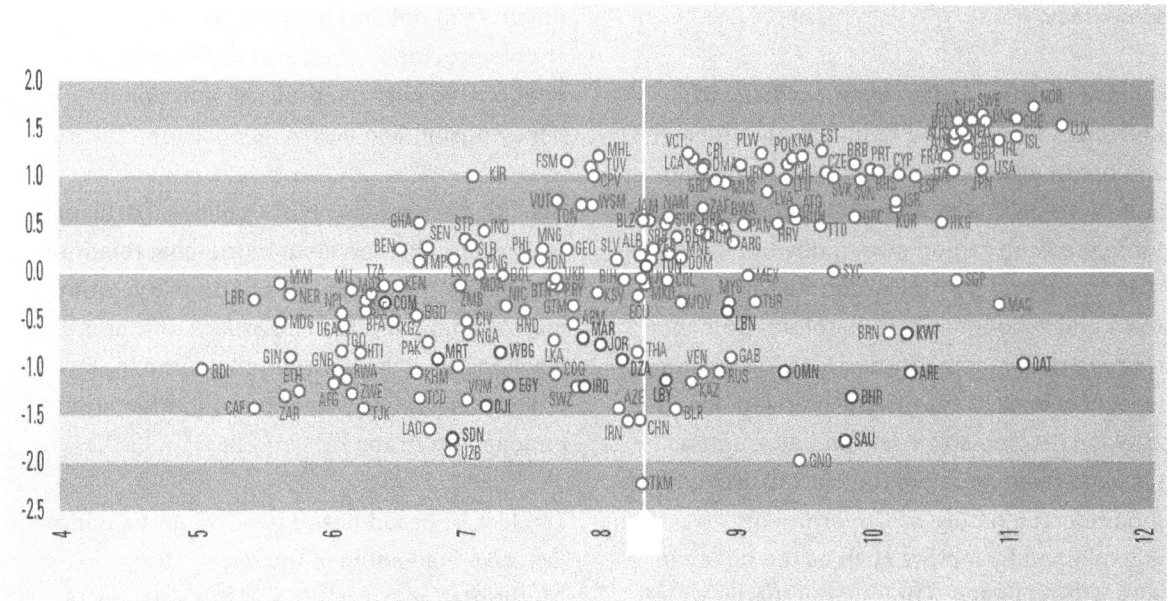

Source: Authors' calculations based on Kaufman, Kraay and Mastruzzi, 2014.
Note: Vertical and horizontal lines represent sample averages. Countries are designated by their ISO codes.

Figure 3.6 Rising income but declining voice and accountability

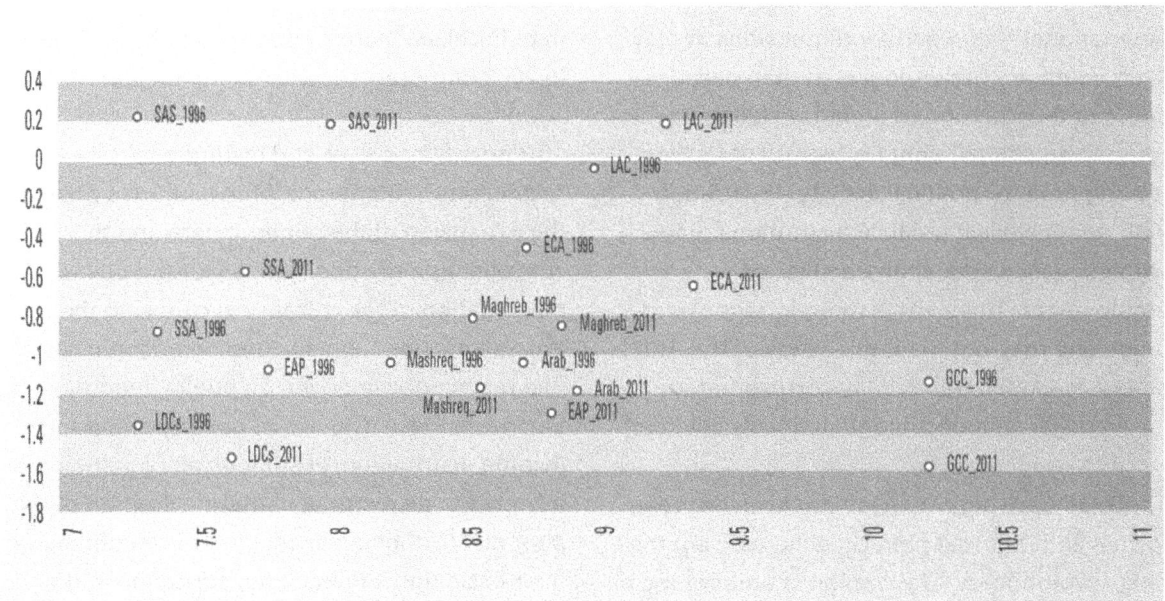

Abbreviations: EAP: East Asia and the Pacific; ECA: Europe and Central Asia; GCC: Gulf Cooperation Council; LAC: Latin America and the Caribbean; SAS: South Asia; SSA: sub-Saharan Africa.
Source: World Bank, 2015d.

4. Human rights abuses

The notion of a trade-off between stability and human rights is common in many countries. The authors of this report maintain that human rights may not be subject to any such compromise. Human rights abuses have been a terrible constant in many Arab countries and have become more rampant still amid the recent turbulence in the region.

One of the most persistent examples of violation of international humanitarian law and human rights remains the many actions taken by the State of Israel in the Occupied Palestinian Territory, as pointed out in United Nations Economic and Social Council resolution 2013/8 on the subject. Israeli occupation has been accompanied by institutionalized discrimination through a range of laws, policies and military orders. The Palestinian people are subjected to the often arbitrary nature and application of laws, curtailing their human rights and the economy of Palestine: decades of potential human development progress have been lost, exacerbating the problems of poverty and undernourishment. Illegal Israeli settlements and infrastructure built on Palestinian lands for the exclusive use of Israelis and Israeli settlers constitute a flagrant form of discrimination based on religion or ethnic origin.[149] There have also been systematic abuses of human rights of children in Israeli detention, where children are "subject to physical and verbal violence, humiliation, painful restraints, hooding of the head and face in a sack, threatened with death, physical violence, and sexual assault against themselves or members of their family, restricted access to toilet, food and water", and more.[150]

It is possible to assess human rights abuses in the region quantitatively. The Political Terror Scale (PTS) project combines the tallies of human rights infringements reported by Amnesty International, the United States State Department and Human Rights Watch.[151] Another source is the Cingranelli-Richards (CIRI) Human Rights Database. They look at torture, extrajudicial killing, political imprisonment, disappearance (Physical Integrity Rights Index), as well as the possibility of foreign and domestic movement, freedom of speech, freedom of assembly and association, workers' rights, electoral self-determination, and freedom of religion indicators (Empowerment Rights Index). They also examine women's economic and political rights.[152] For all indicators, the averages of 2010 up until the most recent year are taken.

All the countries are ranked on their calculated scores. On the Political Terror Scale, we find 6 Arab countries amongst the worst 20: the Sudan, the Syrian Arab Republic, Somalia, Iraq, Libya and Yemen, with the first two ranking in the worst five countries overall. All in all, 16 Arab countries are ranked in the worst half of all countries (180 with available data). The record on women's rights is worse, with 8 countries among the worst 20. Of all the countries with data (173), 15 are in the worst half.

Disregard for human rights is perhaps most blatant in the Syrian Arab Republic, where men, women, children, detainees, the sick and wounded, medical and humanitarian workers, journalists, human rights defenders, and internally displaced persons are all abused. State and non-State actors treat civilians, particularly those from other religious and ethnic groups, with brutality, and "victims of torture and other cruel, inhuman or degrading treatment languish in official and makeshift detention facilities".[153]

In Libya, rebels and forces loyal to the former leader Muammar Qaddafi committed violations of human rights and crimes against humanity. The International Commission of Inquiry, established by the Human Rights Council in February 2011, cites murder, torture, enforced disappearances and acts of sexual violence as part of a widespread or systematic attack against the civilian population by government forces. Anti-government fighters carried out extrajudicial executions, torture, enforced disappearance and indiscriminate attacks against civilian population.[154]

In Yemen, fighting has taken a heavy toll of the civilian population and led to breaches of humanitarian law. Human rights violations were occurring even before the conflict erupted, and included alleged executions or threats of execution of minors, and violence against women and people of different religious groups.[155]

In the Gulf, there has been persistent mistreatment of migrant workers, who "experience decent work deficits and face abuse and exploitation, including in situations akin to forced labour".[156] Similar problems are prevalent in other States using the kafala (sponsorship) system. In Lebanon, a survey found that more than one third of women migrant domestic workers had been physically, sexually or verbally abused.[157]

In several Arab countries, protests met with a violent response from State security forces. National and regional human rights bodies, such as the Arabic Network for Human Rights Information and the Office of the High Commissioner for Human Rights, have tracked a litany of human rights violations in the vast majority of Arab countries.

In its latest annual report, Human Rights Watch[158] globally reviews human rights issues at the country level and emphasizes the main governance challenge:

"The once-heralded Arab Spring has given way almost everywhere to conflict and repression. Islamist extremists commit mass atrocities and threaten civilians throughout the Middle East and parts of Asia and Africa. [...] Many Governments have responded to the turmoil by downplaying or abandoning human rights. Governments directly affected by the ferment are often eager for an excuse to suppress popular pressure for democratic change. Other influential Governments are frequently more comfortable falling back on familiar relationships with autocrats than contending with the uncertainty of popular rule. That subordination of human rights is not only wrong, but also short-sighted and counterproductive. Human rights violations played a major role in spawning or aggravating most of today's crises. Protecting human rights and enabling people to have a say in how their Governments address the crises will be key to their resolution. Particularly in periods of challenges and difficult choices, human rights are an essential compass for political action."

Ideally, commitments to human rights are anchored in national constitutions, although de facto protection of human rights can work even without strong legal provisions, albeit mostly in democratic systems with an independent judiciary. Few countries in the region have gone far with either approach, and policymakers appear unable to translate core human rights values into action.

In a region where traditional, discriminatory views still predominate, abuses of women's rights are a particular cause for concern. Progress in countries such as the Comoros and Oman is overshadowed by the poor state of women's rights in Iraq and Saudi Arabia.[159] Although most Arab States are parties to the Convention on the Elimination of All Forms of Discrimination against Women, many maintain reservations to it.[160] Gender-based violence remains a problem, and the "the status of women and girls in the region continues to be challenged by traditional discriminatory attitudes and harmful practices".[161]

Many constitutions in the region, such as that of the Syrian Arab Republic, contain provisions on human rights and equality, but they are frequently ignored or violated in practice.

C. Roads to 2030

The report uses the WGI to project two possible paths to 2030 – a business-as-usual scenario and a vision scenario. A variant of benchmark country comparison and forecasting is used, where the Arab countries are compared to benchmark countries that either failed to improve their WGI between 1996 and 2013 or improved them considerably. In the business-as-usual scenario, each Arab country was compared with benchmark countries with deteriorating governance, and in the vision scenario, with improving governance. The average slope of deterioration or improvement of the benchmark countries was used to project the expected degree of deterioration and improvement for Arab countries between 2015 and 2030. The benchmark countries were selected based on income per capita and oil riches.

There are caveats to any benchmarking exercise, such as: (a) is the governance quality measured the same in all countries; (b) does it correlate well with income per capita; (c) is what constituted good governance in the past valid for the future; and (d) how do external factors affect progress on governance?

Governance indicators also rely on different, mainly subjective, data sources, so the evaluation of governance in different countries is dependent on their culture. Nevertheless, that does not influence the dynamics we are interested in extrapolating. Although, in the past, the Arab region constituted an exception to the general rule that suggests that the quality of governance is correlated with per capita income (figures 3.5 and 3.6), that does not preclude benchmarking the countries on the basis of income per capita as well, as a proxy for a variety of economic and developmental variables. All WGI comparisons and matching exercises are relative. Exogenous factors are not taken into account, as there is no meaningful way to determine such shocks in the future. Forecasts for all six governance indicators are examined below.

Beyond Kuwait, Oman, Qatar and the United Arab Emirates, control of corruption in the region is poor. In individual countries, corruption is expected to progress to -0.2 under the vision scenario, or deteriorate to -1.15 under the business-as-usual scenario by 2030, depending on the rigour of reform. Figure 3.7a depicts the projections. Starting at a level of -0.6 in 2013, countries would need to increase institutional control and overall accountability, and break the tight ties between businesses and people in power to attain the -0.2 level. If they persist with business as usual, corruption will reach even more depressing levels.

Figure 3.7b splits the region into different country categories. In the conflict-affected countries and LDCs (the Comoros, Djibouti, Iraq, Libya, Mauritania, Palestine, Somalia, the Sudan, the Syrian Arab Republic and Yemen), the failure to undertake serious efforts to combat corruption will have devastating consequences. Under business as usual, on average, conflict-affected countries might deteriorate to a level of -1.7 by 2030. Such high levels of corruption are currently experienced only in sub-Saharan African countries with extremely low levels of development, high poverty, low education, civil conflict, and low overall growth. Similar concerns can be envisaged in low- and medium-resilience countries, such as Egypt, Jordan, Lebanon and Tunisia. Based on projections, it is possible for such countries to perform relatively better, and reach 0.03 in 2030. But if no structural reforms take place, corruption will intensify, pushing their score down to -0.8 by 2030. Projections for higher-resilience countries show that, by 2030, they can advance in fighting corruption,

reaching an estimated score of 0.3. Corruption could worsen if no structural public sector reforms take place.

The effectiveness of government in the Arab region could reach acceptable levels by 2030, performing at almost -0.3, if countries improved institutions, public administration, infrastructure and public financial management. Without concerted efforts, the situation could deteriorate drastically (figure 3.8a).

There is little room for effective public policy in conflict-affected countries, such as Iraq, Libya, the Syrian Arab Republic and Yemen, and the emphasis in countries such as the Comoros, Djibouti, Mauritania, Palestine and the Sudan is on humanitarian issues. Even in the best of scenarios, such countries might score only -0.9 for effective government by 2030 (figure 3.8b). If the political situation continues to worsen, quality will plummet as low as -1.5. If low- and medium-resilience countries slip into conflict in the coming years, they could find themselves on a par with countries affected by conflict today. Higher-resilience countries that improve institutions and administration could reach a level of 0.3. States such as Saudi Arabia and the United Arab Emirates have recently taken measures such as e-government programmes to streamline bureaucracy. Additional work is required to avoid the risks of deterioration presented in figure 3.8, however.

Political instability affects the entire region. If the situation continues on its present path, the results could be catastrophic (figure 3.9). There is little sign of a potential positive turn in events

Figure 3.7 Corruption

a. Gap analysis

Business as usual — Vision 2030

b. Average for each group

■ Vision 2030   ■ Deterioration in the business-as-usual scenario

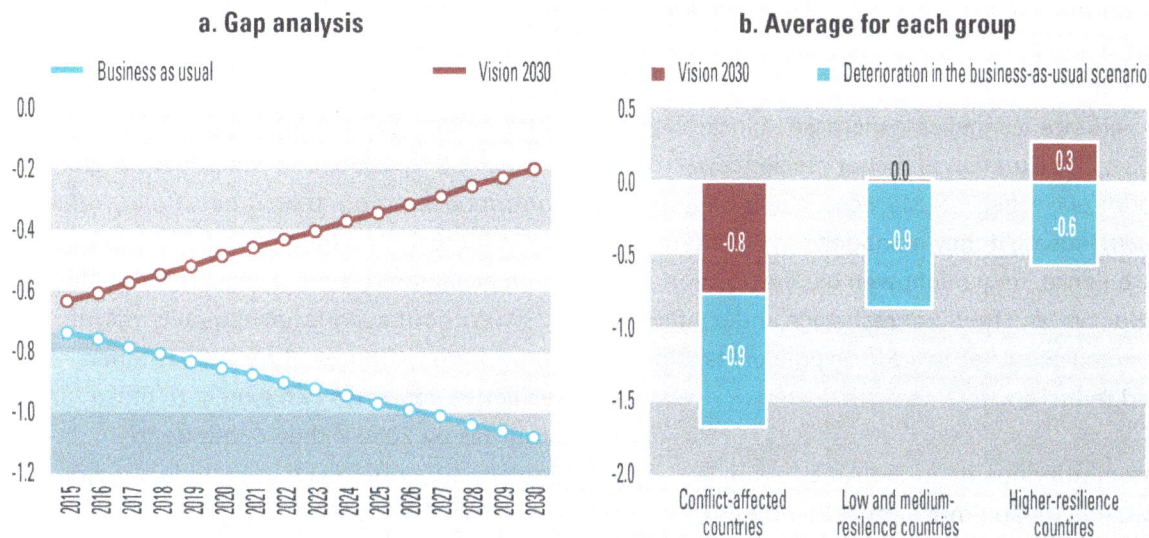

- Conflict-affected countries: -0.8 / -0.9
- Low and medium-resilence countries: 0.0 / -0.9
- Higher-resilience countires: 0.3 / -0.6

Source: Authors' calculations.

Figure 3.8 Government effectiveness

a. Gap analysis

Business as usual — Vision 2030

b. Average for each group

■ Vision 2030   ■ Deterioration in the business-as-usual scenario

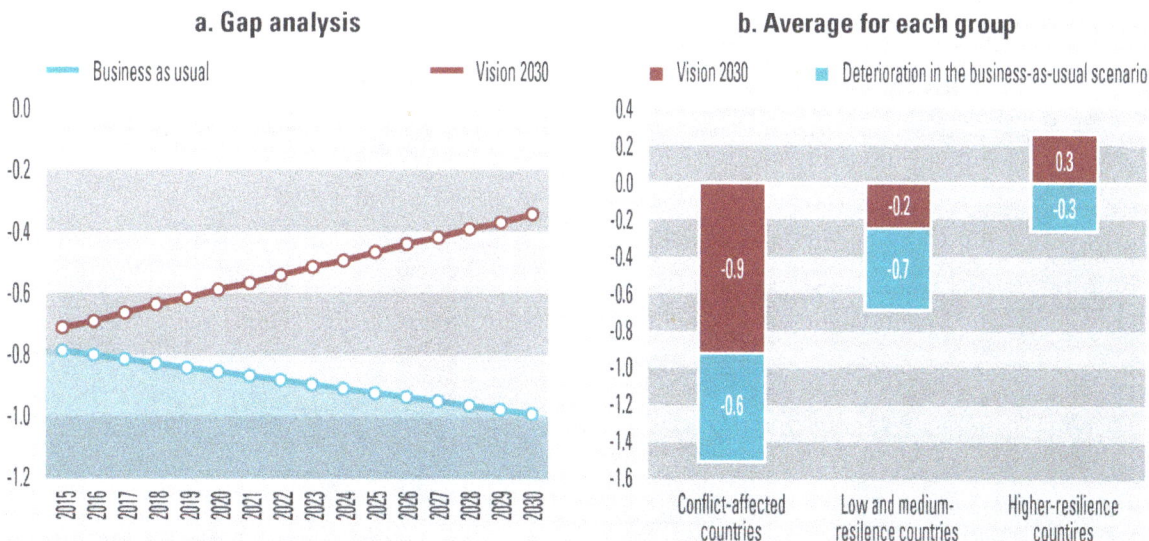

- Conflict-affected countries: -0.9 / -0.6
- Low and medium-resilence countries: -0.2 / -0.7
- Higher-resilience countires: 0.3 / -0.3

Source: Authors' calculations.

in the near future. Low- and medium-resilience countries, such as Jordan and Lebanon, are under constant threat of contagion from conflicts along their borders, and could experience a significant increase in instability by 2030. The situation in higher-resilience countries, especially Morocco, could improve by 2030. Indeed, if they manage to avoid internal turbulence, they might well be in a position to help low- and medium-resilience and conflict-affected countries to address political tension and terrorism.

Regulatory quality in the Arab region is inadequate and much must be done to promote competition, industrialization and financial sector flexibility, ease the conditions for doing business, set effective tax rates, and improve environmental sustainability. Failure

to act could result in a score as low as -1.19 by 2030 (figure 3.10). In the best-case scenario, conflict-affected countries will reach only the 2013 regional average. Alarmingly, if present patterns persist, regulatory quality will drop as low as -1.6 by 2030, and the private sector will contract even more than it has. Policy reform could lift low- and medium-resilience countries to an acceptable level of regulatory quality by 2030. Without such reform, quality might deteriorate to almost -1 by 2030. Higher-resilience countries can expect to make further progress by 2030 if they continue to implement strategies that include a major overhaul of institutions. However, if that does not happen, they could, in the business-as-usual scenario, end at a level of around -0.6 and close to low- and medium-resilience countries.

Figure 3.9 Political instability

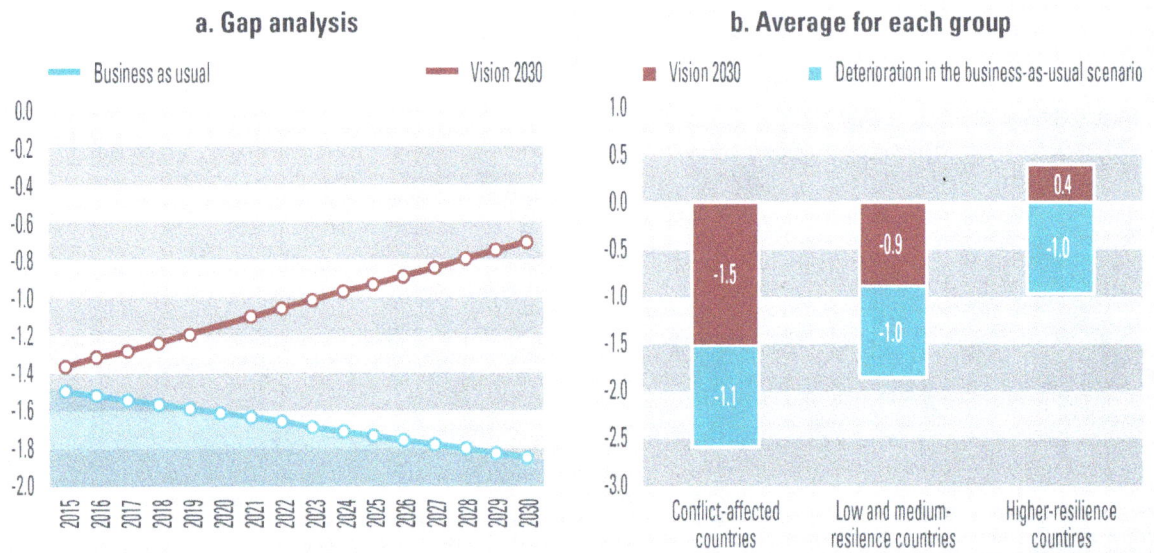

a. Gap analysis

b. Average for each group

Source: Authors' calculations.

Figure 3.10 Regulatory quality

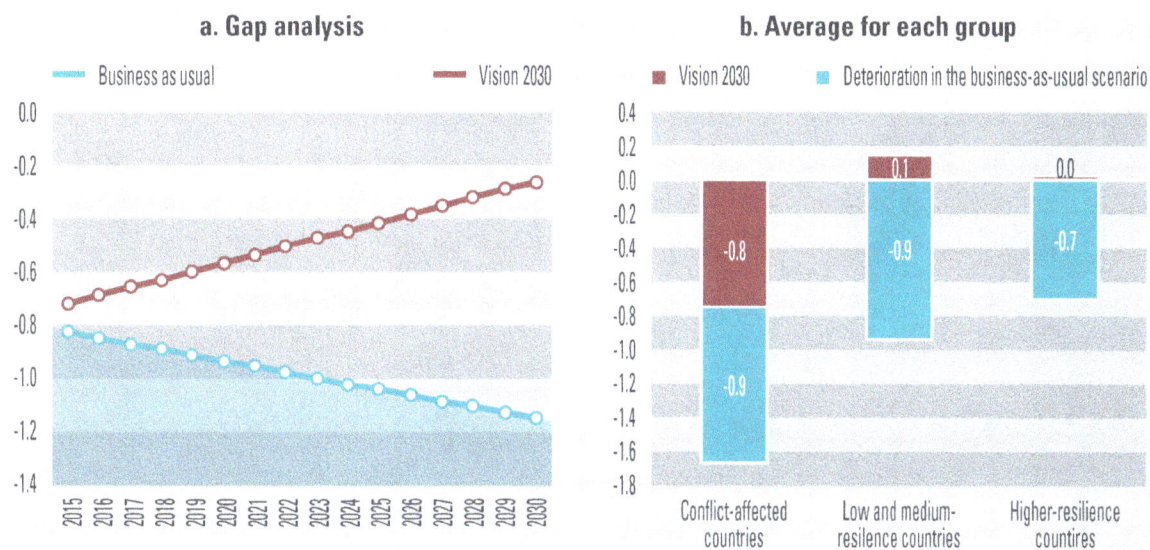

a. Gap analysis

Business as usual — Vision 2030

b. Average for each group

Vision 2030 — Deterioration in the business-as-usual scenario

Conflict-affected countries: -0.9, -0.8
Low and medium-resilience countries: -0.9, 0.1
Higher-resilience countires: -0.7, 0.0

Source: Authors' calculations.

The indicator for rule of law starts off at a low level of -0.72 in 2013 (figure 3.11a). The region could reach 0.05 by 2030, but only if countries strengthen and improve the quality and responsiveness of law enforcement institutions. Conflict-affected countries need to rebuild the judiciary and other law and order institutions, possibly through extensive national dialogue. To reach a level of around -0.5 by 2030, they would need to do much better than they are doing now (figure 3.11b). Failure in that regard could encourage the rise of competing factional powers, with each jurisdiction ruled by a tribal, religious or militia government.

Low- and medium-resilience countries could even overtake higher-resilience countries and reach a level of 0.5 in 2030. To do so, they require more reforms to reduce political interference in the judicial system and improve access to justice. They should also strengthen law enforcement, contract execution and property rights in order to avoid a potentially major deterioration under the business-as-usual scenario. Higher-resilience countries have excellent potential to progress by 2030, given the current quality of rule of law. Further reform could propel them to a score of 0.42, but inaction could induce a decline to -0.5 by 2030.

The region can hope to catch up with the rest of the world in terms of voice and accountability only through concerted efforts to strengthen democracy, freedom of speech, free media, checks and balances, and political participation. With the right reforms, the region might advance to -0.6 by 2030 (figure 3.12a). Failure to act would be harmful, especially at a time of growing militarization. Unfortunately, political turbulence encourages people to assume that stability should take precedence over progress towards democracy. The region might drop to -1.7 in 2030 without democratic reform.

58

Figure 3.11 Rule of law

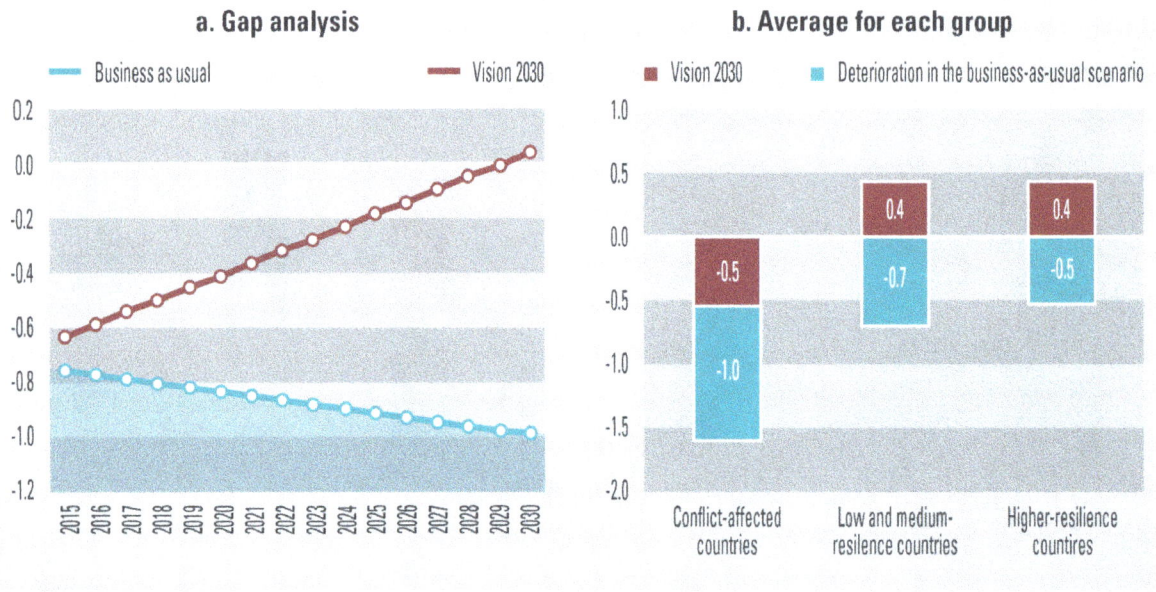

a. Gap analysis

Business as usual   Vision 2030

b. Average for each group

Vision 2030   Deterioration in the business-as-usual scenario

Source: Authors' calculations.

Figure 3.12 Voice and accountability

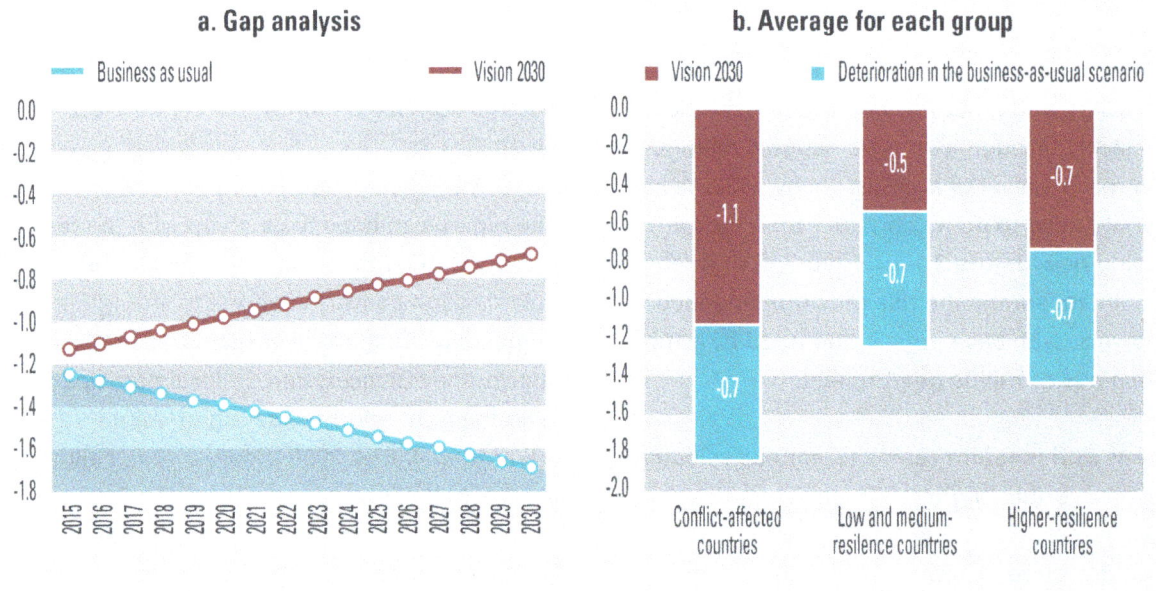

a. Gap analysis

Business as usual   Vision 2030

b. Average for each group

Vision 2030   Deterioration in the business-as-usual scenario

Source: Authors' calculations.

Among conflict-affected countries and LDCs, the status quo will lead to a level as low as -1.81 by 2030 (figure 3.12b). Efforts to move towards democracy, daunting as they may appear, would help such countries to advance to -1.1. Low- and medium-resilience countries could reach -0.5 by 2030 with additional initiatives to enhance democratic institutions and checks and balances. Without these, they could be dragged down to -1.3. Higher-resilience countries, especially GCC countries, could reach -0.7 if they pursued reforms linked to transparency, accountability and political participation. Remaining on their current path, however, would take them to a score as low as -1.5.

D. Policy recommendations

The policy recommendations set forth hereunder are rooted in the Charter of the United Nations and the Universal Declaration of Human Rights.

Governance is part of the 2030 Sustainable Development Agenda (Goal 16) and also figures in the discussion of Arab States playing leading roles in setting the 2030 Agenda.

Tracking progress in Arab countries, especially those in transition, on democratic governance is also important. Specific issues to be monitored include the following: constitutional reform; effectiveness of institutions; status of women; human rights; political transformation; instability and conflict; economic management; and public service provision.[162]

The political, economic, social, and environmental considerations in individual countries are more complex than the three broad country categories set forth in this report might suggest.

Achieving high and sustainable growth and inclusive development will be challenging, especially for those Arab countries that are not rich in natural resources. Only 13 countries have achieved growth rates of 7 per cent or higher annually for over 25 years, namely Botswana, Brazil, China (including Hong Kong), Indonesia, Japan, the Republic of Korea, Malaysia, Malta, Oman, Singapore, Taiwan and Thailand. Their success cannot be attributed to any one set of policies, but they have had capable administrations committed to growth and economic inclusion, not as an end in itself, but as a means of managing the benefits of development and distributing them throughout society.[163]

Almost half of those countries set up 'reform teams' of technocrats who reported directly to top national decision makers. They have been mainly responsible for developing inclusive development strategies, formulating and harmonizing policies across different sectors, liaising with donors, coordinating with the private sector, ensuring the effective implementation of policies, and formulating a vision for the future. Countries with sustained high growth rates have made serious efforts to combat corruption.

There can be no one-size-fits-all recommendation but the 'reform teams' approach provides one option where there is sufficient political will. All governance reform plans need to include elements from each of the four dimensions: good quality governance across the board; political systems conducive to development; participatory political systems; and human rights.

Conflict-affected countries and LDCs have the worst indicators, under the business-as-usual or vision scenarios. They need to work on basic improvements, first in terms of security and stability (political stability is the dimension of governance on which they have the lowest scores), and then address legal, political and economic institutions. Low- and medium-resilience countries could advance considerably on all indicators except political instability by 2030. Higher-resilience countries start with average or above average values for all indicators but voice and accountability, and could improve on all of them. They are likely to remain below average on voice and accountability unless they make significant reforms, such as to end exclusion and protect free speech.

1. Strong State institutions leading to good governance

Higher-resilience and low- and medium-resilience countries need to move towards a competitive political environment and implement public accountability reforms and anti-corruption initiatives as part of poverty reduction strategies. Such reforms could include regulation of financial disclosure, conflict of interest, freedom of information and formal immunity provisions. Other reforms could: improve the running of State-owned enterprises; reform public administration; stimulate formal labour markets to provide more employment, especially for youth and women; foster entrepreneurship and a business climate with reliable rules; and mitigate the

impact of economic migration on education, health systems and housing.

Conflict-affected countries should, after bringing conflicts to an end, replicate, in the medium term, measures taken by the other two groups in the short term. In the short term, they should also help displaced populations, rebuild education and health systems, provide housing, and focus urban agendas on the provision of shelter, water and sanitation, and social infrastructure.

Over the medium to long term, all countries should launch inclusive growth strategies based on broad consultative processes, rather than relying on the advice of small groups of experts. Management of public finances must be reformed, and the gaps revealed by public expenditure and financial accountability assessments addressed.

Open budget processes that are consistent and transparent are less susceptible to petty theft, patronage in funding allocation and general misuse of public assets, and are more responsive to demands from citizens. Budget formulation remains fragmented in many Arab countries. The split in competencies between ministries of planning and ministries of finance, for example, may be justifiable in order to protect development expenditure, but it could hamper a comprehensive overview of public finances.

An open budget process should entail ensuring full integration of recurrent and capital budgets; introducing a medium-term perspective to inform annual budget planning; and presenting a comprehensive and clear budget that is closely linked to policy, for instance by means of a budget strategy paper at the outset of the budget calendar.

Statistical offices and analytical capacity need to be expanded to provide more in-depth economic analysis. A number of missing core indicators, particularly those concerning conditions of work and informal employment, should be assembled. Data on company, real estate and land ownership should be collected and made publicly available online.

The independence of the judiciary must be ensured, antitrust laws enforced and independent regulatory and legal frameworks strengthened. Regional support initiatives can reinforce national governance, particularly in natural resource-based economies. Online initiatives such as Publish What You Pay and the Extractive Industries Transparency Initiative can help policymakers in striving for greater transparency.

Transparency can be increased through packages linking legislation and data provision. One example is Project Transparency, run by Slovenia's Commission for the Prevention of Corruption. It increases public accessibility to information regarding Government-private contacts by providing a list of contacts with lobbyists, the financial status of members of the Commission and, most importantly, a free online application called Supervizor (Supervisor). It provides information on business transactions between public bodies and private firms and other entities, thereby greatly enhancing the transparency of financial flows between the public and private sectors, contributing to the more efficient use of

public finances and limiting systemic corruption.[164]

National anti-corruption commissions should be set up and appropriate legislation passed. Government officials should be required to declare their total wealth and financial interests to such commissions at the start and end of their terms in office. Discrepancies unaccounted for would then be investigated.

Better governance of the financial sector would allow for more competition in the banking sector by permitting foreign banks to enter domestic markets, since they are often the first vehicle for FDI. This should not, however, be equated with total financial liberalization. Moves to free up the sector should remain consistent with a wider macroeconomic strategy, but FDI should not be associated with loose environmental regulation. Studies have failed to demonstrate that weak environmental regulation attracts FDI. Rather, it tends to result in a race to the bottom.[165]

Stricter disclosure rules, a legal framework guaranteeing the independence of central banks and stronger supervisory powers will also lend solidity to the financial system. Credit concentration needs to be reduced gradually, and banks exposed to high credit concentration risk should be subject to additional capital requirements.

The poor performance on lending in the Arab region underlines the need to build a stronger framework governing collateral and bankruptcy. Better access to credit history through public credit registries or private credit bureaus should be promoted in order to encourage disciplined borrower behaviour, reduced information asymmetries, and improved analysis of credit risk among banks. Protecting investors at the corporate governance level, such as through enhanced transparency or shareholder rights, improves the revenue and profit performance of firms by discouraging the use of corporate assets for personal gain. Tightening bankruptcy regulations can help prevent premature liquidation. Bankruptcy proceedings should be shortened and the recovery rate for creditors improved.[166]

The region can do much to improve operational governance. Streamlining processes for obtaining electricity grid connections, construction permits, paying taxes and starting a business, and cutting the time lag and costs of such processes, would encourage private sector-led investment and growth.[167]

Financial oversight bodies need to be strengthened. Security market regulations can spur competition by establishing caps on the size of allocated bids and opening non-competitive auctions to large public-sector funds in order to enhance control of debt among investors.

Inclusive decision-making in industrial policy can be reflected in consultation with the business community, and inter-agency coordination would support more effective planning. Horizontal industrial policies, which are long-term in nature, should be favoured over vertical ones, as they tend to adjust more easily to changing economic conditions. Everything possible should be done to level playing fields across industries, increase transparency, and discourage backroom politics

and the formation of lobbies intent on keeping acquired privileges.

2. Development-friendly political systems

Winston Churchill once said: "It has been said that democracy is the worst form of government, except for all those other forms that have been tried from time to time."[168]

The emergence and survival of democracy depend on many factors, and democracy itself takes a variety of forms. The institutions conducive to development have to evolve at the same pace in order to facilitate transition from one political system to another.

In the short term, initial measures for higher-resilience and low- and medium-resilience countries, especially those rich in natural resources, include application of the rule of law to all, without exception, and strengthened checks and balances in order to foster accountability for financial windfalls acquired through natural resources. Those checks and balances will enable a shift in higher-resilience countries towards more participatory government. High-income Gulf countries, in particular, would be suited to such a transition.

Low- and medium-resilience countries, conflict-affected countries, and those with considerable resources, should start by strengthening State institutions, placing checks and balances on the executive, fostering an independent judiciary, and promoting professionalism among public servants, before moving gradually to more participatory forms of democratic government.

Low- and medium-resilience countries in transition should redesign administrative processes and structures, and change the way in which policymakers and citizens interact.

In the medium to long term, low- and medium-resilience countries should replicate reforms pursued by higher-resilience countries in the short term, and conflict-affected countries should follow the example of those undertaken in low- and medium-resilience ones. Both categories could look at additional options, such as reforming political institutions.

All Arab countries should work on improving access to information and fostering the constructive exchange of views, including through independent and pluralistic media. The formation of political parties should be allowed. Accountability targets should be set for the public administration.

Any democracy should be inclusive and based on equal citizenship irrespective of religion or ethnic origin. Beliefs and religious rights for all should be respected and protected by law. Arab countries should aim for parliamentary democracy with electoral systems based on proportional representation. Institution-building in transition should be complemented by the forging of a national identity and with involvement of the middle class.

Poverty reduction should also be an objective of improved governance. The maximum possible social benefits should be made available to poorer classes, who also need more of a voice in decision-making.

The youth bulge in Arab populations requires policies to improve education, especially at the secondary level. Alternative training and entrepreneurship should be fostered in order to combat youth unemployment and give young people hope for the future.

National infrastructure planning is needed to prevent segregation and the build-up of slums arising from internal and external migration. Water, waste management, transport and mobility, crime and law enforcement, land tenure, social infrastructure, and urban planning require nimble policy responses.

3. Participatory politics

In the short term, higher-resilience countries should: review political institutions and how citizens engage with them to contribute to national development; redesign administrative processes and structures to enhance interaction between policymakers and citizens; allow the formation of civil society organizations, political parties and other forms of association, and their participation in policymaking; encourage the public to vote; and set measurable targets for accountable public administration.

Low- and medium-resilience countries should create a safe environment for peaceful activism; build trust in political systems through increased transparency; leverage the "protest dynamic" to involve diverse stakeholders in decision-making; and build civil society capacity, in particular among marginalized groups such as women and minorities.

In the medium to long term, low- and medium-resilience countries should replicate some of the reforms pursued by higher-resilience countries in the short term, and conflict-affected countries should follow the example of those undertaken in low- and medium-resilience ones. Conflict-affected countries should foster dialogue and the political involvement of marginalized groups, and improve access to information.

All countries need to tackle the scourge of unemployment, ensure economic mobility, establish equality before the law, fight corruption, and guarantee fairer and wider political representation.

4. Human rights

Compliance with human rights law should not be seen as a constraint, but rather as way of establishing a new contract between Governments and people in order to promote a human rights-based approach to sustainable development.[169]

Independent national human rights commissions should be established and, where they exist, their independence protected. Human rights and international humanitarian law should be respected by all. Higher-resilience countries should step up efforts in the short term to participate in and report to the main international human rights treaty bodies, and the other countries should follow suit in the mid to long term. Measures to promote and protect human rights and fundamental freedoms should be taken at the regional level.

Arab countries should adopt frameworks on corporate social responsibility to make sure that multinationals and foreign investors comply with human rights instruments.

Dealing with the aftermath of public uprisings in which lives and/or property are lost, from the point of view of the victims and a nation trying to move forward to a better future, is especially difficult. Proper planning is needed for transitional justice; discussion on it should be public, even during the conflict.
Transitional justice is a key tool for ending conflict and allows for trades of immunity for political change and an end to war.
"Mechanisms and tools of transitional justice need to be selected with sensitivity to country context. These measures include legal frameworks for truth and reconciliation commissions, judicial and non-judicial processes of truth-seeking, punishment, amnesty and reparations."[170]

E. Conclusion

Governance reforms should ensure the freedom of all and respect for basic human rights, safeguard future generations from war, and guarantee the equality of men, women and children.

Any policy mix should lift the quality of governance and the prospects for durable and fair development. It must be domestically owned and its preparation should involve all stakeholders, with the help of domestic and international experts and organizations when needed.

The precondition for governance reform across the board is the cessation of hostilities.

However, even in case of occupation and armed conflict, limited steps can be taken with regard to respect for human rights, in the cause of which as much internal, external and public pressure as possible should be brought to bear, and transitional justice. Frameworks for transitional justice should be established even during the conflict, so as to be ready to start resolving frictions immediately after hostilities cease.

Central to governance reform are the rule of law and public accountability, which together can help to promote a virtuous cycle of governance improvement. The independence of the judiciary is sine qua non, as is a participatory political system, whereby the ability of the people to choose and transparency act as drivers for accountable government.

Governments emerging after uprisings, whether they opt for a liberal democratic or more centralized political system, should remember that only independent and unbiased State institutions will lead to successful transition and ensure their legitimacy. Public servants, whether judges, security officials or bureaucrats, must resist political pressure, uphold the integrity of their offices, and demonstrate by their actions that the role of the State is to serve the interests of all in equal measure.

This chapter does not suggest one-size-fits-all recommendations for better governance, but aims to encourage Arab leaders to move forward to stronger, more inclusive, professional and unbiased State institutions, to the authority of which they themselves would submit.

Keeping in mind the goals of protecting human rights and, where need be, assisting with the coordination of State and private activities, ministries of planning and development should act now, perhaps by creating national reform teams, to launch, maintain and follow up on country-specific governance reform initiatives.

4. Transformational Growth

A. Introduction

Transformational growth is a cumulative process in which economic actors and technology evolve in so as to generate continued innovation that, in turn, contributes to the modernization of production and the economy as a whole, and to the restructuring of markets.[171]

This report sees transformational growth in broad terms as the way forward for economic development in the Arab region to 2030. In looking at how to bring this about, it takes the following considerations into account:

(a) Trade policy is not synonymous with trade liberalization. The latter does not necessarily bring about structural transformation, nor has there been consensus on whether trade openness alone increases growth;

(b) Although capital accumulation can spur innovation in high-tech industrial output, its role in generating employment is not clear;

(c) A developmental State drives transformation through policies designed to shift the economy to higher value, high-tech manufacturing, and promote the necessary productive and technological capacities;

(d) If the main purpose of economic policy is to achieve human development, then transformational growth should emphasize the links between economic growth and income distribution, as well as development outcomes, such as poverty reduction.[172] This report's principal argument is that both the rate and the pattern of growth are crucial for advancing human capabilities.

In the light of the SDGs, this chapter argues that structural transformation and economic development should be based on a sustainable, inclusive growth plan (goals 8 and 12), with the end result being poverty elimination and lower inequalities within and between countries (goals 1 and 10).

Forecasting structural transformation based on extrapolations of average manufacturing shares for a specific group of countries does not provide precise delineations of economic potential. In fact, using such averages tends to amplify the degree of deviation of the trajectories of structural transformation, and can mask important differences among industries.[173] The report therefore considers subsectoral dynamics where possible.

The vision it proposes for 2030 encompasses the following main objectives:

• The Arab region's economy will be concentrated in more advanced sectors, with higher productivity and value added, benefiting workers and creating a broader middle class. Policies will focus on inclusive economic growth, the generation of decent value-added jobs and the equitable distribution of benefits across society. Priorities will include: expanding manufacturing and exports of non-oil commodities; and generating higher productive capacities. Complementary policy reforms in areas such as trade, investment, tax systems, science and technology, enterprises, human-resource training and upgrading, regional development, providing social transfers, and expenditure will be critical;[174]

- The lack of decent work is a major problem in the region. In the long term, economic growth will come with technological advances, leading to economic transformation with higher value-added sectors, better jobs and higher wages;

- Environmental sustainability will be fundamental to the welfare and, in some cases, the survival of Arab societies. An integrated policy model will draw upon principles of economic growth, embracing a new development model that relies more on cleaner and more efficient energy sources and the efficient use of accessible water resources. It will be based on sustainable production and consumption patterns.

A distinction must be made between countries rich in natural resources (mainly oil) with ample fiscal space, and those that are resource poor. This chapter classifies countries in those two categories and argues that structural transformation is essentially a process of delinking from oil-led growth.

B. Structural transformation and resource sustainability challenges

The Arab region has achieved relatively high growth rates (7.7 per cent in the 1960s, 8.1 per cent in the 1970s, 1.4 per cent in the 1980s, and 5.1 per cent in the 1990s and the first decade after 2000), but without the corresponding relatively equal improvements in the well-being of most citizens. Crises and political instability have devastated many countries, with the poor and vulnerable often suffering the most. Inequality has risen and poverty levels are high.[175]

Aside from the destruction of development gains in recent years, key economic development challenges include oil dependence and the concentration of economic activity in informal, low productivity sectors. Structural imbalances and employment deficits have resulted from decades of "rentier" growth. However, with low oil prices, even Saudi Arabia, the biggest player in the Organization of the Petroleum Exporting Countries (OPEC), may have only five years of financial assets remaining at the level of current spending.[176] Other problems include complex trade agreements, poor integration, insufficient energy networks and growing scarcity of water (for most countries) and energy resources (for oil-poor countries).

1. Volatile growth, high unemployment and fragile economic structures

Figures 4.1a and 4.1b show the economic structures of oil-rich and non-oil-rich countries since the 1990s. Oil, gas and mining dominate in oil-rich countries. Non-oil-rich countries have more diversified structures, but their share of manufacturing is low. Overall, more than 30 per cent of the region's economy is reliant on extractive industries.[177] Since 1990, in both groups, the share of the service sector has increased, while that of agriculture has fallen or remained negligible. The ballooning "other services" category includes high and low value-added informal jobs, but is skewed to the latter. Nevertheless, Egypt, Jordan and the United Arab Emirates are listed among the top 20 countries in the world for the most accessible offshore services, according to the Global Services Location Index, offering high levels of education, relatively strong technology services and low costs.[178]

The region's lack of structural transformation has made its productivity gains the slowest in the world (figure 4.2). Between 1991 and 2012,

the productivity growth rate barely exceeded 1 per cent, and was particularly low in oil-rich countries. Although GDP growth in the 1970s shot up by 8 per cent a year, it slowed in the following decades, ranging from 1.4 per cent in the 1980s to 5.1 per cent in the 2000s. Higher growth rates, however, have not yielded larger incomes equally for people in the region.

Growth in the Arab region has suffered from high volatility, especially in low-income and oil-rich countries. Conflict and political confrontation have exacerbated this instability, particularly since 2010. Today, Iraq, Libya, Palestine, Somalia, the Sudan, the Syrian Arab Republic and Yemen are in crisis. The influx of refugees has had a negative impact on inflation, employment, the fiscal deficit and the overall economy in Egypt, Jordan, Lebanon and Tunisia, which also face domestic political difficulties.

Figure 4.1 Sectoral shares of GDP in Arab countries (percentage)

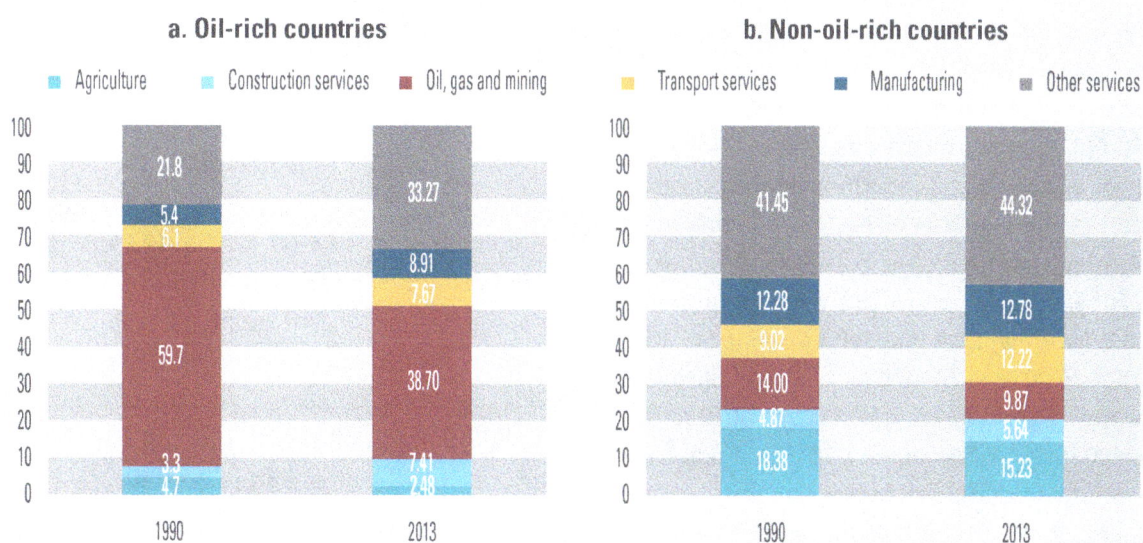

a. Oil-rich countries

Agriculture · Construction services · Oil, gas and mining

	1990	2013
Other services	21.8	33.27
Manufacturing	5.4	8.91
Transport services	5.1	7.67
Oil, gas and mining	59.7	38.70
Construction services	3.3	7.41
Agriculture	4.7	2.48

b. Non-oil-rich countries

Transport services · Manufacturing · Other services

	1990	2013
Other services	41.45	44.32
Manufacturing	12.28	12.78
Transport services	9.02	12.22
Oil, gas and mining	14.00	9.87
Construction services	4.87	5.64
Agriculture	18.38	15.23

Source: Authors.

Note: Calculations are based on national accounts estimates of main aggregates. Agriculture includes agriculture, hunting, forestry and fishing; transport services include transport, storage and communication; oil, gas and mining include mining and utilities; and other services include wholesale, retail trade, restaurants and hotels.

Figure 4.2 Productivity growth rate (percentage)

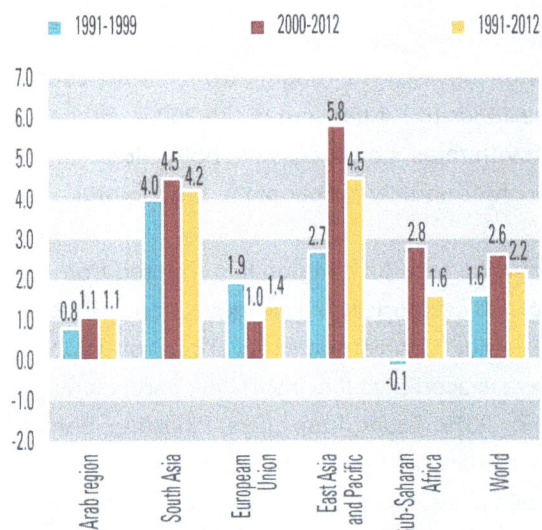

Legend: ■ 1991-1999 ■ 2000-2012 □ 1991-2012

	Arab region	South Asia	European Union	East Asia and Pacific	Sub-Saharan Africa	World
1991-1999	0.8	4.0	1.9	2.7	-0.1	1.6
2000-2012	1.1	4.5	1.0	5.8	2.8	2.6
1991-2012	1.1	4.2	1.4	4.5	1.6	2.2

Source: ESCWA, 2013b.

Conflict in Libya has damaged energy installations and reduced refinery output, undercutting business and consumer confidence and reducing public resources. To maintain living standards, the Government spent 22 per cent of its 2014 budget on subsidies; a pattern that cannot be sustained without boosting oil exports.[179] Additionally, a series of strikes and security breaches at oil sites has hobbled the oil sector, resulting in an estimated contraction of real GDP by 24 per cent in 2014, in addition to a 13.6 per cent drop in 2013. Nominal GDP thus fell by half, from $82 billion in 2012 to $41.2 billion in 2014, as did income per capita, from $12,800 in 2012 to $6,600 in 2014. Throughout 2015, the real economy was affected by the fighting, destruction of physical capital and heavy disruptions in the oil sector on which it relies.[180]

In Yemen, a recent report shows that conflict has led to a contraction in GDP of 12.9 per cent,

a rise in inflation to more than 20 per cent and a dire humanitarian crisis affecting 12.2 million. With a 47 per cent increase of government overdraft since December 2014, and no buyers for central bank treasury bills, fiscal needs greatly exceed the potential sources.[181]

The Palestinian economy continues to suffer because of the Israeli occupation. The 2014 military operation in the Gaza Strip caused major human and economic losses. The destruction of tunnels on the border with Egypt has further crippled the economy.

In Iraq, conflict has wiped out generations of economic achievements. If the security situation continues to deteriorate, especially in the Mashreq, the repercussions for the regional economy will be grave.

High unemployment, a lack of decent work and low wages are hallmarks of the Arab labour market (figure 4.3). The region had the highest overall unemployment in the world before 2010, and conflicts since then have exacerbated the situation, even in countries not directly affected. At the end of 2014, unemployment reached 11.6 per cent among Saudi nationals in Saudi Arabia, 12.9 per cent in Egypt, 12.3 per cent in Jordan and 9.7 per cent in Morocco.[182] The supply of skilled labour is relatively high but demand for it is low, given that most investment is directed at the capital-intensive oil sector, low value-added services, construction and real estate.

By 2013, youth unemployment in the region far exceeded the world average of 13 per cent, with 30.2 per cent in Arab countries in North Africa and 28.3 per cent in the rest.[183]

Figure 4.3 Unemployment rate across regions, 1992-2013 (percentage)

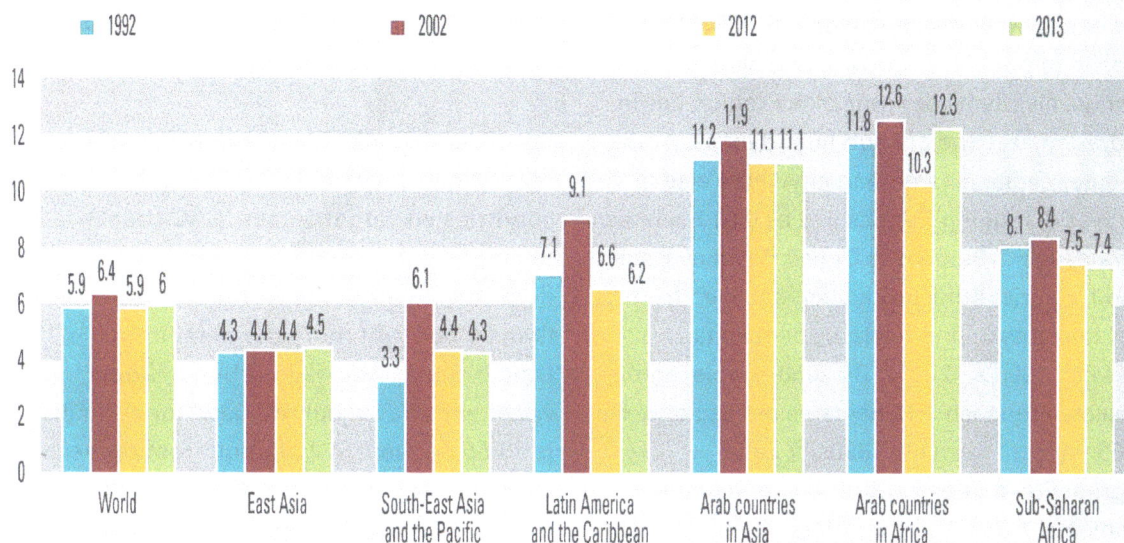

Source: ILO, Global Employment Trends 2014: supporting data sets. Available from www.ilo.org/global/research/global-reports/global-employment-trends/2014/WCMS_234879/lang--en/index.htm (accessed 30 November 2014).

The regional average of jobless young women was 46.1 per cent, compared with 24 per cent for men. In several countries affected by the post-2010 crises, particularly in North Africa, unemployment shot up in 2012 and 2013.

Around 60 million jobs need to be created by 2030 even if the current low rate of women's participation in the labour market continues.[184] Increasing their participation rate in line with developing country average raises the number to almost 100 million.[185] Those estimates do not take into account recent violence in the region. Investment would have to rise to around 50 per cent of regional GDP to provide jobs for everyone and increase women's labour force participation from 17 per cent to 35 per cent.[186]

2. Water scarcity and energy abundance

Water resources in the Arab region are scarce. Half of its population faces water stress and scarcity because of infrequent rainfall, high levels of vaporization and droughts. With the population expected to increase to 500 million by 2025, water availability per person is expected to fall by 50 per cent by 2050.[187] In 2011, average water availability per capita reached a worrying rate of 743.5 cubic metres per year, below the water poverty line of 1,000 cubic metres. Twelve Arab countries face severe scarcity at 500 m³, and seven have an average availability of 200 m³.[188] Annual precipitation is less than 1,000 mm across all 22 Arab countries, and less than 100 mm for GCC countries, excluding Oman.

72

Renewable freshwater resources, measured per capita, are only one tenth the world average and expected to decline by one third by 2025 as a result of population growth and climate change. Nearly 90 per cent of the region lies in arid, semi-arid and dry sub-humid areas. Arable land per capita is rarer than anywhere else in the world, ranging from as low as 0.01 hectares in Palestine to 0.36 in the Sudan.[189] On average, land for agricultural production declined from 0.24 hectares to 0.16 hectares per capita between 1990 and 2012. By 2050, arable land is projected to reach 0.12 hectares per capita, a fall of 63 per cent from the 1990s.[190] Land degradation and desertification are daunting problems. About three quarters of agricultural land has been affected by degradation,[191] including soil erosion and salinity, which will be further exacerbated by climate change.

Moreover, freshwater supplies in many countries originate outside their territory, leaving them vulnerable to upstream dam construction or redirection.[192]

Seven Arab countries use water at rates exceeding renewable supplies, and most countries waste resources. GCC countries have the highest per capita consumption of domestic water in the world, namely more than 50 per cent more per person than in the United States. Waste in urban systems, due to water withdrawn but not used for agriculture, is 40-50 per cent.[193] Pollution from domestic, industrial and agricultural waste is a further threat.[194] Annual freshwater withdrawal is intensifying pressure on scarce supplies, which are diminishing in most countries (figure 4.4).

Figure 4.4 Total annual freshwater withdrawals (billions of m^3)

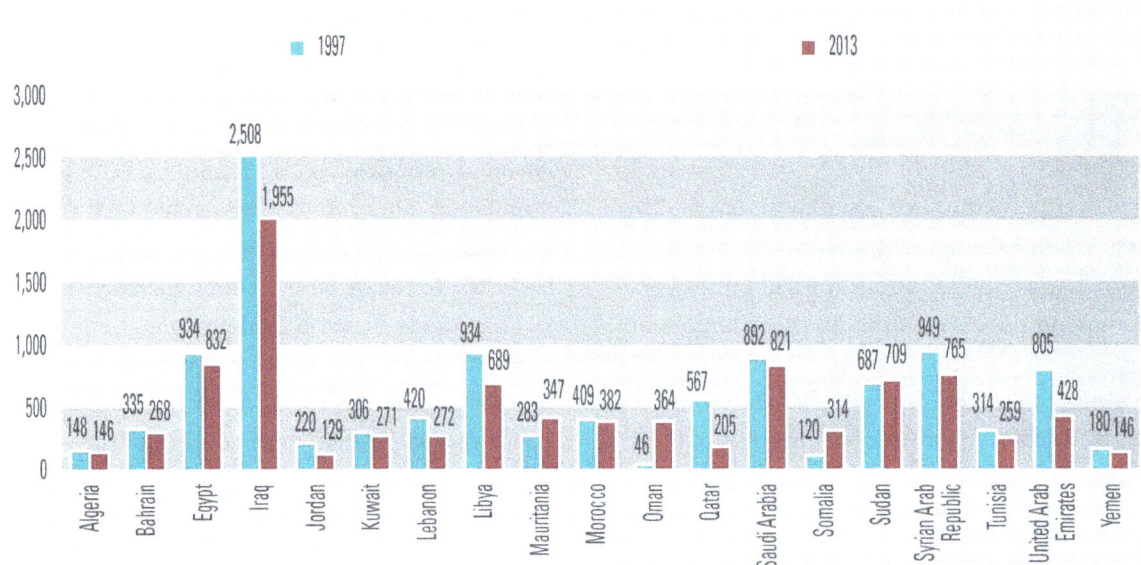

Source: FAO, 2015a.

Figure 4.5 Primary energy use per capita

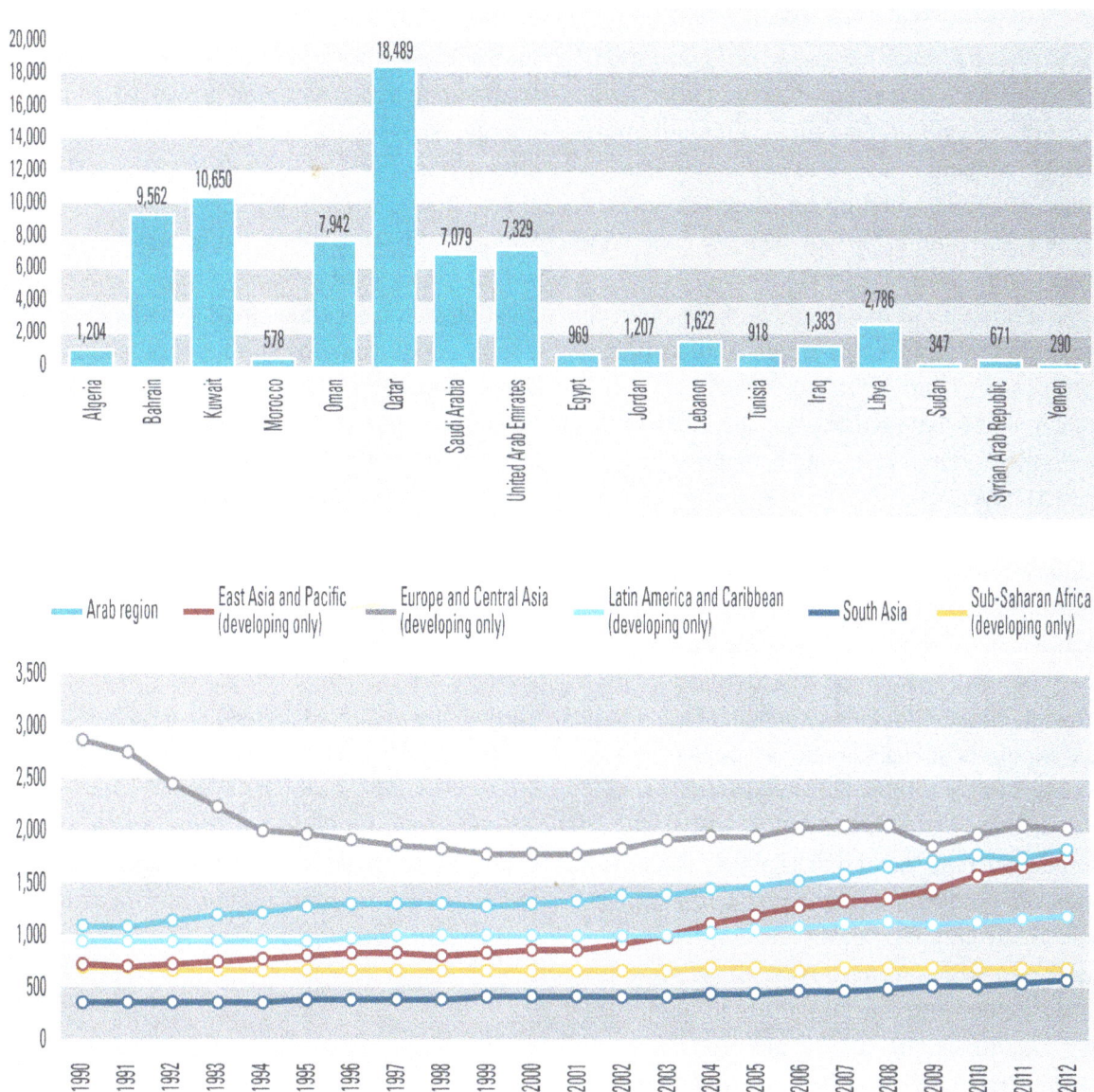

Bar chart: Primary energy use per capita (2012)

- Algeria: 1,204
- Bahrain: 9,562
- Kuwait: 10,650
- Morocco: 578
- Oman: 7,942
- Qatar: 18,489
- Saudi Arabia: 7,079
- United Arab Emirates: 7,329
- Egypt: 969
- Jordan: 1,207
- Lebanon: 1,622
- Tunisia: 918
- Iraq: 1,383
- Libya: 2,786
- Sudan: 347
- Syrian Arab Republic: 671
- Yemen: 290

Line chart legend:
- Arab region
- East Asia and Pacific (developing only)
- Europe and Central Asia (developing only)
- Latin America and Caribbean (developing only)
- South Asia
- Sub-Saharan Africa (developing only)

(Line chart years 1990–2012, values 0–3,500)

Source: World Bank, 2015d.
Note: Data on Arab countries are for 2012.

Agriculture accounts for more than 80 per cent of the region's freshwater consumption, and that figure is expected to increase by a further 40 per cent by 2020. The region has failed to meet its water-related MDGs. Around 15 per cent of the Arab population lacks access to improved drinking water sources and 18 per cent lacks access to improved sanitation facilities.[195] To reduce water consumption, some Arab countries have resorted to importing food or producing it abroad, thereby raising concerns about food security (chapter 5).

Arab oil and gas producers, particularly the GCC countries, consume more primary energy per capita than most other parts of the world.[196] There are wide disparities in energy consumption within the region. Although more than 99 per cent of the Arab population has access to modern energy services, 48 per cent of the population in Yemen, 65.5 per cent in the Sudan and 11 per cent in Kuwait do not.[197] Almost one fifth of the 370 million people in the region rely on non-commercial fuels for various energy uses.[198] In 2013, Qatar consumed 15,020 kWh of electricity per capita, while the Sudan and Yemen consumed less than 212 kWh.[199]

Primary energy use per capita in the region is increasing faster than in the rest of the world (figure 4.5), except for East Asia and the Pacific. Arab countries importing fossil fuels face growing demand for energy at high prices. Fossil fuel exporters are using national supplies to meet energy demands, thus reducing export stocks.

Some have now found that domestic demand outpaces production, creating a gap that must be filled by imports. Kuwait and Dubai import liquid natural gas from Gulf and other countries, as increased electricity demand in the summer has outstripped their natural gas production. Algeria, Iraq, Libya, and GCC countries, are the most energy intensive in the region and among the most energy intensive in the world. Bahrain and Libya, for instance, have five times the energy intensity of Hong Kong and more than twice the intensity of most non-oil-rich and European countries.

Energy inefficiency is increasing, making the region the only one where energy intensity rose from 100 kg of oil equivalent per $1,000 in GDP in 1990 to almost 116 kg in 2011. East Asia and the Pacific, the only region that has outrun the Arab region in consumption growth of primary energy, witnessed a 43 per cent decrease in energy intensity.

Energy in the Arab region is produced almost entirely from fossil fuels, with little diversification since the 1990s. As a percentage of total primary energy supply, fossil fuels increased from 94.5 per cent in 1990 to almost 95 per cent in 2013.[200] The Arab region provided 48 per cent of global energy subsidies and continued to use environmentally harmful and non-renewable energy sources.[201]

A regional shift to renewable energies would help to eradicate poverty through increased access to energy. Improving access to energy, particularly in a region where around half of all countries have a rural electrification rate below 50 per cent, would provide a lever for future economic growth.[202] In energy importing and exporting countries, fossil fuel reliance, inefficient energy consumption and increasing demand threaten energy security.

C. Future scenarios: transformation or stagnation

This section projects the future growth, productivity and employment prospects of Arab economies by presenting two growth scenarios: business as usual and Vision 2030. The transformational growth narrative is based on practices that have influenced past growth in developing economies. Given the set-up of the model used in this chapter, most of the projections are until 2025, although some extend beyond 2030. They are, nevertheless, in line with Vision 2030 and the strategic planning necessary to achieve it.

1. Choice of transformation

In a typical developing economy, structural transformation takes place over a long period. Progress is measured by changes in the relative contributions of different economic sectors, typically involving a decline in the share of agriculture and increases in importance of industry, services and manufacturing.[203] A key to the Arab transformative economic vision will be identifying the kinds of manufacturing and services, and subsectoral activities that will drive growth.

Past experience can offer insight. In successful East Asian economies, increases in the overall share of manufacturing were matched by a decline in two activities known for their lower value-added and productivity growth, namely the textiles and food industries (figure 4.6a). In Malaysia and the Republic of Korea, machinery and other manufacturing activities, which include high-tech consumer durables, constitute the bulk of manufacturing output.

Manufacturing activities benefit from economies of scale and can therefore rapidly increase output, but they can also quickly exhaust their ability to create jobs. Over the past two decades, jobs in developing countries have been created mostly in the service sector,[204] but with varying

results. Employment and productivity growth in the service sector occurred simultaneously in the successful economies of East Asia and the Pacific; for the rest, jobs were created at the expense of efficiency.

Although most countries increased their services share, there are different pathways to structural transformation. The Republic of Korea, unlike the other countries, increased its share of construction, which is generally a low value-added sector, and saw a significant reduction in its social services share. Malaysia, however, increased its share of social services, wholesale and retail trade and tourism. The latter stagnated in Tunisia and declined in the Republic of Korea. All three countries, however, increased their share of transport, communication and financial services, which are generally assumed to include a higher concentration of high value-added service activities. The combined share of these high value-added services has, in most cases, greatly exceeded the average growth rate for all other services, as illustrated in figure 4.7.

Arab countries do not necessarily need to pursue the same path. However, it is not sufficient to promote manufacturing growth without clearly identifying leading industries and considering how their expected contributions will drive shares of aggregate sectors. Economic planners must also focus on subsectors and activities within them.

Figure 4.6 Manufacturing

a. Evolution of the GDP share of manufacturing activities for Korea

b. Percentage share of food and textiles in total manufacturing

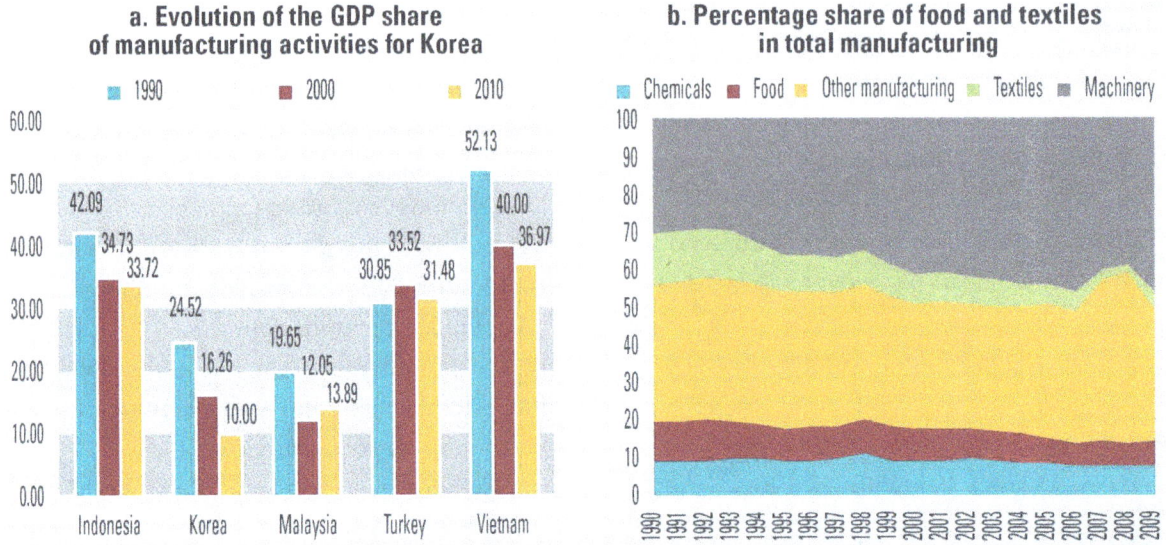

Source: Authors' estimates based on data from the World Bank, 2015d.

Note: On account of missing data, the share of chemicals is held constant in the period 2007-2009, and subtracted from other manufacturing.

Figure 4.7 Service activities

a. Evolution of service activities (percentage of GDP)

b. Service activities (share of GDP)

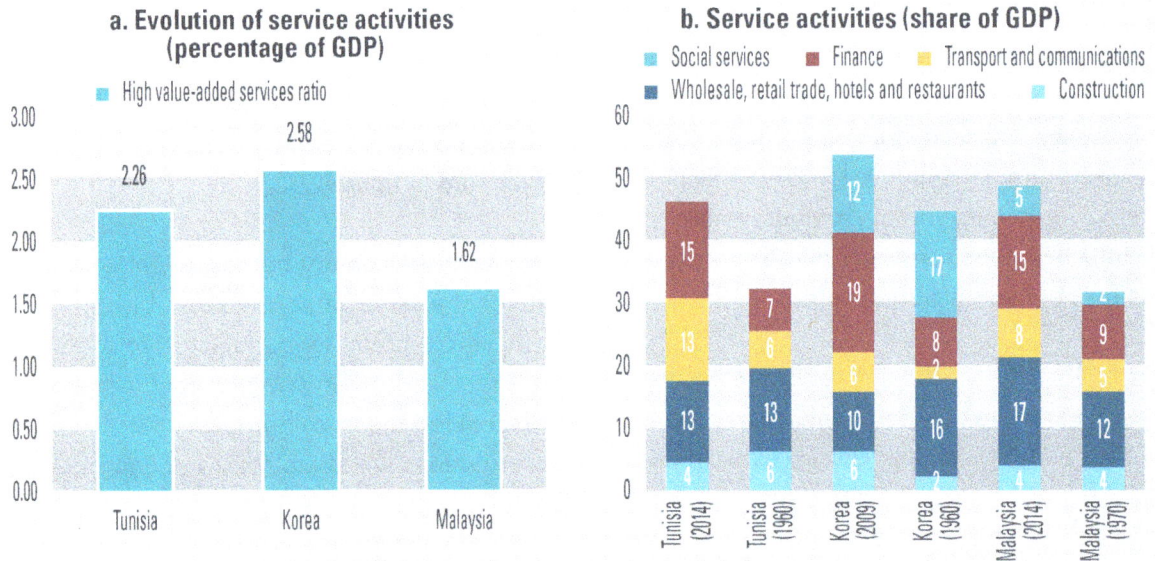

Source: Authors' estimates based on data from United Nations, Department of Economic and Social Affairs, National Accounts Main Aggregates Database. Available from http://unstats.un.org/unsd/snaama/Introduction.asp (accessed 20 June 2014).

Note: No data for social services in Tunisia.

2. The macroeconomic model

(a) Model components

The three main components that underpin the business-as-usual and vision scenarios are political stability and good governance (chapter 3), manufacturing-led growth and regional integration (chapter 6).[205]

Studies on the growth impact of governance shifts have shown that a 1 per cent increase in the standard deviation of a governance indicator on institutions results in a 1.9 per cent increase in the growth rate of total output.[206] With regard to manufacturing-led growth and structural transformation, this report argues, in the light of the East Asian experience (box 4.1), for the promotion of emerging industries, capital subsidies, public investment, and research and development. Greater regional integration offers enormous growth potential for the Arab region.

This modelling exercise divides Arab countries into three groups: the Maghreb, GCC countries and Mashreq. Egypt is dealt with separately, given its demographic weight. However, due to the nature of the analysis, much of the data presented is displayed using other country groupings, or at the individual country level.

(b) Business-as-usual scenario

The business-as-usual scenario is based on the assumption that the region's lack of political stability will continue, negatively affecting production, governance and public investment.

Box 4.1 What Arab countries can learn from East Asia

Asian policymakers nurtured infant and other industries that would have failed if left to the free market. Amsden[*] points out that government intervention "led the market", which was "getting the prices wrong" on its own. She suggests that interventionist features can be viewed as a natural response to late industrialization, when enterprises in developing countries have to compete with more technologically advanced firms in developed countries.

The Asian approach comprises the following four main features:

(a) Massive public investment: growth was supported by a significant increase in savings and investment rates driven by public investment;
(b) Protection of emerging industries: their technological development was assisted, allowing them to produce globally competitive products;
(c) Capital subsidies and targeted credit for productive sectors: capital subsidies granted exporters access to raw materials and technical equipment at the lowest cost, while directed lending policies, monitored by specialized financial authorities, were crucial in achieving export goals;
(d) Research and development as a central driving force of innovation: manufacturing support policies accompanied higher levels of spending on research and development.

[*] Amsden, 2001.

Public investment will shrink by about half in Egypt, the Maghreb and the Mashreq, as weaker financial positions will limit their ability to borrow in international markets and cause interest rate hikes. Most of those countries, with the exception of Algeria and Libya, already suffer from limited fiscal space. Continued instability could result in populist spending policies with little return on productivity.

GCC countries, which enjoyed inflated financial surpluses from higher oil prices in the past and can still finance their fiscal expenditures through accumulated oil funds regardless of price falls, will keep their investment rates at levels predating the Arab uprisings, so as to sustain economic activity and contain any potential social unrest. Spending on research and development and policies to protect manufacturing-led growth will be stifled, while further fragmentation in the region will drive up the cost of shipping between Arab countries by about 50 per cent (table 4.1).

(c) Vision scenario

The vision scenario assumes conditions that will enable an economic take-off. First and foremost, armed conflict will cease in 2016, governance will improve and regional integration will deepen.

Oil-producing countries will increase public investment rates and achieve strategic growth objectives (table 4.1). Public investment will rise by about 50 per cent in GCC countries, Algeria and Libya, and by 20 per cent in Egypt. The Mashreq's limited fiscal space and large public debt in some countries, such as Jordan and Lebanon, will hinder additional investment, so rates will remain at the same level as before the Arab uprisings. Declines or increases in public investment are necessarily always viewed as relative failures or successes. However, under this model and due to the needs of the region, increased public investment is seen as strictly positive.

To drive industrialization, oil-producing countries will back investments in manufacturing to achieve a competitive advantage in international markets. Spending on research and development will increase by up to 50 per cent in all Arab countries as a result of a regional initiative to fund an Arab strategy for joint research and industrial development. Arab countries will adopt uniform standards to protect emerging industries and provide them with appropriate public support.

From 2015 to 2025, the region will reap growth benefits, but the main focus will be on reforming institutions by putting in place better economic governance structures and implementing regional integration. Those measures will not yield immediate results. Investment in scientific research, for instance, even if properly linked to industrial capacities, will take years to translate into productive sector competitiveness. Likewise, governance reforms cannot be implemented overnight; a shift in behavioural attitudes and accountability systems will occur gradually. A more pronounced structural transformation will thus take place between 2026 and 2035.

Countries with financial abundance, mainly GCC countries, or those able to secure the necessary funding to advance rapid industrialization and regional integration, will initially lead progress. That does not, however, exclude industrial policy support in the non-oil-rich countries, where active macroeconomic policies should be encouraged. It will depend on the measures they take and their ability to attract foreign capital, including from GCC countries.

In short, the first development decade of Vision 2030 will be one of adjustment, with little

structural transformation outside GCC countries. The focus will be on regional integration policies to align incentives and business environments. Spillover effects from early movers in GCC countries are expected to produce a regional development domino effect.

Table 4.1 Main assumptions of the business-as-usual and vision scenarios

Component	Description	Countries	Business as usual	Vision 2030
First	Governance	Maghreb	Significant decline	Significant improvement
		GCC	Medium decline	Medium improvement
		Egypt	Significant decline	Significant improvement
		Mashreq		Medium improvement
Second	Public investment	Maghreb	50 per cent decline in public investment	50 per cent increase in public investment
		GCC	No change	
		Egypt	50 per cent decline in public investment	20 per cent increase in public investment
		Mashreq		10 per cent increase in public investment
	Investment support	Maghreb	No support	Support investment in manufacturing sectors by approximately 10 per cent
		GCC		
		Egypt		No support
		Mashreq		
	Research and development	Maghreb	No change	Increase expenditures on research and development
		GCC		
		Egypt		
		Mashreq		
	Protection of emerging industries	Maghreb	No change	Customs protection policies for all Arab countries
		GCC		
		Egypt		
		Mashreq		
Third	Regional integration	Maghreb	50 per cent increase in transport costs between Arab countries	Decrease of transport costs between Arab countries by 50 per cent
		GCC		Arab Customs Union
		Egypt		Adopt an integration policy to meet labour demands
		Mashreq		

Source: Authors.

3. Macroeconomic model results

(a) Economic growth

In the business-as-usual scenario, the absence of regional integration and poor governance will lead to a drop in growth of GDP, with the greatest burden borne by non-oil-exporting countries (figure 4.8). By 2025, non-oil-producing countries will have an average growth rate of around 3 per cent, and oil producers will lag behind with a growth rate below 2 per cent.

In the vision scenario, economic growth doubles for the region as a whole and is relatively equally distributed between oil-producing countries, which will grow at an average annual rate of 6.2 per cent, and non-oil-producing countries (6.1 per cent).

Poor economic performance in the business-as-usual scenario will lead to a modest 26 per cent increase in total regional GDP (figure 4.9), with the lowest growth in Bahrain and Saudi Arabia. The vision scenario produces an 85 per cent increase in total regional GDP.

These growth projections have implications for the size of the income gap between Arab countries and the rest of the world. Figure 4.10 shows the ratio of per capita GDP in both scenarios in the Arab region compared to the per capita GDP of a selected country. In the business-as-usual scenario, the gap continues to widen. In the vision scenario, the gap narrows, especially in comparison to Turkey. Only in China does projected growth exceed that of Arab countries even in the vision scenario.

Figure 4.8 Growth rate in the Arab region, 2015-2025

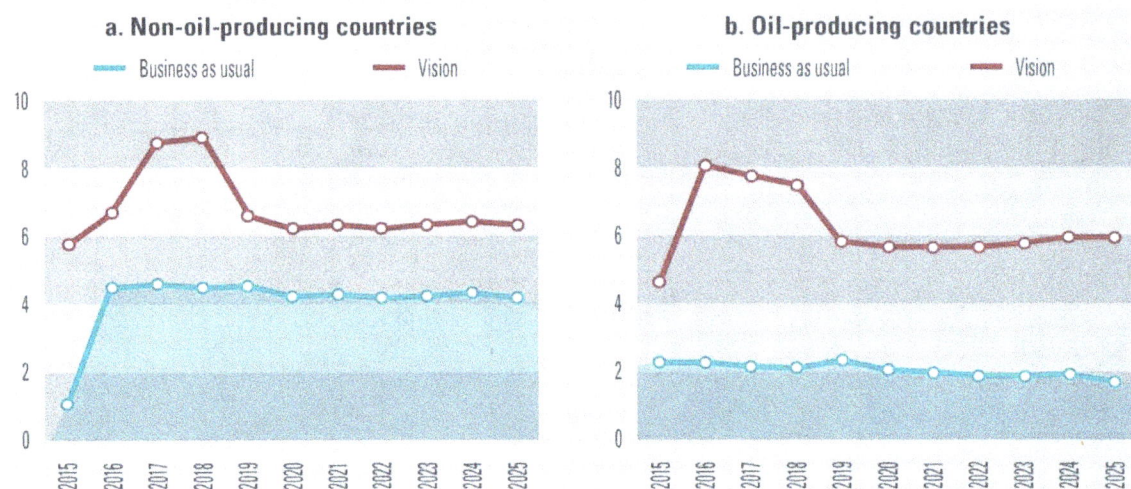

a. Non-oil-producing countries

Business as usual — Vision

b. Oil-producing countries

Business as usual — Vision

Source: Authors' calculations using the Mirage Model (Bchir and others, 2002).
Note: Averages are GDP weighted. Non-oil-producing countries are Egypt, Iraq, Jordan, Lebanon, Morocco, Tunisia and Yemen; and oil-producing countries are Algeria, Bahrain, Kuwait, Libya, Oman, Qatar, Saudi Arabia and United Arab Emirates.

Figure 4.9 GDP increases at the national level, 2015-2025 (percentage)

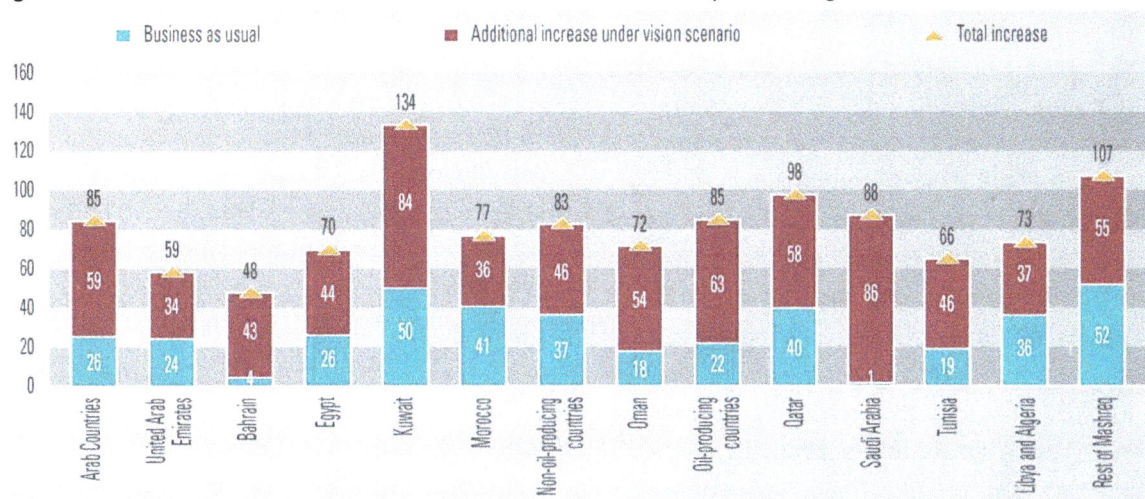

Legend: Business as usual · Additional increase under vision scenario · Total increase

Source: Authors' calculations using the Mirage Model (Bchir and others, 2002).

Figure 4.10 Per capita GDP in Arab countries compared with other countries

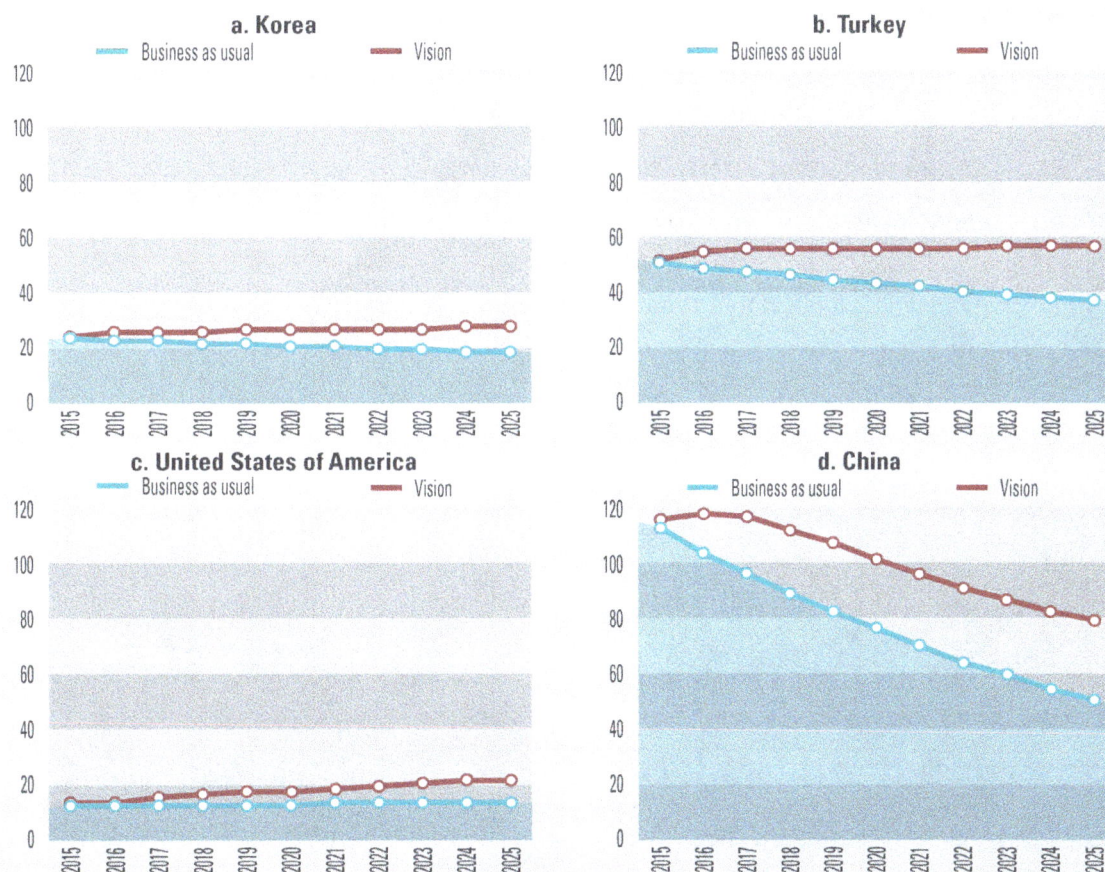

a. Korea
b. Turkey
c. United States of America
d. China

Source: Authors' calculations using the Mirage Model (Bchir and others, 2002).

(b) Employment

Under the business-as-usual scenario, faltering employment demand, internally due to low growth and externally due to poor regional integration, will raise the regional unemployment rate by around 8 per cent. Non-oil-exporting countries will be more vulnerable, with unemployment reaching 21 per cent for unskilled labour and 18 per cent for skilled labour. In oil-producing countries, unemployment in both categories will reach 14 per cent and 13 per cent, respectively. In the vision scenario, productivity enhancements and increased demand for Arab labour in oil-exporting countries will enable the region to reach full employment by 2025.

In the business-as-usual scenario, Saudi Arabia and Egypt will record the largest

increases in unemployment: 8.8 per cent and 6.75 per cent for unskilled workers, and 7.38 and 6.02 per cent for skilled workers, respectively. In the vision scenario, Tunisia and Egypt will record the largest drops in unemployment, by -10.89 per cent and -7.74 per cent for unskilled workers, and -11.12 per cent and -7.19 per cent for skilled workers, respectively.

(c) Productivity, trade and sources of growth

Productivity growth will decline in the business-as-usual scenario, particularly in GCC countries; Bahrain, Qatar and Saudi Arabia will record negative total productivity growth between 2015 and 2025. Conversely, in the vision scenario, productivity enhancement will be noticeable in all countries, particularly in the Maghreb.

Figure 4.11 Unemployment rates for non-oil-producing countries

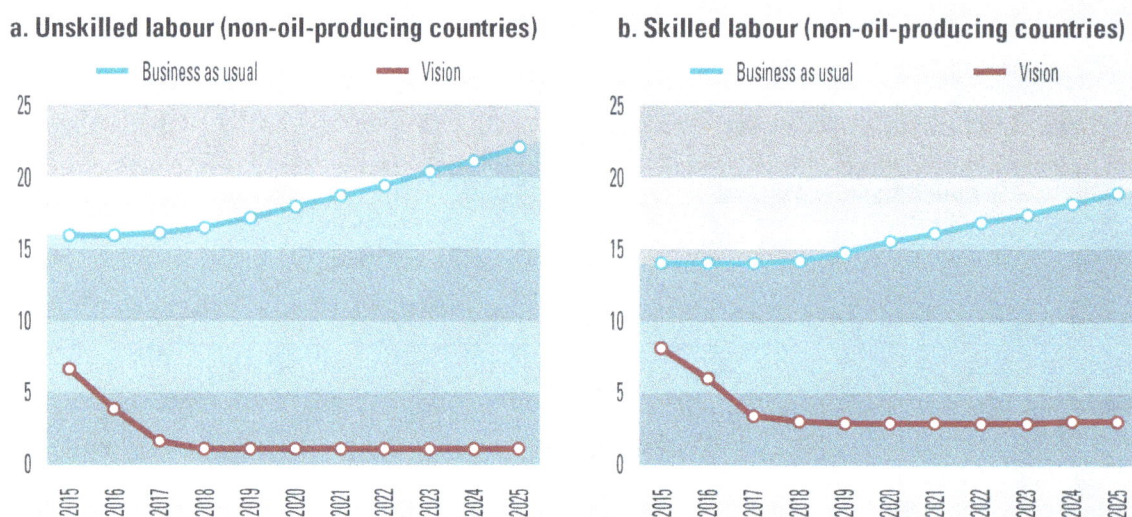

a. Unskilled labour (non-oil-producing countries)

b. Skilled labour (non-oil-producing countries)

Source: Authors' calculations using the Mirage Model (Bchir and others, 2002).

Figure 4.12 Unemployment rates for oil-producing countries

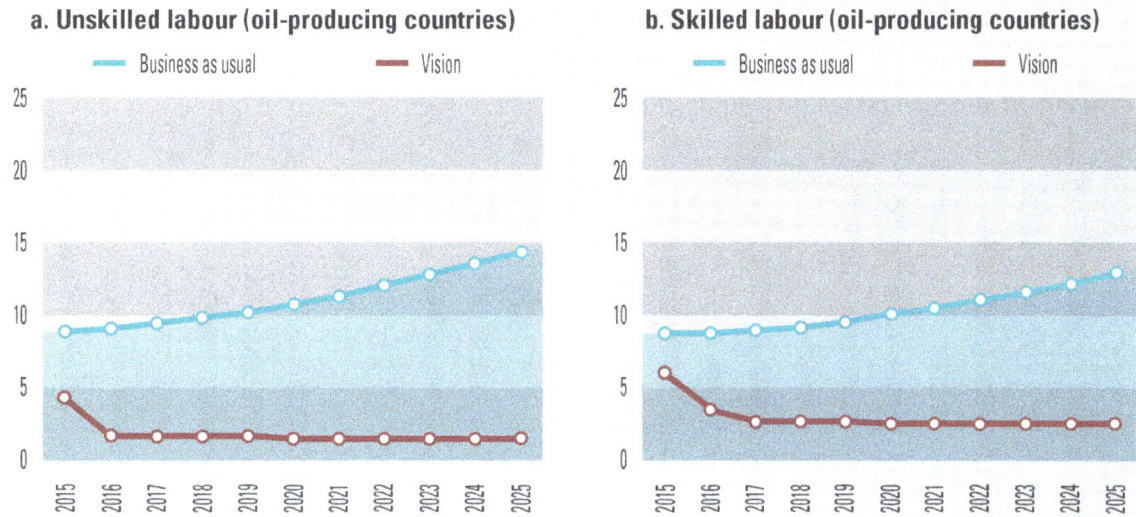

a. Unskilled labour (oil-producing countries)

b. Skilled labour (oil-producing countries)

Source: Authors' calculations using the Mirage Model (Bchir and others, 2002).

Figure 4.13 Percentage change in unemployment rates by 2025

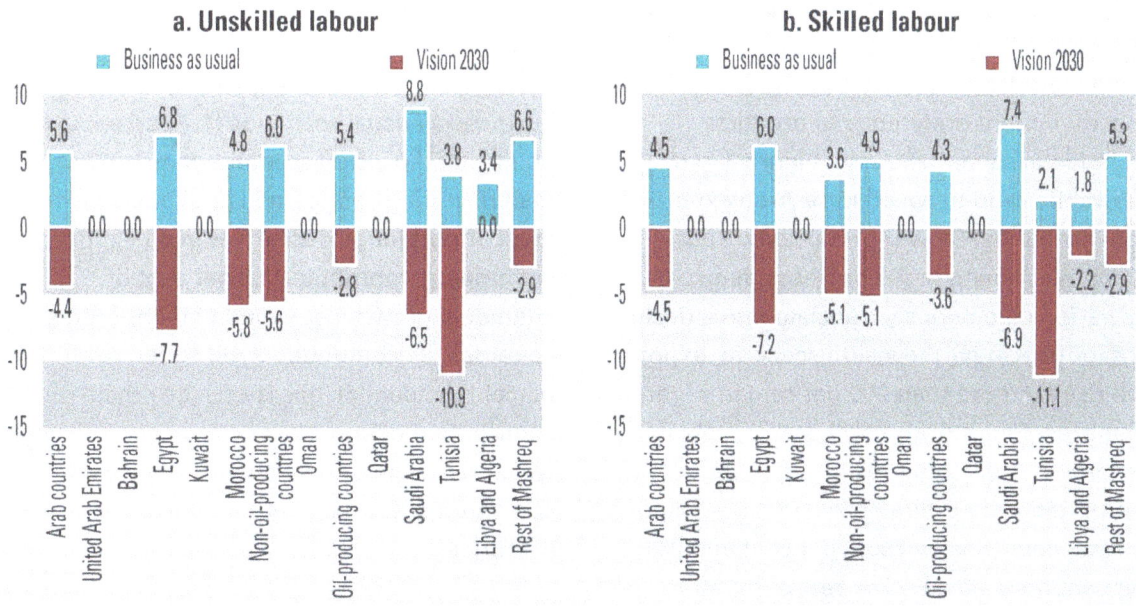

a. Unskilled labour

b. Skilled labour

Source: Authors' calculations using the Mirage Model (Bchir and others, 2002).

Note: Rest of Mashreq stands for Iraq, Jordan, Lebanon and Yemen.

Figure 4.14 Productivity growth and intra-Arab exports

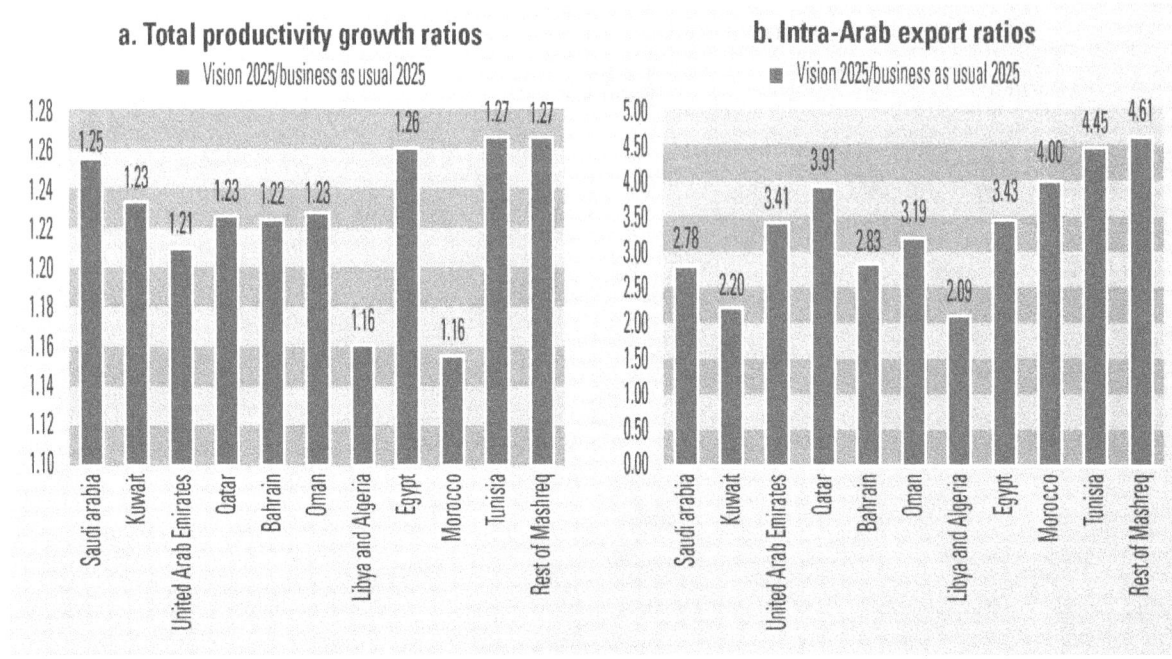

Source: Authors' calculations using the Mirage Model (Bchir and others, 2002).

Figure 4.14a shows the gains in productivity growth in the vision scenario. Arab countries will benefit from regional trade policies that give maximum preference to products manufactured in the region. Figure 4.14b shows the ratio between intra-Arab exports for both scenarios. Slower productivity and economic growth in the business-as-usual scenario will obviously translate into a decline in exports. Under the vision scenario, exports will rise by more than 200 per cent in several countries. Saudi Arabia will nearly triple its exports to Arab countries by 2025. Qatar and the United Arab Emirates will increase exports to Arab countries by 290.8 per cent and 241.2 per cent respectively. The rest of the Arab Mashreq, Egypt, Morocco and Tunisia, given their more diversified economic base, will more than triple exports to Arab countries, as compared to the business-as-usual scenario.

When analysing growth sources, as shown in figure 4.15, productivity differences explain much of the gap between the vision and business-as-usual scenarios (1.7 percentage points). In the vision scenario, the manufacturing sector (industrial policy) is the most important growth driver in oil-exporting countries; it contributes 2.3 per cent of additional growth per year. In oil-importing countries, its contribution will be far lower (0.2 percentage points); this is offset by the higher contribution of improved governance indicators, which raises growth by about 1.2 per cent compared to 0.2 per cent for oil-exporting countries.

(d) Structural transformation

By 2025, the vision scenario assumes considerable improvements in the effectiveness of institutions, public investment, fiscal space, scientific research, and policymaking. Closer regional cooperation will promote joint projects in research and development as the engine of industrial transformation. Given that industrial development and macroeconomic policies are closely tied to fiscal space, growth in the manufacturing sector will be triggered first in countries with financial abundance and those able to secure funding for economic advancement, while making use of labour skills and expanded regional markets. Open capital accounts, with policies aimed at attracting FDI, will assist in bridging the capital gap in countries with tighter fiscal space.

Figure 4.15 What fuels the gap in average growth rates of Arab countries between 2015 and 2025

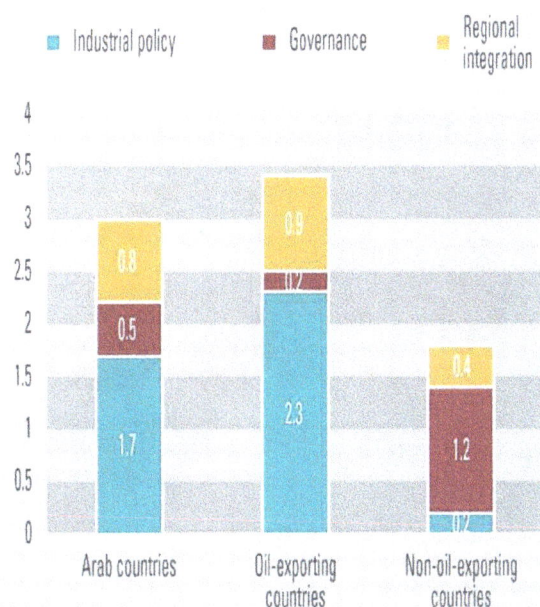

Source: Authors' calculations using the Mirage Model (Bchir and others, 2002).

The business-as-usual scenario leaves economic structures in most Arab countries unchanged, except in Bahrain and Qatar, where the share of manufacturing will grow significantly. In contrast, under the vision scenario, the manufacturing share will increase moderately, by 2.69 percentage

Points, in Tunisia, with smaller increases in Algeria, Libya and the rest of the Mashreq (Iraq, Jordan, Lebanon and Yemen). However, in aggregate, sectoral distribution in non-oil-producing countries will change little. In the oil-producing countries, the share of the oil and gas sector will contract by 4.5 per cent, while manufacturing will increase by 3.6 per cent. Manufacturing in Qatar and Saudi Arabia will expand by 5.9 per cent and 3.9 per cent.

More importantly, the first decade of the vision scenario lays a foundation for establishing economies with higher value-added sectors and activities after 2025. Asian countries provide some insights. Benchmark Asian countries for the oil-rich Arab countries are Indonesia and Malaysia. For the non-oil-rich countries, benchmarks include the Republic of Korea, Turkey and Viet Nam.

For each benchmark country, the best structural transformation decade was identified.[207] Taking average growth rates of sectoral shares and recalculating them into yearly growth rates yields the results in table 4.2, where the growth rates of sectoral values are shown for the period 2026-2035. Although all sectors will grow in terms of their absolute values, sectoral shares of oil, gas and mining will shrink in oil-producing countries, and agriculture and other services will contract slightly in non-oil-producing countries. Following this methodology, oil-producing countries will increase their total value added by 5.7 per cent, and non-oil-producing countries by 5.3 per cent. In both cases, the manufacturing sector will grow considerably, by 9.3 per cent for non-oil-producers and 10.9 per cent for oil-producers, on an annual basis from 2026 to 2035.

Table 4.2 Sectoral growth rates in structural transformation, 2026-2035 (percentage)

	Oil-producing countries	Non-oil-producing countries
Total value added	5.73	5.30
Agriculture	3.70	1.78
Construction services	6.90	6.85
Oil, gas and mining (with utilities)	2.06	5.91
Transport services	9.24	8.86
Manufacturing	10.93	9.33
Other services	6.82	5.17

Source: Authors' calculations based on data from United Nations, Department of Economic and Social Affairs, National Accounts Main Aggregates Database. Available from http://unstats.un.org/unsd/snaama/Introduction.asp (accessed 20 June 2014).

Figure 4.16 Vision for long-term structural transformation

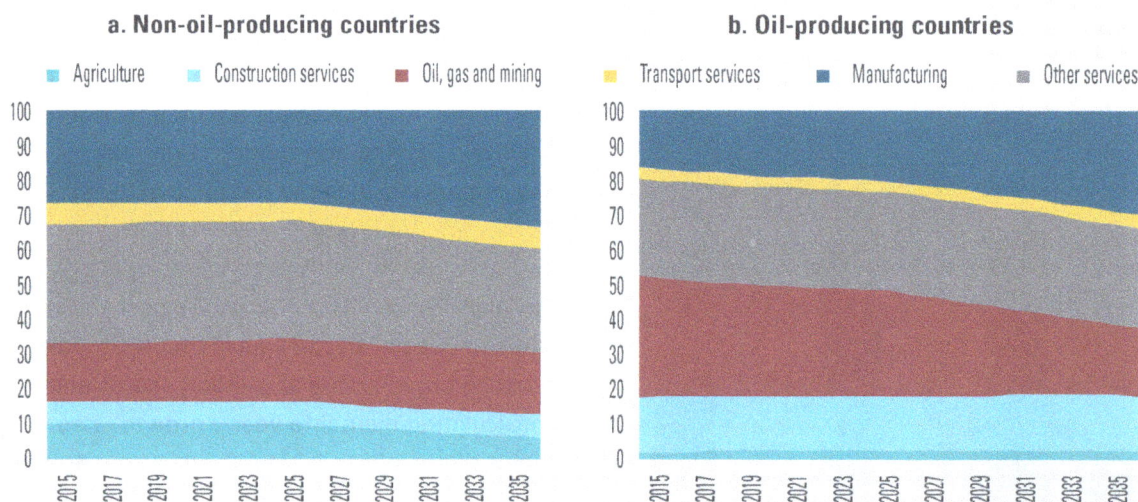

a. Non-oil-producing countries   b. Oil-producing countries

■ Agriculture   ■ Construction services   ■ Oil, gas and mining   ■ Transport services   ■ Manufacturing   ■ Other services

Source: Authors' calculations using the Mirage Model (Bchir and others, 2002); and data from United Nations, Department of Economic and Social Affairs, National Accounts Main Aggregates Database. Available from http://unstats.un.org/unsd/snaama/Introduction.asp (accessed 20 June 2014).

Note: The data from the Global Trade Analysis Project (GTAP) used in the computable general equilibrium model are based on national sources. A different methodology is used by the United Nations Statistics Division (UNSD), resulting in considerably different sector sizes. The UNSD methodology is linked to the GTAP disaggregation to match it as much as possible, and UNSD sectoral growth rates are then applied to the shares of GTAP sectors.

Applying these sectoral growth rates of the two groups of countries and their sectoral shares[208] yields an additional developmental decade of structural transformation, as seen in figure 4.16, which builds on existing structural transformation under the vision scenario for 2025. Oil-producing countries could boost manufacturing shares from 27 per cent in 2025 to 37.6 per cent in 2035, by increasing the value added of manufacturing and reducing the share of oil, gas and mining by more than eight percentage points. Structural transformation for non-oil producers would also be strong, with the manufacturing share rising by almost 8 per cent and agriculture falling by 3.5 per cent. A mixture of low (such as wholesale and retail trade) and high (such as financial mediation) value-added services would decrease by 1.3 per cent in the case of oil producers and by 4.5 per cent for non-oil producers. However, this hides variations within the service sector, which should lean towards higher value-added services, especially in oil-producing countries.

4. Water and energy

The business-as-usual scenario assumes a continuation of historical patterns of water availability and demand, and of energy consumption and production, resulting in water shortages and unsustainable energy intensity.

In addition to water insecurity owing to natural aridity, climate change will make the region increasingly vulnerable to drought. If current conditions prevail, the quality of water services will decline as a result of increasing demand and weak infrastructure.[209] According to the World Bank, the region will face a severe water shortage in the next 10 years; 20 per cent of the

gap will result from climate change and 80 per cent from population pressures and rising per capita consumption.[210] The recent Paris Agreement on climate change should, however, alleviate the pressure.[211]

As people move to urban areas, where the population is expected to increase from 57 per cent of the total in 2011 to 70 per cent by 2030, water infrastructure will come under considerable pressure. The gap between water supply and demand, estimated at more than 43 km^3 per year in 2009, is expected to reach 127 km^3 per year by 2030.[212] Desalinated water, mainly found in GCC countries, is projected to increase from 1.8 per cent of the Arab region's water supply to 8.5 per cent by 2025. "Arab countries are expected to desalinate about 19 billion m^3 in 2016 and about 31.4 billion in 2025 — 30 per cent of unmet demand".[213] Arab climate predictions for the end of the twenty-first century indicate an even warmer and drier climate, emphasizing the need for immediate measures.[214]

Projections for GCC countries indicate that total annual demand for water will rise from 26 billion m^3 in 1995 to 49.4 billion m^3 by 2025. Agricultural demand will continue to dominate. However, in 2025, projected availability of water in GCC countries stands at 18.2 billion m^3. The water deficit in GCC countries, currently estimated at 15 billion m^3, will continue to increase, reaching around 31 billion m^3 by 2025 on present population and consumption trends.

Figure 4.17 shows the extent to which per capita water supplies in the region will have fallen by 2025 compared with 1960. Many countries are already tapping non-renewable groundwater sources. Overexploitation of groundwater will continue, accelerating the depletion of aquifer reserves, the deterioration of water quality and the growing salinity of agricultural land. Under such circumstances, large-scale food imports will be unavoidable.[215]

Primary energy demand has mostly been met by the region's two chief energy resources: crude oil and petroleum products, and natural gas. Combined, they account for more than 98 per cent of regional energy consumption. Burning crude oil and fuel oil in the summer to overcome shortages in domestic supplies of natural gas in some Gulf countries has become the norm, with vast losses in revenue. They will soon have to consider whether they can continue consuming rising shares of finite energy resources at the same rate.

Under the business-as-usual scenario, energy demand will rise due to rapidly increasing population, increased travel and widespread energy subsidies. Energy intensity will increase in most Arab countries.[216] Total energy consumption and energy consumption per capita will grow at an annual average of 3.7 per cent and 2.1 per cent.[217] Energy intensity, already high

Compared to other regions, is set to deteriorate (increase) even further in several Arab States (figure 4.18). Domestic oil consumption in the Arab region could reach European Union (EU) levels before 2030, even though its population is expected to be half and its economy only one fifth the size of those of the EU.[218] If Saudi Arabia does not curb domestic energy demand and diversify its electricity generation profile, it could be a net oil importer by 2038 (figure 4.19).

Figure 4.17 Annual per capita water supply forecast for 2025

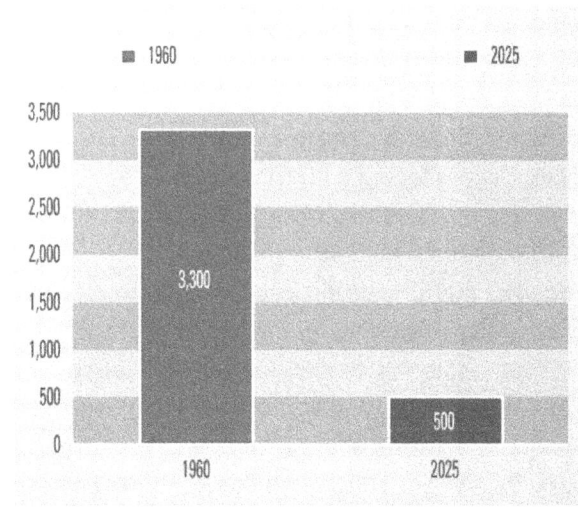

Source: IFAD, 2009.

Looking forward along the business-as-usual path, forecasts on energy consumption are telling. The starting point mix of energy in the region is completely reliant on liquids and natural gas, while quite diversified in the world as a whole. Expected dynamics are even worse, as the consumption growth for the region for liquids and natural gas is almost twice as large as global growth in those two energy sources. The share of renewables on the global level is expected to reach almost 6 per cent by 2030, but stay below 1 per cent in the Arab region (figure 4.20). This consumption pattern is neither efficient nor sustainable.

Several proposals have been put forward for achieving sustainable water and energy consumption, including from the Arab High-level Forum on Sustainable Development, held in Amman in April 2014, and the Arab Ministerial Council Meeting on the Sustainable Development Goals, held in Sharm al-Sheikh in October 2014. The following proposals refer to the water sector:

(a) Achieve universal and equitable access to safe and affordable drinking water for all by 2030;

(b) Substantially increase water-use efficiency across all sectors and ensure sustainable withdrawals and supply of freshwater to address water scarcity, and substantially reduce the number of people suffering from water scarcity by 2030;

(c) Integrate water resources management at all levels, including through transboundary cooperation as appropriate by 2030.

With regard to the energy sector, the following is suggested:

(a) Ensure access to sustainable energy for all and raise the share of renewable energy to 20 per cent of total energy consumption in the region by 2030;

(b) Phase out all fuel subsidies by 2020;

(c) Ensure universal access to affordable, reliable and modern energy services by 2030;

(d) Double the global rate of improvement in energy efficiency by 2030;

(e) Strengthen resilience and adaptive capacity to climate-related hazards and natural disasters in all countries.

Even with natural gas playing a larger role in the energy mix, particularly in North African countries, failure to substitute oil in the power sector will be damaging. Maintaining today's fuel mix will mean an extra 2 million barrels per day of oil used in the region's power sector by 2035, representing a financial drain on the region's fiscal balances (although partly alleviated if oil prices increase correspondingly) and a drop in its oil exports.[219]

Figure 4.18 Energy intensity (ton per $1 million 2005 GDP)

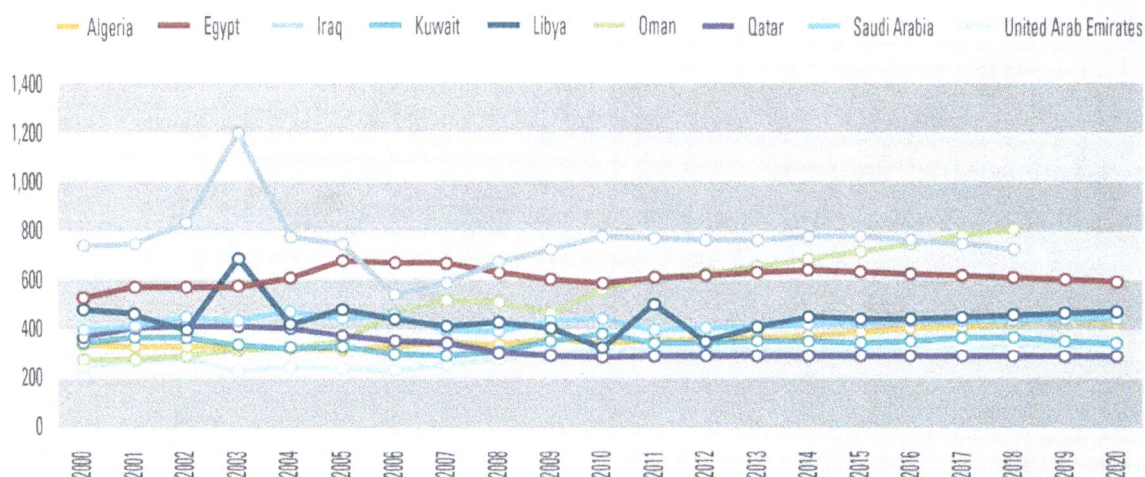

Source: Economist Intelligence Unit, 2014.

Figure 4.19 Saudi Arabian oil balance on the business-as-usual trajectory

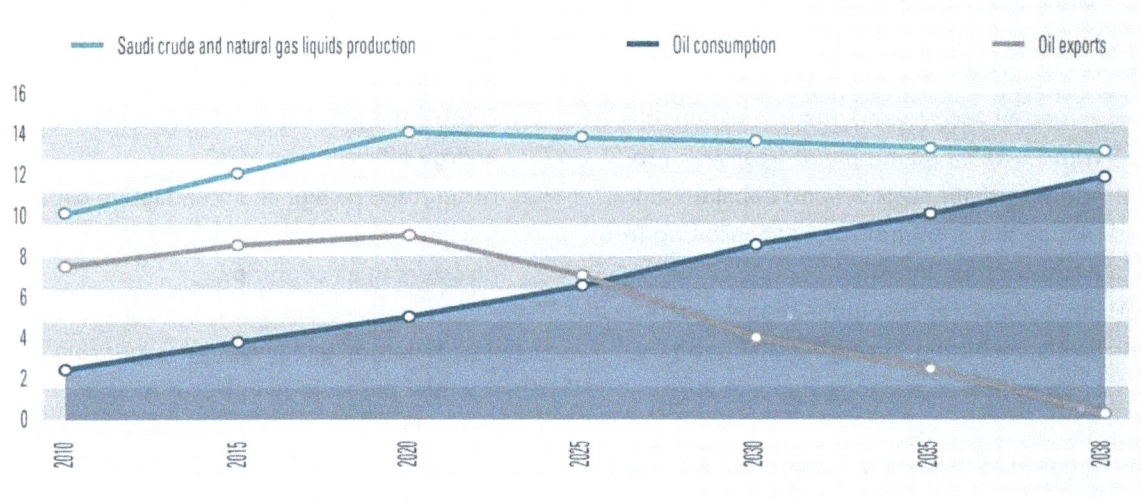

Source: Lahn and Stevens, 2011.

Figure 4.20 Total energy consumption by fuel type

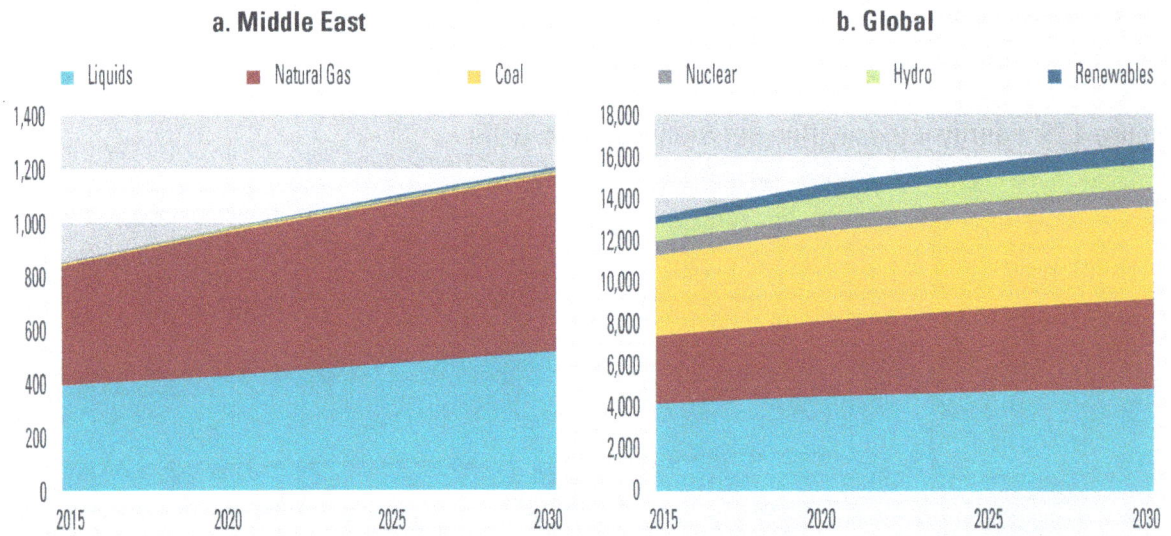

Source: British Petroleum, 2015.

Note: Countries included are Bahrain, the Islamic Republic of Iran, Iraq, Israel, Jordan, Kuwait, Lebanon, Oman, Qatar, Saudi Arabia, the Syrian Arab Republic, the United Arab Emirates and Yemen.

D. Policy recommendations

Potential for structural transformation in the Arab region is linked to the global economy, and the institutions and rules that govern it. This section considers how macroeconomic policies can be used to promote structural change.

1. Macroeconomic and sectoral policies

Macroeconomic policy should be used to advance economic growth, industrial development and diversified employment, rather than to favour a minority through rent-oriented activities.[220] The global sustainable development agenda provides an important reference point for charting such a course.

A number of policy ingredients and other conditions characterize countries with consistently high growth rates, including macroeconomic stability achieved through manageable fiscal deficits, relatively low or moderate inflation, manageable debt, high savings and investment rates, sound domestic markets, integration in world markets, the adoption of new technologies, and mobile labour and capital. Deeper regional economic policy coordination can contribute to industrial growth and sectoral development.

(a) Quality public investment, financial incentives and structural transformation policies

Government capital expenditure should play a significant role in investment. In the early 2000s, public investment in East and South-East Asia reached 24 per cent of total investment (32 per cent in Viet Nam). Public spending can have a "crowding-in" effect on private investment by loosening supply constraints on long-term growth and creating the fundamentals, such as infrastructure, for a market economy to prosper.

Crowding-in multipliers can be substantial, helping to increase labour productivity and capital. In contrast, there is little evidence of the "crowding-out" of private by public investment through changes in interest or exchange rates;[221] crowding-out is minimized when moderate monetary expansion accompanies increased government investment. Public resources can also help to redirect investment to poor regions and groups that otherwise might remain outside market reach. China invested in its poorer western regions under its National Poverty Alleviation Strategy, and Indonesia helped spread the benefits of urban manufacturing growth into rural areas.[222]

Public investment in the Arab region is higher than in other developing regions and the OECD average. Nevertheless, it is essential to make careful choices for optimal investment levels and allocations across sectors in order to boost economic growth that benefits broad sections of society.[223] Investments that promote structural transformation and shift labour from low to high value-added sectors are particularly beneficial. Evidence from 52 developing economies suggests that, between 1990 and 2013, countries that have experienced growth by moving toward high-value added sectors such as manufacturing, trade and transport, and communications have made significant progress in reducing poverty.[224]

In many cases, public investment in the region should branch out from large-scale projects into smaller initiatives, especially in rural areas, and aim at increasing social impact and improving opportunities for the poor. More must be done to relax credit policies for private enterprises that provide high quality jobs, and for small and medium enterprises,[225] which are the backbone of many economies. Public investment in research and development will spur innovation at reduced costs, with potentially large spillover benefits. Public-private partnerships can leverage private-sector financing and participation in larger projects, especially in infrastructure.[226]

High national savings are needed for public investment in critical areas such as infrastructure, health and education. Liberalization and deregulation should be approached with caution. States should consider industrial policies covering directed credit, trade protection, export subsidies and tax incentives. More importantly, they should encourage public-private sector cooperation, which does not mean creating protected bubbles vulnerable to crony capitalism. Industrial policy should emphasize the policy process as one of discovery, "where firms and the Government learn about underlying costs and opportunities and engage in strategic coordination".[227]

(b) Monetary policy

Mainstream economic doctrine calls for low inflation, at close to 2 per cent, but there is little empirical evidence to suggest that inflation rates above that level, or even above 10 per cent, hamper growth in developing countries. Threshold values for inflation differ between developed and developing countries, with values for industrialized countries around 2 per cent and exceeding 19 per cent in non-industrialized countries.[228]

Arab countries need more independence in monetary policy that can control inflation sufficiently to protect poorer groups from its worst effects, while allowing it to rise enough to promote rapid economic expansion and structural transformation.

The choice of an exchange rate regime depends on country specifics. Monetary measures can be used to manage flexible exchange rates in response to adverse demand or supply shocks. This also remedies the risk of companies being priced out of a market because of drastic exchange rate changes. A more flexible exchange rate is especially effective before export diversification. After export diversification and more regional integration, using monetary policy to stabilize the exchange rate can become more useful.

(c) Technology development and building productive capacities

Total investment in research and development in Arab countries is half that of Singapore and a quarter of what is invested by Israel.[229] Economic and development strategies in the region should therefore aim to boost such investment significantly.

Part of the solution lies in creating centres of excellence and coordinating Arab scientific research programmes. The region can learn from the EU, whose member States have adopted a coordination plan, created the European Joint Research Centre together with the Massachusetts Institute of Technology

Foundation, and adopted a programme for research and technological development.[230]

Specific industrial policies may be needed to promote agro-industry and rural non-farm activities.[231] Policies aimed at positioning industrial firms at the right stage of global value chains (GVCs), so they can profit from increases in international trade in intermediate and semi-finished products, are crucial, as is infrastructure development. The Arab region could capitalize on its natural resources through commodity-based industrialization, whereby upstream linkages are used to replace raw materials as exports with more highly valued processed goods in the same branch. There are several examples of this in Africa: Botswana has added value to diamond exports by conducting high-level processing internally; in Ethiopia, 95 per cent of leather exports are now processed domestically; South Africa has taken advantage of its mining sector to enlarge the manufacturing sector through the production of mining equipment.[232]

Refining capacity in Arab countries rose between 1973 and 1990 from 2.7 million to 5.2 million barrels per day, but has since stagnated. However, as domestic demand increases, renewed interest has been shown in establishing new refineries and expanding old ones.[233] Building upon this initial value addition to crude oil, the region can move further into other related high-value industries and so achieve long-term transformation.

(d) Knowledge economy and growth

In the long term, high-income Arab countries (oil exporters) need to break the shackles of oil dependence, while their low and middle-income counterparts need to move away from traditional labour-intensive industries. By enhancing education and research opportunities, the region can ensure that the human capital needs of high-tech industry and services are met. Progress in service sectors will also improve prospects for entrepreneurship and economic growth in other sectors, as financial market distortions decrease and the matching of finances to productivity-enhancing activities improves.[234] The Arab region could benefit from service-sector clustering in burgeoning cities through information sharing and local innovation networks.[235] Education policy needs to include the long-term aim of reducing reliance on external sources for technological expertise in the region.

The Saudi experience provides some useful indicators on how to proceed. In 2007, a five-year communications and information technology plan was launched to help build the knowledge economy. Basic legal and regulatory frameworks on intellectual property rights and patents were brought into line with international standards. Educational reforms, focused on ICT-related human capital, have been designed to meet growing demand for technical workers. The Government is investing in ICT infrastructure and encouraging more widespread use of broadband Internet and smart phones. In 2011, the Saudi Arabian General Investment Authority built upon these efforts to develop a 20-year plan for ICT investment. The country already controls much of the region's telecommunications and information technology markets, and aims to push growth through further investment in state-of-the-art infrastructure and support for e-commerce activities.

(e) Employment generation

Greater social dialogue and policies are needed to stimulate job creation, increase the quality of jobs and introduce universal social protection. Reforms are needed to facilitate the formation and growth of small and medium enterprises, including through access to credit and financial services. Labour market policies to establish employment and job counselling services and to support small and medium enterprises, will help to meet market demand and better integrate certain groups, such as young people and women.

The use by GCC countries of low-cost migrant labour dampens labour productivity and wages, and encourages nationals to seek employment in an increasingly bloated public sector.236 Macro and sectoral policies favouring greater productivity and the creation of high-wage jobs attractive to nationals should be implemented. Balances in social costs and benefits should be considered under migration policy.

To achieve full employment by 2030, the non-oil-producing Arab countries would require total investment of $4.4 trillion (in constant 2005 prices), substantially higher than available domestic savings in these countries. In the Vision 2030 scenario, complementarities in growth and employment between oil-poor and oil-rich economies are essential since, with stronger regional integration, the former are provided with demand for their surplus labour, and the latter have an opportunity to upgrade their economic structure and use the expanded Arab market to promote emerging industries.

Most Arab countries have achieved gender parity in education but need laws prohibiting discrimination against women and removing barriers to them in the labour market.[237]

2. Water and energy policies

(a) Efficient usage

Modern irrigation methods cover only 27 per cent of irrigated land in Egypt, 16 per cent in Morocco and 11 per cent in Tunisia.[238] Broadening their use will reduce water loss and increase productivity. High-density vertical growing systems, for example, are well suited to desert environments; Arab countries with limited arable land must look to them if they are to feed a population expected to double in the coming 40 years. Producing saltwater tolerant varieties of strategic crops, particularly in low-lying parts of northern Egypt and other coastal areas, where salinity is rising, could prove crucial.[239]

A regional research and development fund with a long-term budget could be the best agricultural investment for the region. Greater integration and a regional farming policy could make food self-sufficiency feasible, at least to a certain degree.

(b) Water pricing

Efforts should be stepped up to bring water prices closer to actual cost, establish decentralized water management associations and encourage traditional water conservation in rain-fed areas. Price incentives can improve irrigation efficiency. Morocco and Tunisia have reduced irrigation subsidies and are using volumetric pricing, thus charging farmers by the amount of water used instead of the number of cultivated hectares. Jordan has imposed a graduated tariff on water supply services. Such steps can only slow the rate of resource depletion; other fundamental interventions, such as reuse of treated wastewater and improved water governance, are necessary.

(c) Water desalination and reuse

Large-scale desalination has been taking place in the Arab region for more than 50 years and the most commonly used techniques are considered efficient and reliable. The region produces 44 per cent of the world's supply of desalinated water, and this is expected to rise.[240] In 2013, Algeria, Kuwait, Libya, Qatar, Saudi Arabia, and the United Arab Emirates were among the top 10 desalinating countries globally.[241]

However, they are all oil rich and their desalination processes require costly energy from petroleum and natural gas, although new technologies are driving the cost down. In the long term, solar energy will become one of the cheapest sources of power and increase capacity for desalination.[242] The cost of desalination will also decrease as techniques become more efficient.[243]

Treated wastewater reuse has great potential. Around 55 per cent of total wastewater in the region is treated and 15 per cent is treated and reused in agriculture, landscape irrigation, industrial cooling and environmental protection. Water reuse helps recharge groundwater in some countries. Egypt, Saudi Arabia, the Syrian

Arab Republic, and the United Arab Emirates are the largest gross users, accounting for 75 per cent of regional domestic water reuse. Jordan, Kuwait, Qatar, the Syrian Arab Republic, and the United Arab Emirates were the top five Arab countries in terms of water reuse per capita in 2010. However, economic, institutional, health, and environmental problems restrict the sustainable and safe reuse of wastewater. Concerted efforts, supported by regional and international organizations, are required to boost the volume of treated water that is reused.[244]

(d) Water governance

Reforms are needed to better redistribute access to water. Ensuring sustainable use requires a policy shift from increasing supply to managing demand.[245] Measures could include metering and tariffs on groundwater extraction. Regulations, institutional reform, tax exemptions, pricing subsidies on technology, and capacity-building for farmers could encourage the adoption of water-efficient agricultural techniques.[246] Public-private partnerships are used to manage water supply networks in Jordan and Morocco, and construct water supply and sanitation systems in Algeria, Egypt, Qatar, Saudi Arabia and the United Arab Emirates. Raising public awareness of water-saving practices in agriculture, industry and households can bring about considerable savings in water consumption.

Further improvements in water governance require greater national, regional and international cooperation. Two thirds of water resources in the region are transboundary. Arab countries with international rivers, such as

Egypt, Iraq, Jordan, the Sudan and the Syrian Arab Republic, need adequate agreements with other riparian countries, particularly those upstream.[247] The Arab Ministerial Water Council, established in 2008, has attempted to implement region-wide programmes for water and sanitation monitoring and a unified strategy for shared water. It has failed to address the issue of fair utilization of shared resources.[248] A lack of good governance has inflamed conflict between Israel and Arab countries, since the Jordan River, shared by Israel, Jordan, Lebanon, Palestine and the Syrian Arab Republic, has been mostly controlled by Israel since 1967.[249]

(e) Renewable energy and fossil fuel subsidies

The Pan-Arab Renewable Energy Strategy 2030 has projected increases in renewable energy from 12 gigawatts of power generation capacity in 2013 to 75 gigawatts by 2030. Arab countries have reached broad consensus on a long-term renewable energy target, in partnership with the private sector, but it does not go far enough.[250]

Europe also needs a secure, affordable and clean electricity supply, suggesting potential for the two regions to develop an integrated power system. The idea that renewable electricity could be produced in areas with optimal resources and exported to regions with high demand has become known as the Desertec vision.[251] Europe could source some of its electricity production from the southern Mediterranean deserts, which have excellent solar and wind resources and are sparsely populated. By importing up to 20 per cent of its electricity from renewable energy resources in Arab countries, Europe would meet a carbon

dioxide emissions reduction target of 95 per cent in the power sector.

Arab countries could supply this market and meet their own energy needs from abundant solar and wind resources, while reducing emissions in the power sector by 50 per cent, even with a massive increase in demand. Exports could be worth up to €63 billion annually. Europe and Arab countries would profit from a 40 per cent drop in the marginal cost of emission reductions in the power sector.[252]

To stimulate the use of renewable energy resources, the region should phase out fuel subsidies and use part of the resulting savings to support renewable projects and subsidize related research and development. Removing subsidies would also curb problems such as wasteful consumption and encourage the switch to renewables. If fuel subsidies are phased out by 2020, there will be more opportunities for growth, taking into account that some compensatory measures may be required to facilitate the process. A recent ESCWA study explored renewable energy growth in Jordan, driven by public-private partnerships.[253]

(f) Nuclear power

In 2012, the United Arab Emirates started building the region's first nuclear power plant. Egypt has also begun building such a facility.[254] Algeria, Jordan, Libya, Morocco and Saudi Arabia are studying the nuclear option. Growing demand and higher standards of living justify interest in nuclear power, which could also be used for desalination. In Saudi Arabia, for instance, around 9 per cent of total annual electricity production is used for desalination and groundwater extraction.[255]

(g) Regional energy solutions

Structural transformation of the energy sector is best tackled at the regional level. The Arab Ministerial Council for Electricity, established in 1994, developed the Pan-Arab Strategy for the Development of Renewable Energy 2010-2030, but cooperation remains weak. There are only two regional natural gas pipelines, the Dolphin and Arab Gas Pipelines, and cross-border electrical connections provide exchanged energy of only 2.7 per cent of total electricity production. Studies indicate that, by 2020, an increase of 135 gigawatts of generating capacity will be required to meet the region's growing energy needs; with an integrated approach, only 102 gigawatts would be needed.[256] Enhancing regional cooperation to supplement shortfalls in non-renewable energy would also stimulate progress on the use of renewable energy resources.

E. Conclusion

Rentier economics and oil dependency have largely doomed past economic policies in the region to failure. Structural transformation is the only viable way out of many of the region's problems. Reliance on extractive resources holds back Arab countries from inclusive and productive growth, resulting in import-based economies with predominantly low value-added, service-based activities. They are unable to benefit from technological change and do not have the incentive to invest in dynamic industries that generate high-skilled labour and well-paid jobs.

Arab States will need to play a more active policy role and ensure a larger revenue base in order to finance capital expenditure and generate employment. The multipliers for public investment can be substantial if it boosts the productivity of labour and capital. Manufacturing-led economic policies should go hand in hand with efforts to improve governance and deepen regional integration.

The business-as-usual scenario is economically and environmentally unsustainable. Oil dependency leads to a highly energy-intensive pattern of production and consumption. Tackling energy waste and water scarcity is a matter of economic survival. Structural transformation, technological progress and development of renewable energy sources will mark the way forward.

5. Human Development and Social Justice

A. Introduction

Advancing economic growth has been at the centre of public policy since the establishment of the gross national product (GNP) measurement. Although designed to measure economic progress only, it was also used as an indicator of general well-being until 1990. The limited application of economic growth to human lives was revealed by the human development concept and its associated human development index (HDI). The HDI is a summary of achievements in health, education and income, where the latter is seen as a means rather than as an end in itself.[257] The concept of human development is broader than the HDI and encompasses crucial aspects of human life, such as dignity, freedom, equity, sustainability, and opportunities, all of which are absent in GNP.

The HDI challenged the notion that economic growth is a sole prerequisite for improvements in human well-being in terms of health and education. Cross-country evidence during 1970-2010 shows that, although HDI improvements and income growth across countries are associated, there is no definitive pattern linking income growth to improvements in non-income dimensions of HDI (education and health).[258] That implies that improvements in health and education are possible without high income growth. Sen[259] compared GDP per capita and life expectancy at birth in Brazil, Mexico and the Republic of Korea (each with incomes above $1,500 and a life expectancy of 63-65 years) with China and Sri Lanka (with incomes of $290 or less and a life expectancy of 64 years or more), utilizing data from 1980. He argued that "if the Government of a poor developing country is keen to raise the level of health and the expectation of life, then it would be pretty daft to try to achieve this through raising its income per head, rather than going directly for these objectives through public policy and social change, as China and Sri Lanka have both done".[260]

Development patterns across the world indicate that wealthier countries in terms of GDP per capita are not necessarily better off in terms of human development.[261] Belonging to a "non-poor" household does not guarantee avoiding malnutrition or receiving an education, particularly in places with few or no public services.[262]

The link between HDI and income needs to be understood conceptually.[263] Economic growth contributes to human development through consumption growth in core indicators of HDI, such as nutrition and education. High economic growth can lead to high human development only if the former is distributed to benefit the poor. The transfer of high human development to high growth occurs through the enhancement of productivity and research and development. For example, improved health and nutrition have been shown to have direct effects on labour productivity, especially among poorer people.[264] Education is associated with additional earnings, whereby the rate of return varies with the level of education,[265] and plays a crucial role in research and development.[266]

The stronger the link between human development and economic growth, the more pronounced the virtuous cycle, with growth feeding into human development, which, in turn, promotes further growth.[267] The weaker the link, the stronger the propensity to enter a vicious downward cycle in which growth may not be sustainable. In the absence of a cycle, countries can enter situations of "human development lopsidedness" (only possible in resource-rich countries, where resource income is lavished on education, health and other areas of human development), with relatively strong human development but weak economic growth, and "economic growth lopsidedness", with relatively weak human development and strong economic growth. Neither situation is sustainable in the long run.

Social, economic and environmental sustainability are underlying principles of human development. Limited food, water and energy resources, and continued reliance on the unsustainable extraction of fossil fuels for economic growth, are major problems for the region. Sustainable production and consumption patterns are essential for balancing human activities and environmental sustainability.

Human development is also tied to the concept of social justice, which includes equal rights and access to resources and opportunities for all. In the Arab region, human development is undermined by discrimination, social exclusion, conflict, occupation and corruption. People in the region have risked their lives in violent protests, demanding an end to segmented social classes, exploitation, political repression, corruption and nepotism. Social justice must be an integral part of any vision for Arab human development.

Quality education, decent jobs, good health care, and honest and responsive governance were the top four priorities of the Arab people for the post-2015 period, according to an online My World Survey on the future they want (figure 5.1). The results reflect demands for basic State services. National consultations in 2013-2014 identified critical areas for consideration,[268] including governance, accountability, peace and security, rights, international partnerships, addressing inequality, and sustainability in all its dimensions. The meeting of the Council of Arab Social Affairs Ministers identified 15 regional development priorities and associated targets in their 2014 Sharm al-Sheikh Declaration.

Although the authors have been guided by the SDGs, data limitations have compelled them to select only a few human development indicators for the projection exercises in this chapter. They are set out in box 5.1, along with normative indicators that do not require exercises. Vision 2030 encompasses the following three interconnected objectives that conform to several SDGs, in particular goals 1-5, 8, 10, 12, and 17.

Figure 5.1 My World Survey votes on priorities for the Arab region

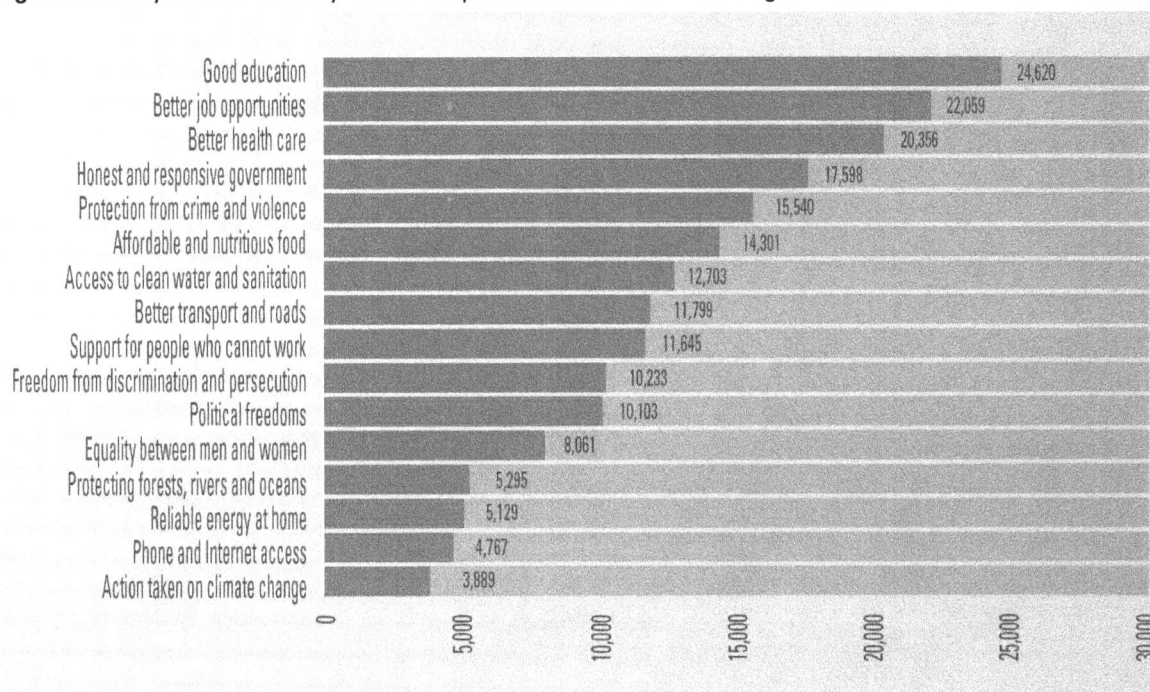

Priority	Votes
Good education	24,620
Better job opportunities	22,059
Better health care	20,356
Honest and responsive government	17,598
Protection from crime and violence	15,540
Affordable and nutritious food	14,301
Access to clean water and sanitation	12,703
Better transport and roads	11,799
Support for people who cannot work	11,645
Freedom from discrimination and persecution	10,233
Political freedoms	10,103
Equality between men and women	8,061
Protecting forests, rivers and oceans	5,295
Reliable energy at home	5,129
Phone and Internet access	4,767
Action taken on climate change	3,889

Source: United Nations, My World Survey data. Available from http://data.myworld2015.org (accessed 30 January 2015).

1. Committing to ending poverty and hunger

Ending extreme poverty by 2030, measured by a poverty line of $1.90 per day (2011 PPP), is the bare minimum. However, that does not cover most poor people in the middle-income countries of the region. Assigning different poverty lines to countries grouped by their standard of living, such as the level of expenditure per capita, can provide more accurate information about the true scope of poverty.[269] The use of national definitions of poverty is therefore a priority. Harmonized data and measurement methodologies across the region are also important to enable comparison of progress between countries.[270]

Non-income aspects of poverty include: inadequate access to electricity and clean water;

social exclusion; a lack of decent employment; and conditions that prevent people from fully developing their capabilities.[271] Hunger and undernourishment are on the rise, despite improvements in income poverty until 2010 and economic growth. Goals for 2030 include adequate food for all, reduced malnutrition and the eradication of stunting.

2. Ensuring equity and environmental sustainability essential for quality growth and human development

Greater emphasis should be placed on making economic growth more inclusive and sharing benefits equitably. Provision of social protection and redistributive expenditure policies can protect incomes and promote social mobility. Sustainability needs to be factored into production and consumption patterns, and consumers need to be aware of the costs and benefits of those patterns, which can affect long-term development paths.

3. Promoting convergence and regional integration

Arab countries should aim for regional convergence in human development. Oil-rich countries have invested heavily in education and health using oil and gas revenues. Arab LDCs, however, and several developing countries in the region face severe fiscal constraints in combating poverty, child and maternal mortality, and undernourishment. Inequality between Arab countries is high and has increased since 2000.[272] For more on the Vision 2030 approach to regional development, see chapter 6.

Box 5.1 Vision 2030: selected targets for human development

- Eradicate extreme poverty
- Reduce poverty by at least half, according to national definitions
- Implement nationally appropriate social protection systems and measures for all, and ensure complete coverage for the poor and vulnerable
- End hunger and guarantee access for all to safe, nutritious and sufficient food all year round
- End all forms of malnutrition, with special attention to eradicating stunting and wasting in children under the age of 5
- Establish sustainable food production systems and implement resilient agricultural practices
- End preventable deaths of newborns
- Reduce under-5 mortality
- Reduce maternal mortality
- Eradicate AIDS, tuberculosis, malaria and tropical diseases, and combat hepatitis and waterborne and communicable diseases
- Ensure access to health, including sexual and reproductive, and psychological care for all
- Provide free, equitable and quality primary and secondary education for all
- Provide quality early childhood development care and pre-primary education for all
- Improve the pupil-teacher ratio
- Ensure that all young people and adults achieve literacy and numeracy
- End all forms of discrimination and violence against women and girls
- Ensure the full and effective participation by and equal opportunities for women at all levels of decision-making in political, economic and public life
- Improve the ratio of female-to-male labour force participation
- Ensure equal opportunities and reduce inequalities of outcome
- Adopt effective fiscal and wage policies and progressively achieve greater equality

Source: Authors, based on the SDGs and related targets, and the Sharm al-Sheikh Declaration on the development priorities of the Arab region under the post-2015 development agenda.

B. Where the Arab region stands today

1. Human development since the 1990s

The Arab region has seen consistent improvements since the 1960s in literacy and school enrolment of boys and girls. The average years of schooling for adults (15 years and above) rose from 1.3 years in 1960 to 5.4 years in the 2000s, and illiteracy rates were halved.[273] There were significant improvements in higher education. In 1940, there were only 10 universities in the Arab region; in 2014, the number of higher education institutions had risen to nearly 1,000.[274] Child mortality has declined significantly and health outcomes have improved since the 1980s.[275] Per capita income has increased, although its growth rate is much lower than it should be, given relatively high

average economic growth since the 1970s.[276] Better education, increased life expectancy and higher income have led to improved capabilities and greater socioeconomic mobility, reflected in a rising HDI score between the 1980s and the early 2000s.

However, the rate of HDI progress has slowed significantly since 1990.[277] In the periods 1990-2000 and 2000-2013, a fall in this rate, measured by the average annual percentage change in the HDI score, was recorded in 11 out of the 14 Arab countries for which an HDI trend was available. A similar pattern was registered for 7 of 13 countries in 1980-1990 and 1990-2000. During the most recent period, 2010-2013, HDI growth was marginal for most countries and negative for conflict-affected countries, such as Libya and the Syrian Arab Republic (figure 5.2).

Figure 5.2 Average annual HDI change in Arab countries (percentage)

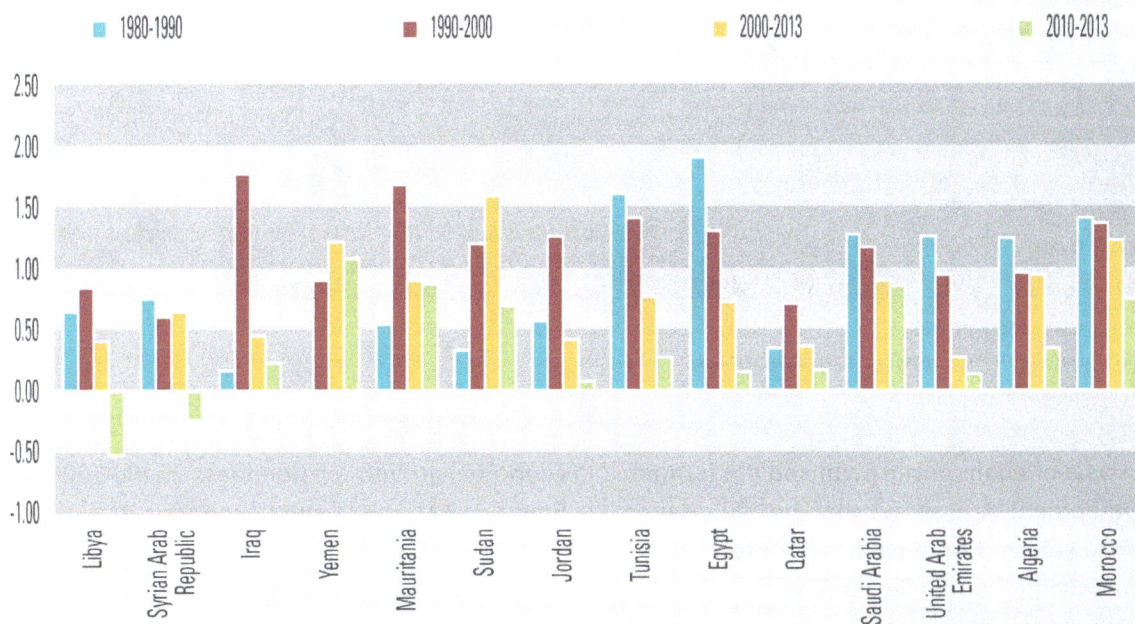

Source: Authors' calculations based on data from UNDP, Human Development Reports Data. Available from http://hdr.undp.org/en/data (accessed 1 November 2014).

Table 5.1 Virtuous, vicious and lopsided performance of Arab countries

	1960-1970	1970-1980	1980-1990	1990-2001	2001-2013*
Algeria	Vicious	Economic growth lopsided	Vicious	Human development lopsided	Growth average improved; HDI pace slowed
Egypt	Economic growth lopsided	Economic growth lopsided	Vicious	Vicious	Growth average slowed slightly; HDI pace slowed sharply
Jordan	-	-	Human development lopsided	Human development lopsided	Growth average improved sharply; HDI pace slowed sharply
Kuwait	Human development lopsided	Human development lopsided	Human development lopsided	Human development lopsided	-
Morocco	Economic growth lopsided	Economic growth lopsided	Vicious	Vicious	Growth average improved sharply; HDI pace slowed
Oman	Economic growth lopsided	Vicious	Virtuous	-	-
Saudi Arabia	Economic growth lopsided	Economic growth lopsided	Human development lopsided	Human development lopsided	Growth average improved sharply; HDI pace slowed
Syrian Arab Republic	Virtuous	Virtuous	Human development lopsided	Human development lopsided	-
Tunisia	Economic growth lopsided	Economic growth lopsided	Human development lopsided	Human development lopsided	Growth average slowed; HDI pace slowed sharply
United Arab Emirates	-	Human development lopsided	Human development lopsided	Human development lopsided	Negative growth average; HDI pace slowed sharply

Source: Ranis and Stewart, 2005.

* The column on 2001-2013 is based on authors' calculations.

Analysis of economic growth and the human development data shows that, by 2001, seven of nine selected Arab countries were experiencing human development lopsidedness, and two were caught up in a vicious downward cycle (table 5.1). No country entered the virtuous cycle or experienced economic growth lopsidedness in 1960-2001. Egypt and Morocco were economic growth lopsided in the 1960s and 1970s, but shifted into vicious cycles in the 1980s and 1990s. This suggests that the benefits of reasonably high economic growth did not translate into human development. In the 2000s, the HDI pace slowed for all countries in the sample, despite improved growth rates, indicating vicious cycles. For example, economic growth in Egypt slowed slightly from 2.7 per cent in the 1990s to 2.5 per cent in the 2000s, but HDI growth slowed from 1.3 per cent to 0.7 per cent over the same period. Taking into account the period 2005-2011, Egypt exhibited a paradox of high growth but increasing poverty.[278]

By 2001, oil-rich countries such as Algeria, Kuwait, Saudi Arabia and the United Arab Emirates were in the human development lopsided category, given that they could sustain heavy expenditure financed by oil revenues. Interestingly, Jordan, the Syrian Arab Republic and Tunisia were in this category too, and among the top MDG performers until 2010, as per the Arab MDGs report 2013.[279] Oman and Tunisia were among the top 10 global achievers in human development between 1970 and 2010.[280] However, the fact that uprisings took place in some of those top performers in 2010-2011 indicates that MDG and human development assessments have ignored significant development deficits and injustices.[281]

2. Poverty, inequality and social protection

(a) Rising poverty since 2010

In most Arab countries, much of the population is concentrated between the global extreme poverty line of $1.25 a day and $2.75

a day (in 2005 PPP). By shifting the poverty line from $1.25 to $2 and then to $2.75, poverty rates for the region increase from 4 per cent to 19 per cent to 40 per cent, respectively.[282] Such spectacular increases are a distinct feature of the Arab region.[283]

The global extreme poverty line, based on living conditions in the world's poorest countries,[284] is inappropriate as a benchmark for living conditions in the Arab region. The poverty rates are much higher when judged by national poverty lines. The report uses two poverty lines at national levels – lower and upper poverty lines.[285] People below the national lower poverty line are considered "poor" and those between the lower and upper poverty lines are "vulnerable" to poverty. Applying this method, 21.3 per cent and 19.5 per cent of people in the region were poor and vulnerable, respectively, based on data prior to the 2011 crises.[286]

Figure 5.3a shows the incidence of poverty according to the latest available household surveys, and figure 5.3b presents estimates taking into account the crises in the Syrian Arab Republic and Yemen. In the former, armed conflict has increased poverty from 12.3 per cent in 2007 to 43 per cent in 2013. In Yemen, even before hostilities broke out, prolonged recession had lifted poverty from 34.8 per cent in 2006 to 54.4 per cent in 2011; the number of vulnerable people in both countries has risen. In Egypt, poverty rose from 16.7 per cent in 2000 to 25.2 per cent in 2011, despite high economic growth rates.

Figure 5.3 Poverty rates in Arab countries in line with national poverty lines (percentage)

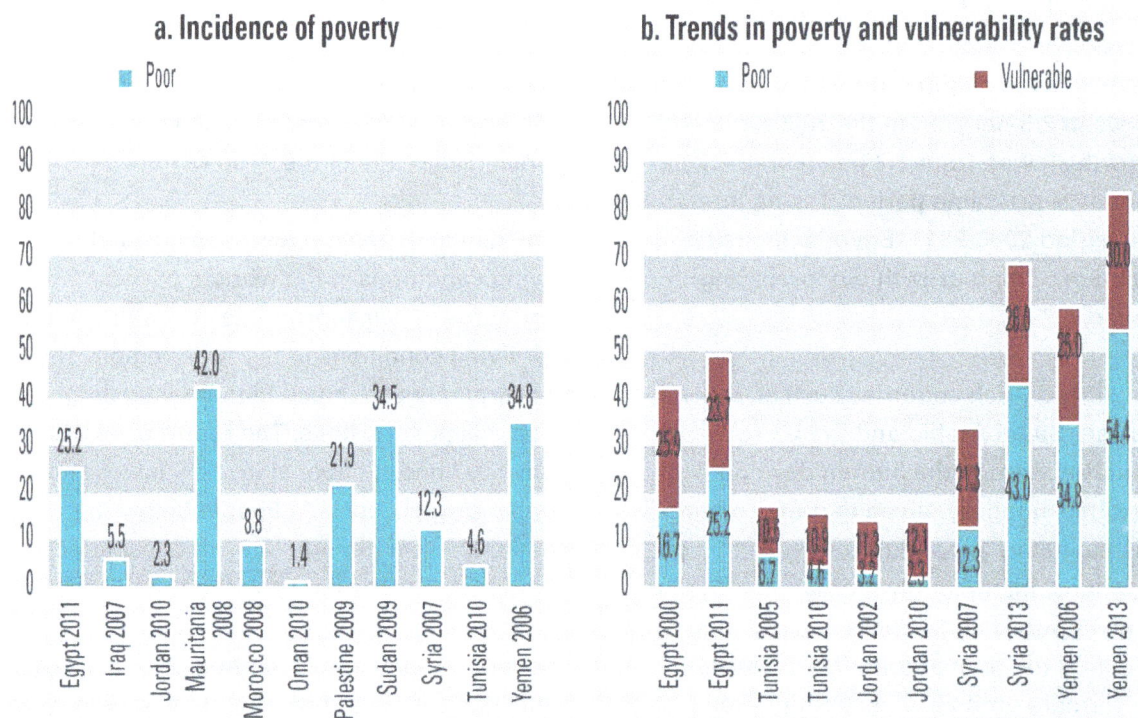

a. Incidence of poverty

- Poor

Values shown (Poor): Egypt 2011: 25.2; Iraq 2007: 5.5; Jordan 2010: 2.3; Mauritania 2008: 42.0; Morocco 2008: 8.8; Oman 2010: 1.4; Palestine 2009: 21.9; Sudan 2009: 34.5; Syria 2007: 12.3; Tunisia 2010: 4.6; Yemen 2006: 34.8

b. Trends in poverty and vulnerability rates

- Poor
- Vulnerable

Values shown: Egypt 2000: Poor 16.7, Vulnerable 25.0; Egypt 2011: Poor 25.2, Vulnerable 22.1; Tunisia 2005: 6.7 / 10.0; Tunisia 2010: 4.6 / 10.9; Jordan 2002: 3.2 / 11.8; Jordan 2010: 2.3 / 12.1; Syria 2007: 12.3 / 21.3; Syria 2013: Poor 43.0, Vulnerable 26.0; Yemen 2006: Poor 34.8, Vulnerable 25.0; Yemen 2013: Poor 54.4, Vulnerable 30.0

Source: Authors' calculations based on data from national household budget surveys of respective countries.

Note: The poverty and vulnerability rates in figures 5.3a and b are based on the latest national household surveys by using a consistent methodology across countries (in line with national lower and upper poverty lines). The poverty rate in the Syrian Arab Republic (2013) and in Yemen (2011) are authors' estimates, taking into account the impact of crises. Jordan's official poverty rate was 14.4 per cent in 2010, in line with the upper poverty line (or vulnerability line) as shown in figure 5.3b.

(b) Widening gap between rich and poor

Disparities in income and wealth across economic classes have increased significantly over the past decade in the Arab region. In Egypt, the Gini coefficient for wealth was 0.8 in 2014, having rapidly increased since 2010.[287] The 20 or so largest companies in the region are owned either by the State or by private family concerns.[288] Unfortunately, high inequality is not reflected in typical household survey expenditures. The Gini coefficient for expenditure remains moderate in Egypt and in most other Arab countries, ranging between 0.30 and 0.45.[289] Lack of reliable data on accounting wealth and expenditure makes it hard to estimate inequality measures accurately. However, the large difference between wealth and expenditure inequality, such as in Egypt, indicates that expenditure surveys fail to capture top incomes. The large and growing divergence between private final consumption expenditure, given by national accounts, and survey-based household expenditure substantiates that hypothesis.[290]

By combining information on expenditure from national accounts and household surveys, the disparity between the average expenditure of the rich and other population classes shows high and increasing inequality (figure 5.4).[291] For instance, in 2011, per capita expenditure of the rich in Egypt was more than 16 times higher than that of the poor, 11 times higher than that of vulnerable groups, 7 times higher than that of the middle class and 2.5 times higher than that of the affluent class. A similar situation was noted in Tunisia in 2010. Furthermore, the average expenditure ratio has increased significantly in most countries over the past decade. In Yemen, the ratio of the average expenditure of the rich to the average expenditure of the middle class doubled between 1998 and 2006; in Egypt, it increased from 5.7 to 7.4 between 2000 and 2011; and in Jordan, it rose from 2.9 to 3.4 between 2000 and 2010. In Tunisia, the ratio was stable at around 4 between 2005 and 2010.

(c) Social protection

Lack of adequate social protection is a major issue that the region needs to address in order to fight poverty and rising inequality. Two broad categories of social protection exist in Arab countries. The first consists of social insurance based on formal employment, which applies to 30-40 per cent of the workforce. The second comprises social assistance, which mainly covers cash transfers and subsidies for energy and food. On the sidelines, civil society organizations provide relief to the poor and destitute through *zakat* funds, for example.

However, social protection in the Arab region is neither universal nor rights-based. Three-quarters of the population do not receive any assistance, a rate similar to sub-Saharan Africa and South Asia.[292] According to the Arab NGOs Network for Development,[293] social protection has shrunk in most Arab countries because of financial constraints. Arab countries have failed to adopt important international social protection laws. For instance, Tunisia has not ratified the ILO Social Security (Minimum Standards) Convention, 1952 (No. 102). In Jordan, a number of international conventions are being ratified, but the right to health and housing are absent from the Constitution.

Figure 5.4 Average expenditure of different population groups

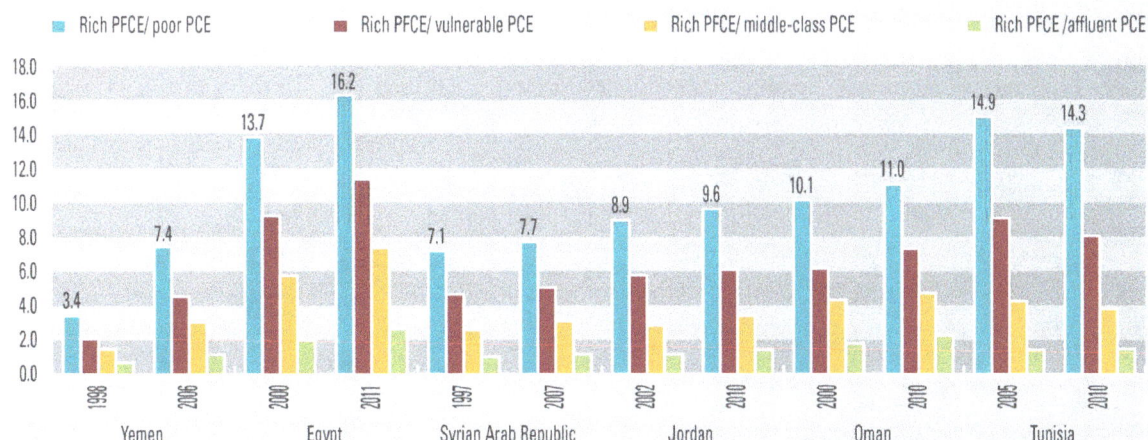

Abbreviations: PFCE, per capita final consumption expenditure; PCE, per capita expenditure.
Source: Authors' calculations based on data from national household budget surveys and National Accounts of respective countries.

3. Food insecurity and undernourishment

Tackling food insecurity is another major challenge for the Arab region. Low agricultural productivity is one of the critical barriers, in particular. For instance, cereal yields in the region are at half the world average (figure 5.5). Other factors, such as the scarcity of arable land and water resources, and low rainfall (chapter 4), make it difficult to produce enough food for a growing and increasingly urban population.

The region depends heavily on food imports, exposing it to fluctuations in agricultural commodity prices, as was the case in 2008. Dependence on cereal imports, high and fluctuating international food prices, and export restrictions in crisis situations put pressure on household and national budgets. The poor suffer most from price shocks, given that they spend 35-65 per cent of their income on food. Climate shocks may add to price pressure in the future unless preventive regional initiatives are taken. Conflicts and political instability have further undermined food security.

Nearly one quarter of people in the region were undernourished in 2014; it is the only region where the prevalence of undernourishment and the number of undernourished have increased. The latter rose from 9.7 million in 1990 to an estimated 22 million in 2015.[294]

Those numbers do not include Somalia and the Sudan. Estimates from the Food and Agriculture Organization (FAO) for 2009-2011 indicate that one quarter of the population in the Sudan and two-thirds of the population in Somalia were undernourished then. Including estimates for those two countries would double the total current number of undernourished people. The rate of undernourishment is particularly high in conflict-affected countries and LDCs. According to estimates in 2015, the rate was 15.9 per cent in Djibouti, 19 per cent in the Syrian Arab Republic, 22.8 per cent in Iraq and 26.1 per cent in Yemen.[295]

Figure 5.5 Cereal yield, world regions (kg/hectare)

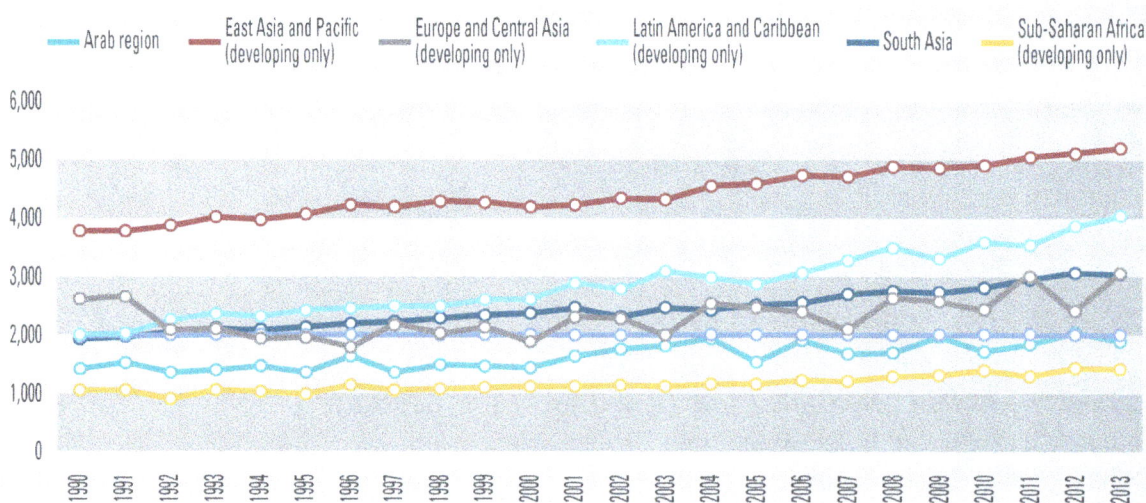

Source: World Bank, 2015d.

Figure 5.6 Stunting (percentage)

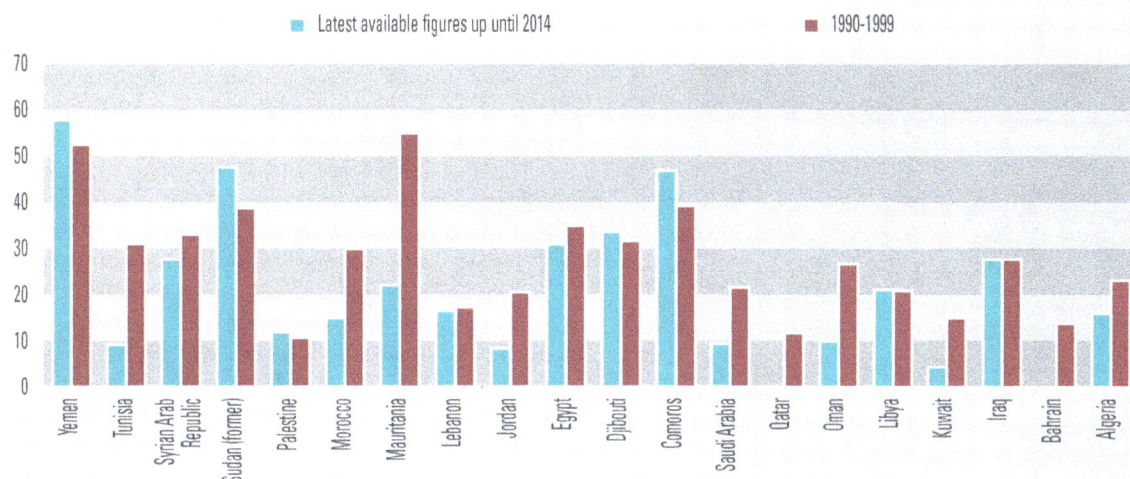

Source: Based on FAO, 2015.

Across the region, the proportion of underweight children aged under 5 increased from 14.5 per cent in the 1990s to 15.3 per cent in 2010.[296] In Arab LDCs, more than one in three children are affected. Chronic malnutrition among children, measured by stunting, has risen in many countries, particularly conflict-affected countries and LDCs such as the Comoros, Djibouti, the Sudan and Yemen (figure 5.6). Stunting is also high in Egypt, Iraq and the Syrian Arab Republic. On average, 22.2 per cent of Arab children were stunted in the year closest to 2014.[297]

4. The impact of crises on MDG gains and fiscal space

(a) Reversals in MDG gains

Crises in the Arab region have exacerbated poverty and other aspects of human development. No section of the population has remained untouched. In some countries, the middle class in particular has suffered. If the middle class accounted for 47 per cent of the region's population in the first decade of the

twenty-first century,[298] by 2013 it had shrunk to 36.7 per cent, largely as a result of the conflicts in the Syrian Arab Republic and Yemen.[299]

Crises have undone much of the region's development progress. By 2010, the Syrian Arab Republic had achieved many MDGs, including those on reducing extreme poverty, extending access to primary education and achieving gender parity in secondary education. It had also made remarkable progress towards other goals, such as cutting malnutrition and infant mortality rates, and boosting access to sanitation. Those achievements have been undone since 2011. Poverty, measured by the national poverty line, increased from 12 per cent in 2007 to an estimated 43 per cent in 2013. The country now struggles to provide health care, food security and education (box 5.2). According to an MDG achievement index, the Syrian Arab Republic was among the high achievers in the Arab region in 2010.[300] In 2013, it trailed behind the Sudan, one of the poorest MDG performers (figure 5.7).

Box 5.2 Impact of the Syrian crises on selected MDGs

1. Poverty and hunger: Applying the $1.25 poverty line, poverty in the Syrian Arab Republic declined from 7.9 per cent in 2007 to 0.2 per cent in 2010, but increased to 7.2 per cent in 2012-2013. Using the lower national poverty line, it rose from 12 per cent in 2007 to 43 per cent in 2013. The percentage of undernourished people climbed to 19 per cent in 2013, compared to a low of 5 per cent in 2011. The percentage of underweight children is estimated to have increased from 10 per cent in 2011 to 12 per cent in 2013.

2. Primary education: The percentage of children enrolled in primary schools fell from 98.4 per cent in 2011 to 70 per cent in 2013, which is the same as in the 1980s. Almost half of those enrolled drop out of school.

3. Child and infant mortality: The conflict has derailed the MDG on under-5 mortality, with the rate increasing from 21.4 per 1,000 in 2011 to 25.1 per 1,000 in 2013. Infant mortality is estimated to have risen from 17.9 per 1,000 live births in 2011 to 23.3 in 2013. Child vaccination rates have plunged from 99-100 per cent across provinces. For most types of vaccines, rates now range between 50 per cent and 70 per cent, and in some areas are near zero.

4. Maternal health: The maternal mortality rate was 52 per 100,000 live births in 2011. It is estimated to have reached 62.7 per 100,000 live births in 2013 due to damaged infrastructure and health facilities and a lack of medicine caused by falling domestic production. Births attended by skilled health personnel fell from 93 per cent in 2011 to 72 per cent in 2013. The international blockade and a lack of road safety, particularly between the countryside and cities in some provinces, are complicating the situation.

5. Diseases: Health, hygiene and environmental indicators have all declined, allowing for the re-emergence of nearly eradicated diseases. For example, after more than 14 years, poliomyelitis has reappeared among children, mostly in the northeast. Infectious and non-infectious diseases are on the rise, including a steady increase in cases of acute diarrhoea, particularly in the countryside around Damascus, Homs, Idlib, Aleppo and Deir al-Zor. The number of measles, typhoid and parotid gland hepatitis patients has also increased. The growing incidence of leishmaniasis, with 41,000 recorded cases in the first half of 2013, stems from heavy pollution and poor hygiene, particularly in the province of Aleppo.

Figure 5.7 MDG index

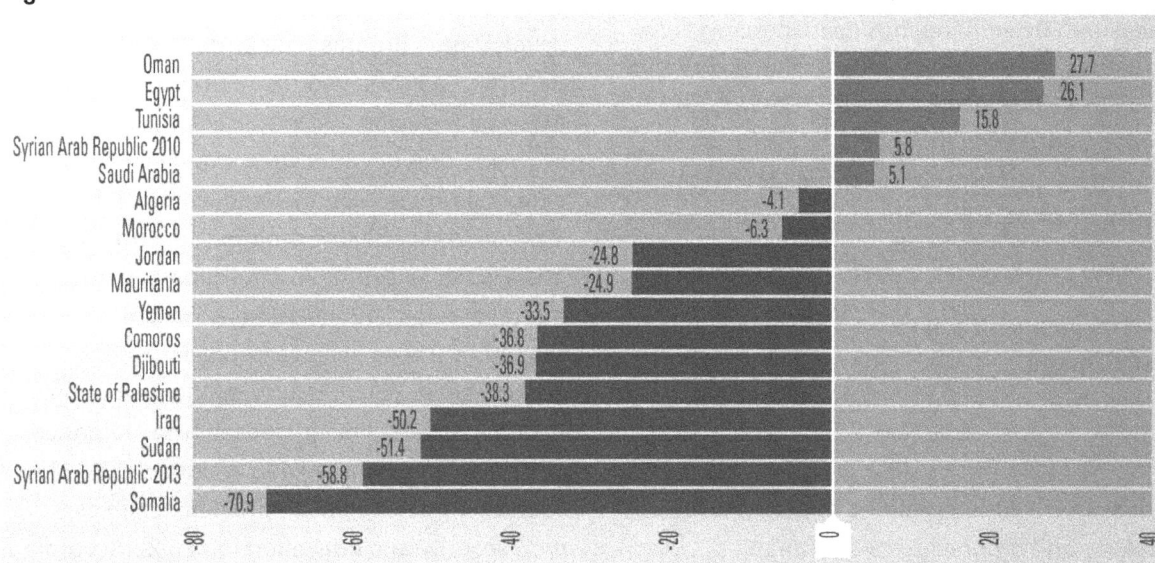

Source: ESCWA, 2014e.

Note: The MDG index reflects national performance in meeting 12 MDG targets by 2015, with 1990 as the base year. If the MDG index is zero, a country is on track to meeting the targets; if the index is higher than zero, the country is an early achiever; if it is less than zero, the country has not yet achieved the target. This index is based on available data at two points in time, the year closest to 1990 and the latest year. They cover the following: children under 5 moderately or severely underweight; undernourished proportion of the population; total net enrolment ratio in primary education; literacy rates of 15-24-year-olds; gender parity in primary level enrolment; gender parity in secondary level enrolment; children under 5 mortality rate; infant mortality rate; maternal mortality ratio; births attended by skilled health personnel; proportion of the population not using improved drinking water; and proportion of the population not using improved sanitation.

Box 5.3 Impact of conflict on poverty and hunger in Yemen

It is estimated that poverty in Yemen today affects more than 60 per cent of the population, and emergency humanitarian relief is needed to deal with hunger and malnutrition. In 2014, the World Food Programme (WFP) found that 10.6 million people, or 41 per cent of the population, did not have food security. Almost half were in severe need of food assistance. The conflict that erupted in 2015 has pushed many more Yemenis into hunger. According to one estimate, more than 12 million Yemenis face food insecurity and that number is likely to increase following an escalation in violence.

Of the 22 governorates in Yemen, 18 are affected by fighting. Telephone land lines and cell phone networks in parts of Aden and Abyan no longer work. A ban on shipping in Yemeni waters is worsening a severe fuel shortage that could be devastating for public health. More than half of the population, around 16 million people, needs humanitarian aid and has no access to safe water. The cost of water has more than tripled, from $13 to $43 per tank, equivalent to one quarter of an average monthly salary. Consequently, large-scale migration from Yemen is expected over the coming months.

Sources: United Nations News Service, 2015a and 2015b; UNHCR, 2015c; Dyke and Mojalli, 2015; and WFP, 2015.

Poverty in Yemen has risen from 34 per cent in 2006 to more than 60 per cent in 2015, due to economic recession and conflict (box 5.3). The unemployment rate in Gaza in the first quarter of 2014 stood at 40.8 per cent. Even as the global community is setting new goals on sustainable development for the post-2015 period, people in these Arab countries are struggling for basic survival.

(b) Fiscal challenges

The macroeconomic and fiscal situation in Arab countries, especially those in political transition, is daunting. After three years of transition, economic growth has plummeted, fiscal accounts have deteriorated and debt has risen. All Arab countries have been affected to varying degrees, either directly or indirectly. Libya, Tunisia, the Syrian Arab Republic and Yemen have experienced internal political crises. Economic growth in the Arab region had reached 4.4 per cent on average in 2000-2010 (population weighted), compared to only 1.6

per cent in 2011-2012 and 3.5 per cent in 2013.[301] Since then, the region has lost around 3 per cent of its economic growth because of political instability. Some countries increased public spending during the uprisings to satisfy protestors' demands for wage increases, subsidies and expanded social assistance. Those commitments have become difficult to reverse for political reasons and increased pressure on government budgets.

Low tax revenue is a significant fiscal constraint for most Arab Governments. Taxes comprise 62 per cent of government revenue worldwide, but only 37 per cent in the Arab region. Tax revenue as a percentage of GDP is around 15 per cent globally; in the Arab region, it varies from as little as 1 per cent in Kuwait to 23 per cent in Morocco. In Algeria, Libya, the Sudan, the Syrian Arab Republic and Yemen, the share is at or below 10 per cent.[302] Government revenues fell during the uprisings. Between 2010 and 2011, revenues declined from 25.1 per cent of GDP to 22 per cent in Egypt and from 31.5 per cent to 30.6 per cent in Tunisia.[303] In the oil-rich countries, the fiscal balance is declining, mainly due to the recent drop in oil prices (figure 5.8a). Most non-oil-rich countries have huge fiscal deficits, particularly due to the lack of fiscal adjustments in expenditure and revenue mobilization (figure 5.8b). Consequently, non-oil rich countries have experienced high and rising public debt, especially since 2010 (figure 5.9).

Official development assistance (ODA) from Development Assistance Committee (DAC) and non-DAC countries to the region, excluding oil-rich countries, which are net donors, declined from around $11 billion in 1990 to $3.3 billion in 2002. Thereafter, it picked up slowly, reaching around $9 billion in 2012. In 2013, ODA increased to $16 billion, mainly due to an increase in aid flow to conflict-affected countries such as the Syrian Arab Republic and Palestine.

The share of DAC ODA to total ODA has declined sharply from 92 per cent in 2010 to 54 per cent in 2013. ODA per capita in the non-oil-rich countries was $73 in 1990. It dropped sharply in the early 2000s and had recovered to $68.2 by 2013 (figure 5.10). ODA to six Arab LDCs has been on the rise, particularly since 2002, and reached $3 billion in 2013 (up from $0.66 billion in 2002). ODA fluctuation reflects the political stance of donors and conflict, as was the case in Iraq after 2002, and Lebanon and Palestine after 2007. An increase in aid to Jordan, Lebanon and the Syrian Arab Republic in 2013 could have been related to the crisis in the latter, and the increasing number of refugees in neighbouring countries. In some Arab countries, ODA represents a sizeable share of foreign capital inflows, but it is unlikely to be sufficient to meet the challenges they face.[304]

Figure 5.8 Government budget surplus/deficit (percentage of GDP)

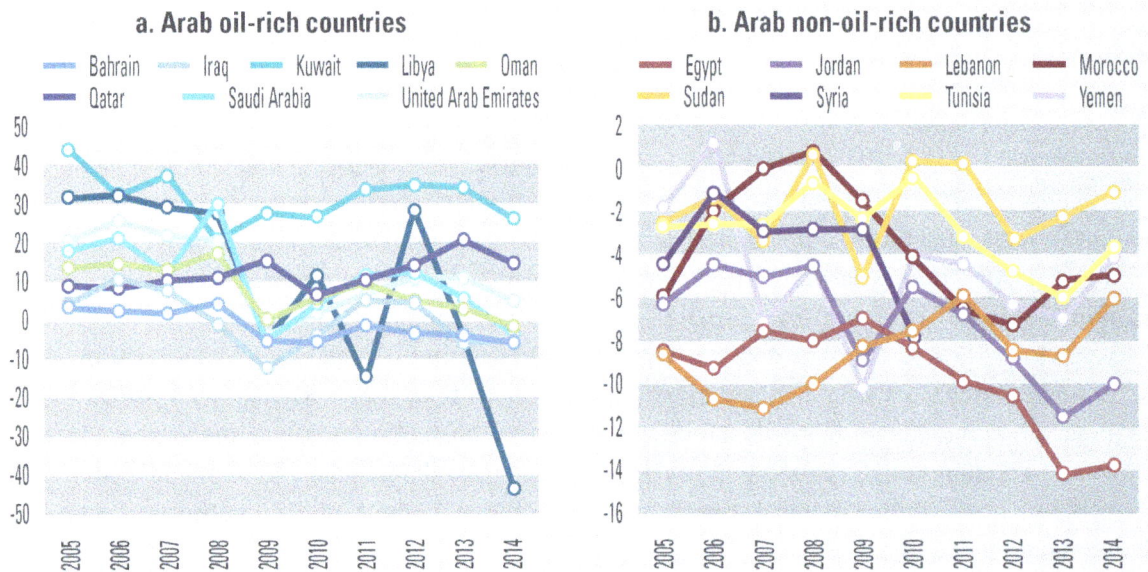

Source: IMF, 2015.

Figure 5.9 Government gross debt (percentage of GDP)

a. Arab oil-rich countries

Bahrain — Iraq — Kuwait — Libya — Oman
Qatar — Saudi Arabia — United Arab Emirates

b. Arab non-oil-rich countries

Egypt — Jordan — Lebanon — Morocco
Sudan — Syria — Tunisia — Yemen

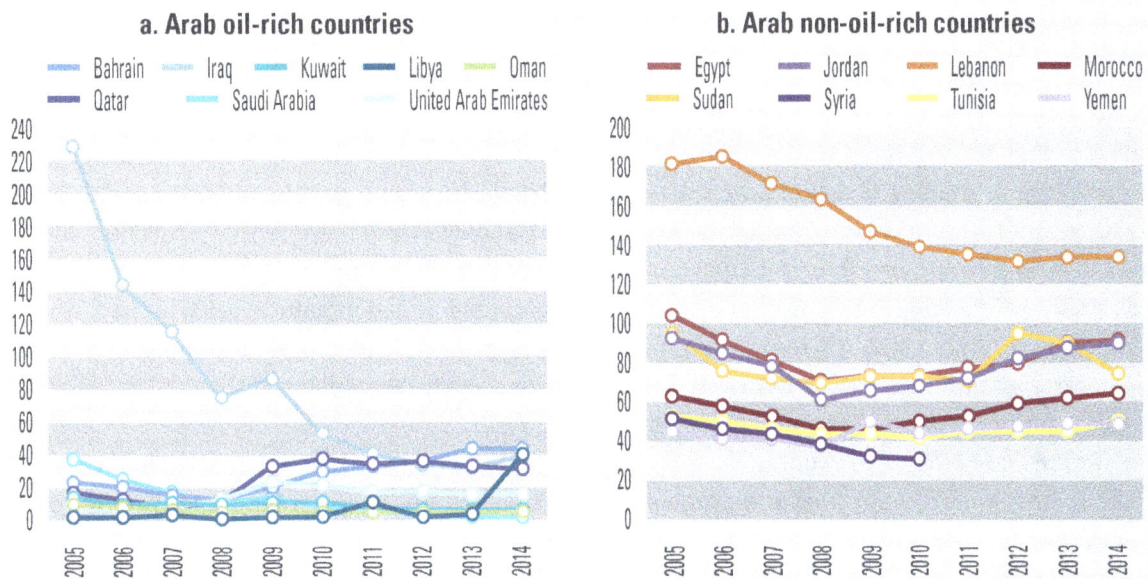

Source: IMF, 2015.

Figure 5.10 Per capita ODA for the Arab region (excluding oil-rich countries), current prices

Non Oil Producing Countries (DAC countries) — Total (DAC + Non DAC)

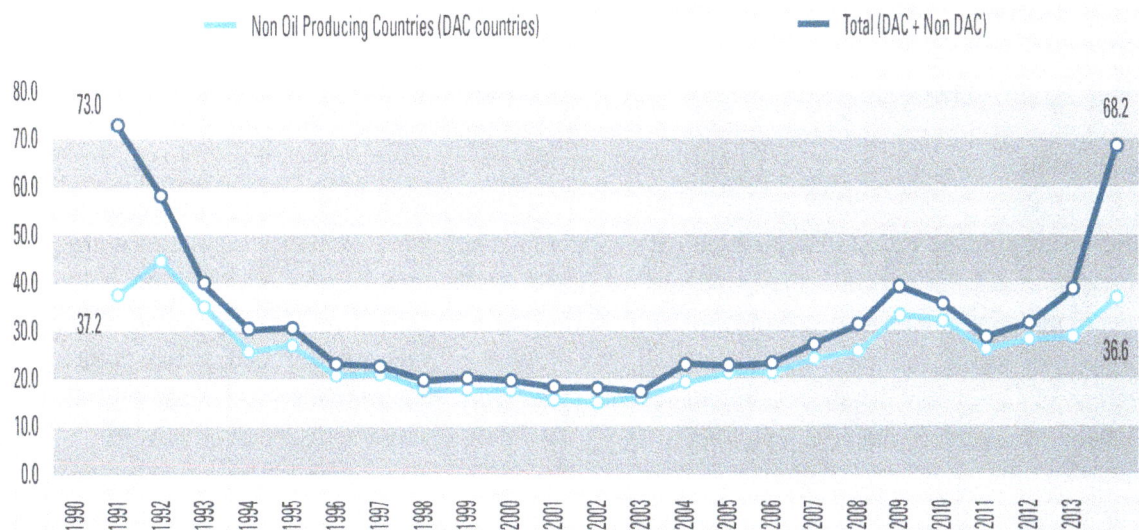

Source: OECD, n.d.a.

5. Gender equality

The region lags behind on gender equality, highlighted by shortfalls in women's participation in the labour market and political decision-making. Progress towards education parity at the primary, secondary and tertiary levels has not translated into job parity. In 2013, the female labour force participation rate was only 21.6 per cent, compared to a global average of 51.3 per cent. The female labour force participation rate rose in the two decades before 2010, but declined from 26 per cent in 2012 to 21.6 per cent in 2013 (figure 5.11). Crises in many countries and associated uncertainties in the labour market may explain the drop. Under normal circumstances, numerous factors already contribute to the low participation rate of women in the labour force, including the lack of day care and public transport, and cultural and religious reasons.

Unemployment is higher for women than men, particularly among young people. In 2013, the rate among young educated women was 46 per cent, compared to 23 per cent for young men.

Differences are also reflected in the types of jobs women do. For example, they hold less than 20 per cent of paid jobs outside the agricultural sector, compared to a global average of 40 per cent. Analysis of middle-class households suggests that, in Egypt, Iraq, the Sudan and the Syrian Arab Republic, most women are in agriculture-based occupations or "other services" within the service sector, which tend to be largely informal and low value-added activities. In Jordan (2010) and Lebanon (2005),

60-76 per cent of employed women held jobs in "other services". In Tunisia, in 2010, however, a reasonably large share of women was employed in the industrial, trade and transport sectors (figure 5.12). It is therefore reasonable to conclude that, in general, women in the Arab region, excluding certain countries and despite significant advances in higher education, are engaged in jobs that are largely informal and low value-added in nature. Such limited opportunities undercut their rights and prospects for well-being.[305]

Women's representation in parliaments is rising, but the region is far behind the rest of the world. Their share of seats rose from 2.6 per cent in 2000 to 12.7 per cent in 2013, compared with around 20 per cent globally and 18 per cent in other developing regions.

Globally, women occupy only 25 per cent of senior management positions, but this number is significantly lower in the Arab region.[306] In countries with available data, the highest share is in Kuwait, at 14 per cent. In most other Arab countries the share is below 10 per cent. Yemen has the lowest rate, at 2 per cent.

Violence against women and girls remains a major problem. Statistics on violence are scarce, but some surveys show that incidence is high. A 2011 global survey provided data on Egypt, Jordan and Morocco, in which 33.2 per cent, 20.6 per cent and 6.4 per cent of women, respectively, reported having experienced violence.[307] Demographic health surveys in Egypt, Djibouti, Somalia and the Sudan reveal that female genital mutilation is widespread, affecting more than 90 per cent of women.[308]

Figure 5.11 Labour force participation rate, 2013 (percentage)

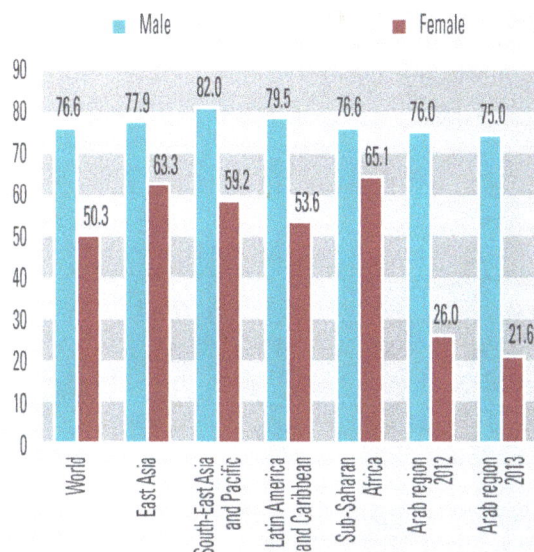

Source: ILOSTAT Database. Available from www.ilo.org/ilostat/faces/oracle/webcenter/portalapp/pagehierarchy/Page137.jspx?_adf.ctrl-state=11m3los537_158&clean=true&_afrLoop=3343162325535317&clean=true (accessed 30 November 2014).

6. Education and the knowledge society

In general, enrolment rates in the region are relatively high, but the quality of education is low. Several countries, such as Algeria, Bahrain, Egypt, Kuwait, Morocco, Oman, Qatar, Tunisia and the United Arab Emirates, are close to universal primary enrolment, with a net rate above 95 per cent. Education quality has not kept pace, however, including in terms of equipping people to compete in the labour market, fostering innovation in research and development and creating a knowledge economy.[309]

Quality in education is hard to monitor, but one indicator is performance in international assessments. Results confirm that Arab countries fall far below international averages. According to the Trends in International Mathematics and Science Study (TIMSS) 2011, none of the 14 participating Arab countries reached the international achievement level of 500.[310] Results of the Programme for International Student Assessment (PISA) revealed that performance in participating Arab countries, namely Jordan, Qatar and Tunisia, was generally poor.

Higher education does not guarantee employment; acquired skills must be relevant to the labour market. In Tunisia, only 33.6 per cent of university graduates were employed in 2013, although this may be partly due to the fact that the economy is dominated by low-skill industries.[311] According to Malik and Awadallah,[312] the skills and preferences of graduates, particularly in oil-rich countries, are geared to jobs in the public sector; the private sector relies mostly on expatriate workers, who are more willing to be part of a competitive job market. Such segmentation in labour markets has profound implications, particularly for private-sector development.

Socioeconomic status, wealth, sex, poverty, and inequality determine access, or the lack of it, to education. In Egypt, only 20 per cent of the poorest children receive primary education, but 100 per cent of the richest complete secondary school.[313] Low-income and conflict-affected countries face particular problems. In the Syrian Arab Republic, for example, the percentage of children enrolled in primary school fell from 98.4 per cent in 2011 to 70 per cent in 2013.

To prepare future generations for a knowledge society,[314] which is the cornerstone of sustainable development, the region must ensure equal opportunities in education and

116

provide young people with a comprehensive set of skills accompanied by values that guide

"youth in their work for the good of humanity and society".[315]

Figure 5.12 Share of middle-class women by sector (percentage)

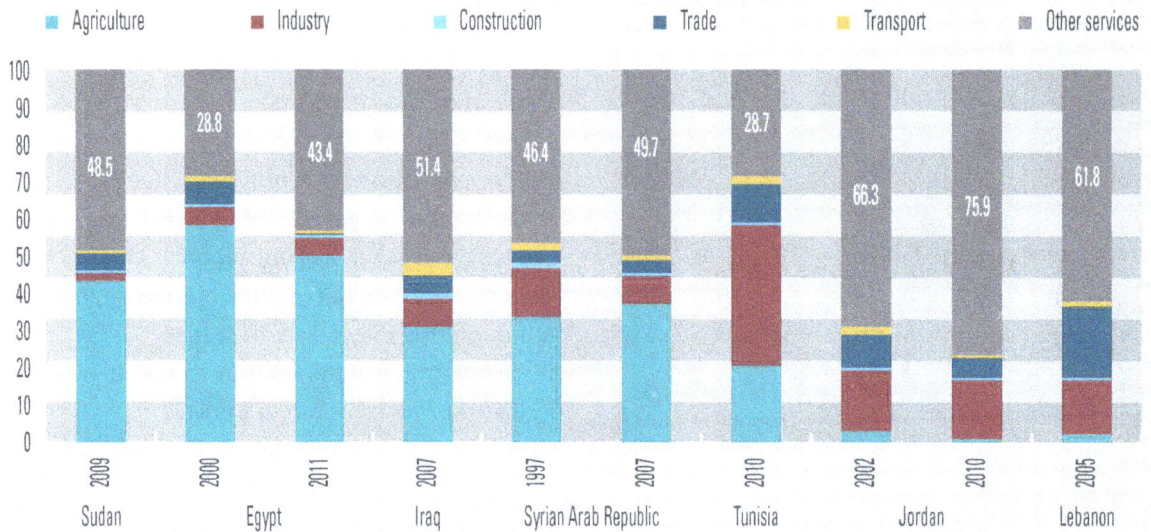

Source: ESCWA, 2014c.

Figure 5.13 Employment of middle-class youth by sector (percentage)

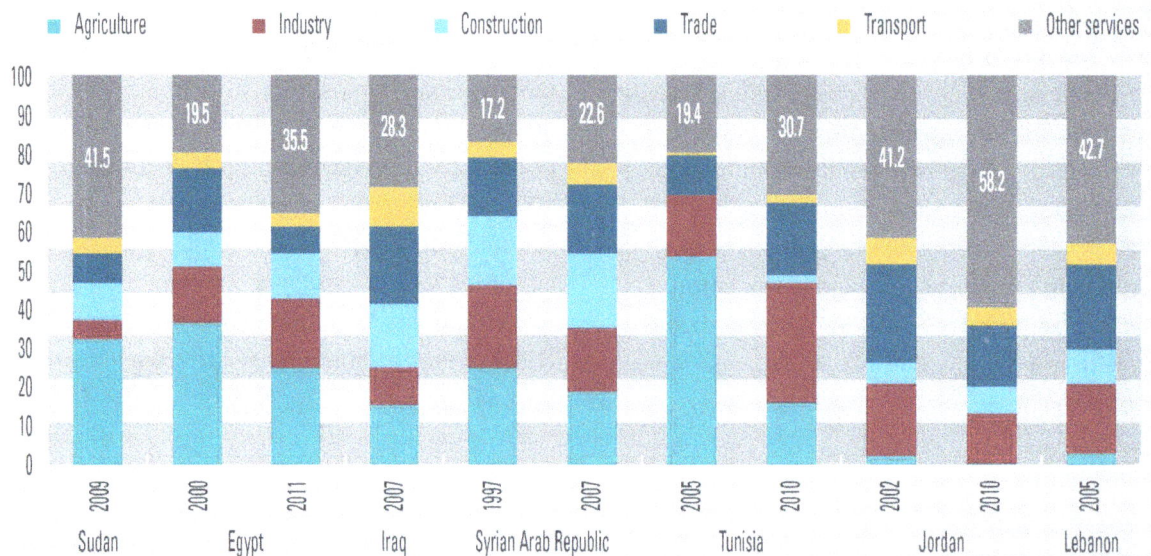

Source: ESCWA, 2014c.

In the decade prior to the 2011 uprisings, the Arab region achieved fairly high rates of economic growth and relatively fast employment creation. However, the impact on quality of life was less evident, particularly because of a lack of decent jobs for educated young people; jobs were largely in the informal, low value-added sectors.[316] According to the latest available household surveys, 35.5 per cent of young people from middle-class households in Egypt in 2011 worked in "other services"; 22.6 per cent in the Syrian Arab Republic in 2007; 58.2 per cent in Jordan in 2010; and 30.7 per cent in Tunisia in 2010 (figure 5.13).[317] Such a pattern results from a lack of economic structural transformation and low productivity,[318] as argued in chapter 4 of this report.

7. Population growth, young people and urbanization

The region's population will continue to grow, but at a slower rate over the period 2012-2025 compared with 1980-2012. It is estimated to reach half a billion by 2030. The fertility rate is expected to remain high; by 2030, just under half of all Arab countries will reach their replacement level of fertility, while many will surpass it. Arab LDCs, however, will not reach their replacement level before 2050.[319] Consequently, the shares of the working age population and young people are growing. Estimates show a slight decline in the percentage of those aged 15-24, from 18.2 per cent in 2015 to 17.5 per cent in 2030. However, in absolute terms, the number of young people will rise. The working age population, aged 25-64, is expected to continue to rise until 2050 (figure 5.14).

Figure 5.14 Demographic dynamics by age group, 1980-2050 (percentage)

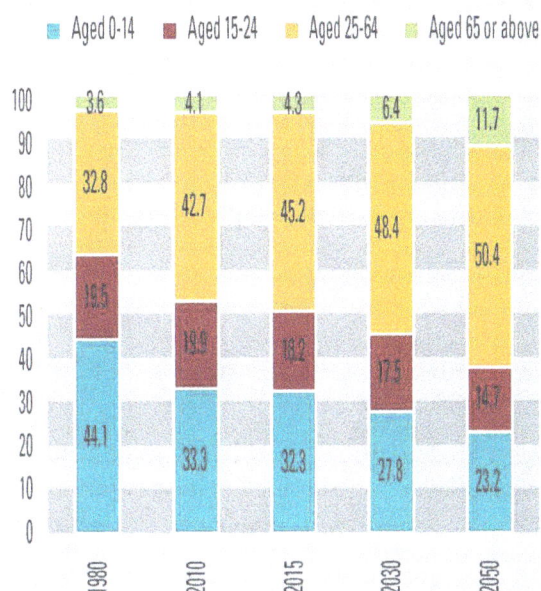

Legend: Aged 0-14 | Aged 15-24 | Aged 25-64 | Aged 65 or above

Year	Aged 0-14	Aged 15-24	Aged 25-64	Aged 65 or above
1980	44.1	19.5	32.8	3.6
2010	33.3	19.9	42.7	4.1
2015	32.3	18.2	45.2	4.3
2030	27.8	17.5	48.4	6.4
2050	23.2	14.7	50.4	11.7

Source: Based on ESCWA, 2013a.

By 2030, half of the region's population will be in the working age group, which could boost economic growth and prosperity if effective socioeconomic policies are implemented. A rise in the Arab world's old-age dependency ratio is also expected, from 7 in 2015 to 10 in 2030 and to 18 by 2050.[320] Social protection expenditure for the elderly is therefore expected to increase. Inclusive social policies need to consider these changing demographics in order to cater for the needs of various population groups. Urbanization levels in the region are well above world averages. By 2025, all Arab countries will experience significant shifts of population to urban areas. In the region as a whole, over 60 per cent of the population will reside in urban areas.[321]

Future population growth and demographic shifts can represent barriers or opportunities, depending on whether policies are adapted to the evolving needs of the Arab population. For instance, food security will be affected by the widening ratio of urban to rural populations, but the concentration of people in cities will provide a chance to enhance access to services previously unavailable or of lesser quality in rural areas.[322]

C. Business-as-usual and Vision 2030 scenarios

Vision 2030 envisages a life in dignity for all by 2030. Full achievement of the vision targets will depend on how countries act. Lessons from other countries, particularly "nearest neighbours" to the Arab countries in terms of development stages and trajectories, indicate varying possible levels of performance. Understanding their experiences can be an entry point for creating a vision road map, along with indicators to guide progress.

Given data availability, selected targets were projected for a business-as-usual scenario and vision scenario. For each indicator, ten "nearest neighbour" countries were selected for comparison, such as those for projecting the HDI (box 5.4). The average development achievements of the top five performers were used to model Vision 2030. The average of the bottom five shows the business-as-usual scenario, which reflects the situation for Arab countries in 2030 if they maintain the status quo, and if conflicts in some countries end in 2015. If conflicts continue, the business-as-usual scenario might deteriorate.

1. Human development

Human development is difficult to measure given the complexity of dimensions such as freedom, empowerment and sustainability. HDI provides a summary of three dimensions that are more readily measurable and capture achievements in basic human well-being: health, education and income. The HDI varies between 0 and 1, with 1 indicating the highest levels of human development.

HDI scores diverge significantly across Arab countries. In 2013, countries rich in natural resources, such as Bahrain, Kuwait, Qatar, Saudi Arabia and the United Arab Emirates, had HDI scores above 0.800. Low-income countries, including Djibouti, the Comoros, the Sudan and Yemen, had scores of less than or equal to 0.500. The regional average was 0.660.

Under the business-as-usual scenario, average HDI for the region could improve to 0.733 in 2030 (figure 5.15). Much of the improvement has to come from low and middle-income countries. Most high-income countries have already achieved very high HDI levels, so further increases will be incremental. However, this business-as-usual scenario will not be achievable if current crises deepen, because low and middle-income countries are disproportionately affected by them.

Under the vision scenario, where Arab countries' performance in achieving development outcomes is as strong as the five top performing nearest neighbours, the HDI average could reach 0.765. That is a significant improvement, given that change at the upper end of the HDI is sluggish because it is capped at 1.

Box 5.4 Nearest neighbours

HDI for Egypt was 0.682 in 2013. The table below lists 10 countries that, in 2000, had scores closest to the HDI for Egypt in 2013. Looking at HDI growth over the period 2000-2013, in order of performance, the scores of Venezuela, Mauritius, Kazakhstan, Sri Lanka, and Brazil rose faster than the other five countries. The average growth rate of those top five countries can be used as a trajectory for the vision scenario, whereas the average change of the bottom five countries shows the business-as-usual scenario.

Projecting HDI by using the performance of nearest neighbours: Egypt

Nearest neighbours	HDI in 2000	Growth rate of HDI 2000-2013
Venezuela	0.677	12.9
Mauritius	0.686	12.4
Kazakhstan	0.679	11.5
Sri Lanka	0.679	10.5
Brazil	0.682	9.1
Belize	0.675	8.4
Peru	0.682	8.1
Fiji	0.674	7.4
Tonga	0.672	4.9
Dominican Republic	0.691	3.8

Source: Authors' calculations.

Figure 5.15 HDI projections for the Arab region

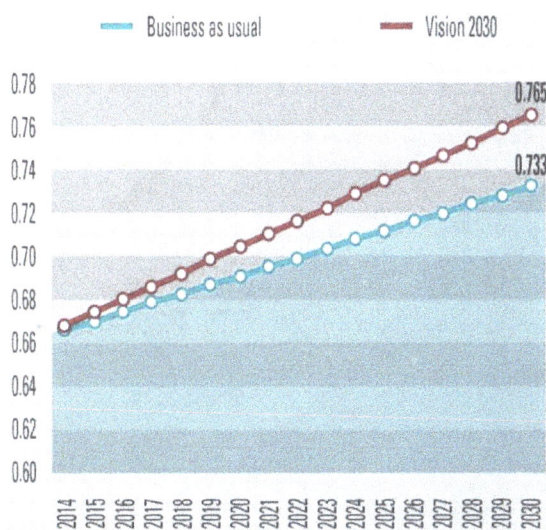

Source: Authors' calculations.

Assuming an end to hostilities, conflict-affected countries can make rapid HDI improvements, given their low base. Improvements in the HDI among low-income countries, such as the Comoros, Djibouti, the Sudan and Yemen, are expected to be moderate; they will remain trapped below the high human development level. The difference between HDI growth in the vision and business-as-usual scenarios is not significant enough to lift these countries into high human development (figure 5.16), because of structural and fiscal constraints.[323] High HDI gains are expected in countries with more diversified economies, stronger and more educated workforces, and a large middle class, such as Egypt, Jordan, Lebanon and Tunisia (figure 5.17). In the vision scenario, these countries, excluding Egypt, are all expected to pass the 0.790 HDI mark by 2030.

120

2. Poverty

In the business-as-usual scenario, extreme poverty persists in Arab low-income countries. In middle-income countries, much of the population will remain trapped between the globally defined extreme poverty line of $1.25 per day and $2.50 per day (2005 PPP), the latter being closer to the national poverty lines of several countries in the region. Poverty incidence has risen since 2010, particularly in countries that had previously witnessed significant reductions in poverty. Under the vision scenario, the aim is to eradicate

extreme poverty and reduce poverty rates by at least half, according to national definitions. The first aim is normative: extreme poverty threatens survival and countries must respond to it with appropriate strategies to ensure that nobody dies of poverty. The second refers to poverty as defined by national authorities, which often classify poverty rates based on lower and upper poverty lines. The lower poverty line represents higher levels of deprivation. Projections for the business-as-usual and vision scenarios use national lower poverty lines to measure poverty rates.

Figure 5.16 HDI improvement in Arab LDCs

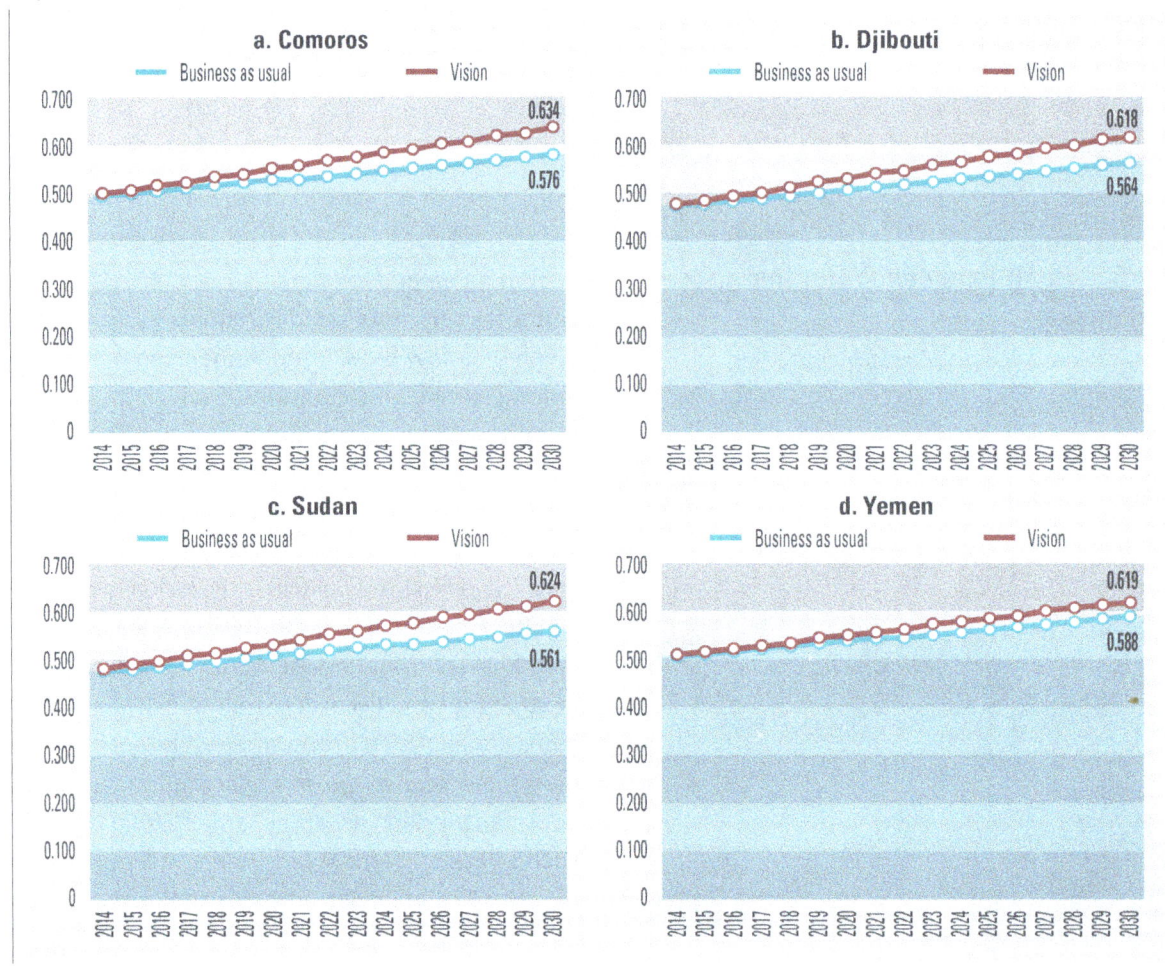

Source: Authors' calculations.

This report has conducted poverty projections based on three different scenarios: business-as-usual, vision with growth only, and vision with growth and a 1 per cent reduction in inequality. The methodology is described in box 5.5. Figure 5.18 shows poverty projections for the region, based on available data from seven countries.[324] The regional aggregate shows that poverty under

the business-as-usual scenario will be 21.2 per cent in 2025, a marginal decline from 21.9 in 2014. If they achieve the vision growth scenario, the poverty rate in 2025 will be 14.7 per cent. If they reduce inequality by at least one percentage point by 2025, the poverty rate will fall further to 12.9 per cent in 2025, an annual reduction of about 4.8 per cent over time. Following that trajectory, the region will go beyond halving national poverty rates by 2030.

Figure 5.17 HDI improvements in more diversified economies

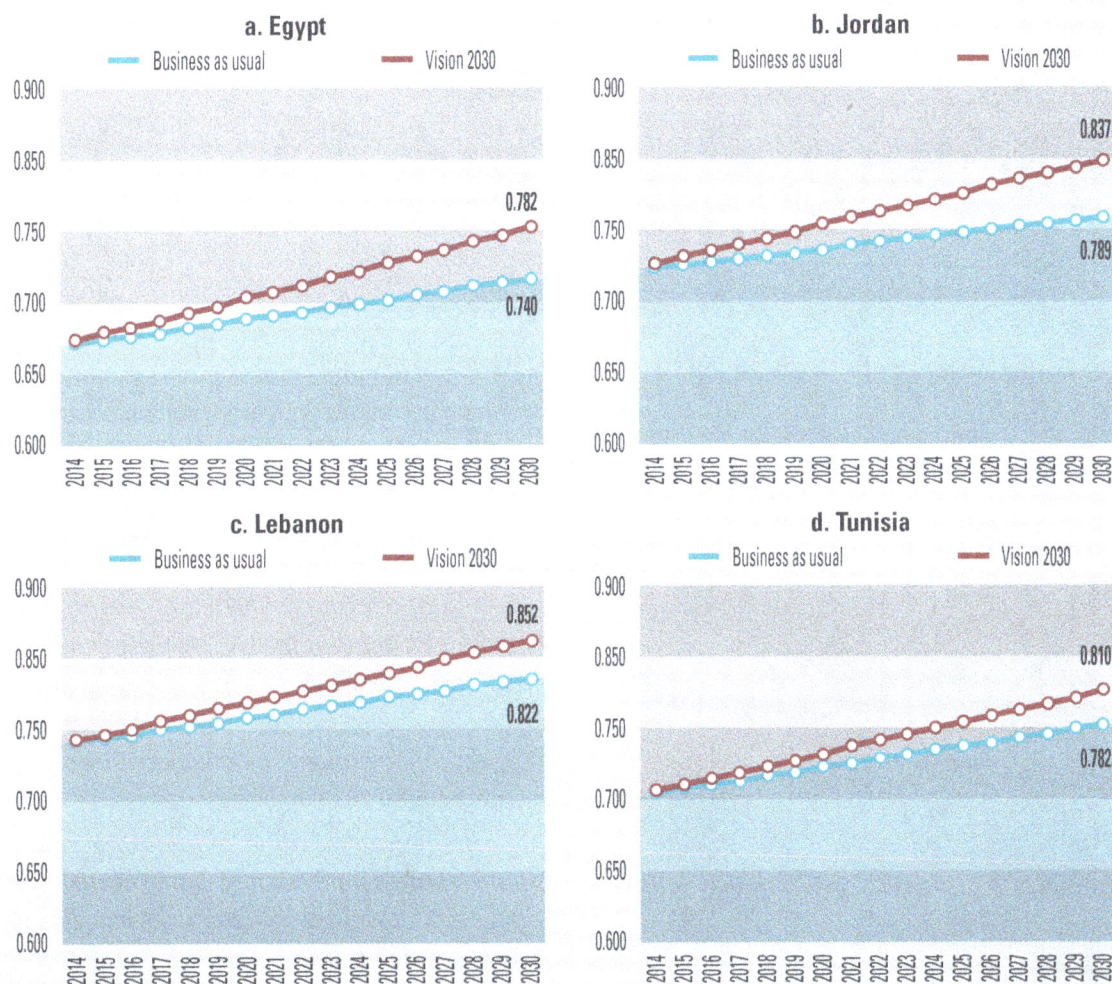

Source: Authors' calculations.

Box 5.5 Poverty projection methodology

Following the approach of Son and Kakwani (2004), change in poverty is affected by growth and income distribution. Assuming that ΔlnPt is the expected percentage change in the level of poverty for the year t (based on the national lower poverty line), ΔlnYt is the expected percentage change in per capita gross domestic product (GDP)[a] for the year t, and ΔlnIt is the expected percentage change in the distribution of income, the projected poverty rates are based on the following equation:

$$\Delta lnP(t) = \theta \times E\,\Delta lnYt + P(t-1)_{+\lambda} + E\,\Delta lnIt + P(t-1)$$

In case of neutrality of distribution, or if λ=0

$$\Delta lnP(t) = \theta \times E\,\Delta lnYt + P(t-1)$$

θ is the growth elasticity of poverty, which is assumed constant over time, λ is the inequality elasticity of poverty,[b] which is also assumed constant over time, and P(t-1) is the level of poverty in the year t-1. In the case of developing countries, targeting inequality in terms of a number is more complicated than targeting poverty as an outcome. Using the framework of Son and Kakwani, this report also examines the extent of poverty reduction, assuming a 1 per cent drop in inequality in respective countries by 2025. It equally divides the 1 percentage point drop in inequality between the period up to 2025 and the latest point of available data.

Source: Authors' calculations.

[a] Theoretically, GDP is related to poverty, but the component of GDP that has a direct impact on poverty is per capita final consumption expenditure, which is impacted by growth distribution. We tried to address this issue in the vision scenario by taking into consideration a hypothetical change in income distribution.

[b] Due to a lack of inequality data for Arab countries, we applied the + average inequality elasticity of poverty (from consumption expenditure) at 2.0 for all countries in the sample. See Fosu, 2010.

Figure 5.18 Poverty in the Arab region

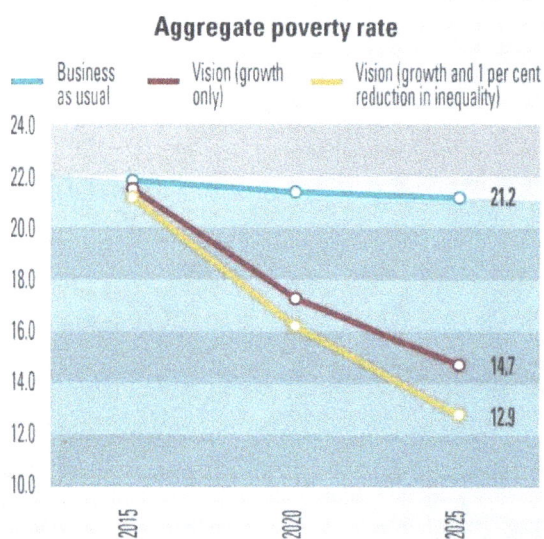

Aggregate poverty rate

Business as usual — Vision (growth only) — Vision (growth and 1 per cent reduction in inequality)

21.2
14.7
12.9

Source: Authors' calculations.
Note: The aggregate poverty rate is derived as a weighted average of national poverty rates.

There are variations across countries, however. In Egypt the national poverty rate increased from 16 per cent to 25 per cent between 2000 and 2011. In the business-as-usual scenario, poverty is expected to increase, despite positive growth.[325] In the vision scenario, poverty will decline to 20 per cent by 2025 from an estimated 24 per cent in 2015. A 1 per cent reduction in inequality by 2025 will cause the poverty rate to fall further to 17 per cent, which suggests that Egypt will be unable to halve its poverty rate by 2025.

Tunisia, Jordan, Morocco and Oman are expected to reduce their national poverty rates significantly under the vision scenario. However, in conflict-affected countries such as Iraq and Yemen, poverty reduction will remain a challenge.

3. Health

This report provides projections on two key health indicators: the under-5 child mortality rate per 1,000 live births and the maternal mortality ratio per 100,000 live births, both indicating the quality and accessibility of health services.

(a) Under-5 mortality

Figure 5.19 shows that, under the business-as-usual scenario, the average regional under-5 mortality rate is expected to fall from over 30 per 1,000 live births in 2014 to 21 per 1,000 live births in 2030. In the vision scenario, it is expected to reach 12 per 1,000 live births, a 60 per cent reduction compared with the present situation. That would still fall short of the SDG on ending under age-5 mortality by 2030.[326]

Figure 5.19 Under-5 mortality rate

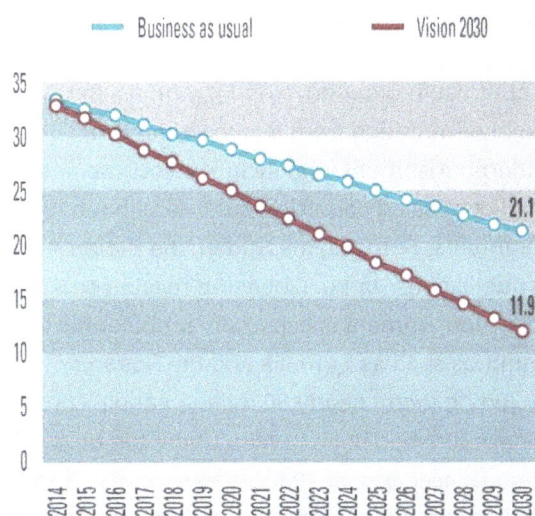

Source: Authors' calculations.

Figure 5.20 Maternal mortality ratio

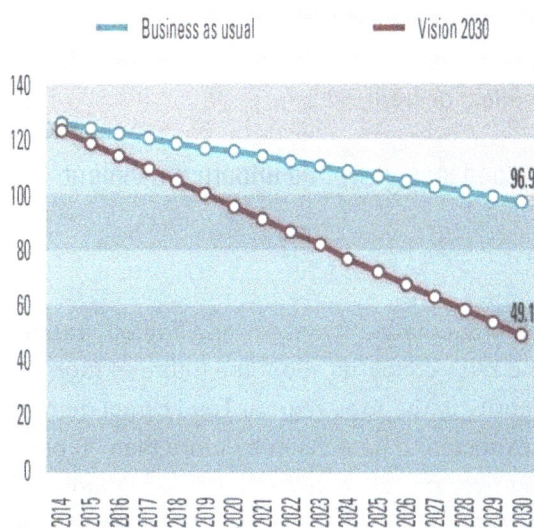

Source: Authors' calculations.

Countries with the highest mortality rates are expected to make the most progress, but when relative reductions are examined, the better performers are likely to be higher-resilience countries like Morocco and the oil-rich States. The smallest improvements in absolute and relative terms can be expected from low- and medium-resilience countries.

(b) Maternal mortality rate

Figure 5.20 shows the average decline in the maternal mortality ratio in the region under the business-as-usual and vision scenarios. In the former case, the rate declines to 97 per 100,000 per live births in 2030 from 125 per 100,000 per live births in 2014. In the latter, it falls to 49 per 100,000 live births, ahead of the global target of reducing maternal mortality to less than 70 per 100,000 live births.[327] Achieving that SDG target could thus be well within the region's grasp.

The largest reduction by 2030 in absolute terms is expected in conflict-affected countries, which currently have the highest ratios, if fighting ends. Higher-resilience countries will see the smallest decreases.

4. Food insecurity and undernourishment

(a) Food insecurity

Rapid population increases and limited arable land raise concerns about the future of food security in the Arab region. Total cereal demand is expected to have risen by more than 70 per cent over the 30 years to 2030.[328] Egyptian demand for imported cereals will increase by an estimated 137 per cent over the same period. Based on a model by the International Food Policy Research Institute (IFPRI), even if cereal production increases by over 80 per cent, the total amount of imported cereal will still rise by 55 per cent.

Figure 5.21 Food Production Index

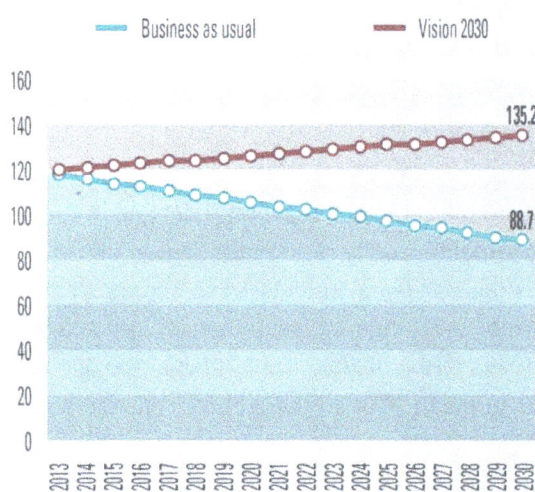

Source: Authors' calculations.

The FAO Food Production Index (2004-2006 = 100) includes edible and nutritious food crops; crops such as coffee and tea are excluded because they have no nutritional value. Figure 5.21 shows that the region's Food Production Index is expected to deteriorate from nearly 120 at present to 89 in 2030 under the business-as-usual scenario, following a drop in productivity and severe water shortages aggravated by conflict. Production in almost all countries is expected to decline, with Djibouti, Jordan and Yemen suffering the most. If the region improves agricultural productivity and pursues sustainable consumption of water and energy, the index could reach 135 in 2030 under the vision scenario. Production will improve more in non-oil rich countries with large tracts of arable land than in the oil-rich countries. Resilient systems for sustainable food production are needed to counteract the pressure of growing population. The wide gap between the business-as-usual and the vision scenario outcomes underscores the need to enhance agricultural productivity.

(b) Undernourishment

In contrast to other developing regions, the Arab region is suffering from increased rates of undernourishment, mainly in low-income and conflict-affected countries, such as Djibouti, Iraq, Mauritania, Somalia, the Sudan, the Syrian Arab Republic and Yemen. Obtaining reliable data on undernourishment is especially problematic in countries such as Somalia and the Sudan. Excluding them, nearly 30 million people could be undernourished in the region under the business-as-usual scenario by 2030. The vision scenario aims to end hunger, ensure uninterrupted access to safe, nutritious and sufficient food for all (figure 5.22) and eliminate all forms of malnutrition, focusing on stunting and wasting in children under the age of 5, by 2030.

5. Quality of education

Based on available data, this report projects the pupil-teacher ratio in primary schools, a crucial indicator of quality education for all (figure 5.23). The ratio could improve to 14 or 11 pupils per teacher on average by 2030 under the business-as-usual and vision scenarios respectively. Already low pupil-teacher ratios are expected to fall further in higher-resilience countries. The ratio will fall somewhat more in low- and medium-resilience countries such as Lebanon and Tunisia. Conflict-affected countries and LDCs with the worst ratios are expected to achieve great improvements, although they will not reach the same levels as higher-resilience countries.

Figure 5.22 Undernourishment

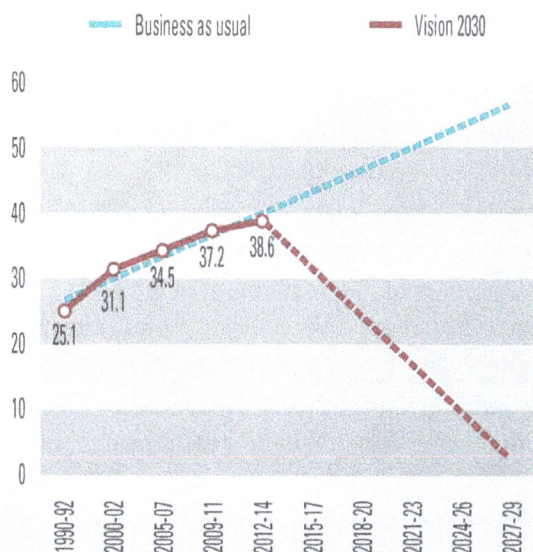

Source: Authors' estimates based on FAO, 2015.

Figure 5.23 Pupil-teacher ratio

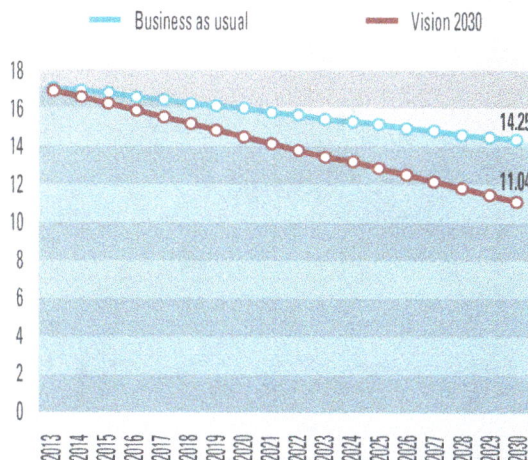

Source: Authors' calculations.

6. Gender inequality

Ensuring gender equality is imperative for sustainable development in all its forms. Projections in this chapter indicate the ratio of female-to-male labour force participation, a key indicator of women's empowerment.

Gender equality accelerates development and economic growth. Men's labour force participation is currently 30 per cent higher than that of women. The business-as-usual scenario envisages marginal improvements to 33.5 per cent by 2030. Under the vision scenario, the rate could rise to 42.5 per cent by 2030 (figure 5.24).

The female rate will still remain far below the male rate, but it will be closer to the global average. Improving the rate of participation by women in the labour force to parity with men could boost regional GDP by 20 per cent and annual per capita GDP by $770. GDP could thus grow by 12 per cent in the United Arab Emirates and 34 per cent in Egypt.[329]

Figure 5.24 Female-to-male labour force participation (percentage)

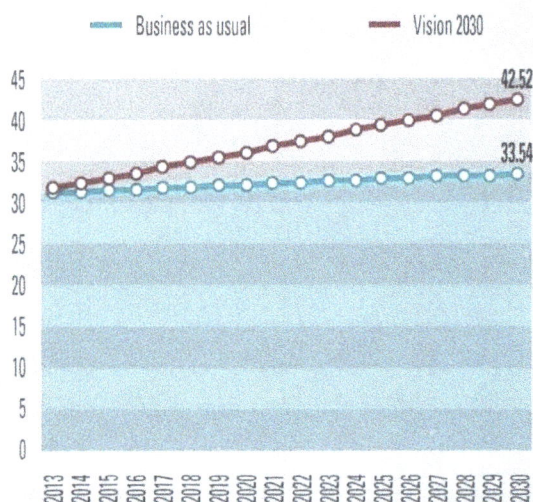

Source: Authors' calculations.

D. Policy recommendations

Public policy should be geared towards improving people's well-being and achieving sustainable development, not just ensuring higher economic growth.

1. Inclusive economic growth

A combination of economic growth and redistribution policies is essential for inclusive growth; countries cannot sustain high growth for long periods without healthy and well educated populations,[330] and if social inequality is rife.[331] Recent evidence from cross-country analysis suggests that "lower inequality is correlated with faster and more durable growth, for a given level of redistribution".[332] Advancing inclusive strategies, such as wage-led growth and cash transfers to the poor, can help to boost economic growth. Wage growth can support demand through consumption effects and induce higher productivity growth.[333] One study argues that keeping real wage growth below productivity growth to increase the international competitiveness of the EU has had detrimental effects, particularly in increasing inequality, lowering the share of wages in national income and supporting an unsustainable growth model.[334] These are good lessons for the Arab countries, which have experienced declining wage shares in national income over the past decade, and where inequality is one of the root causes of conflict.

Arab countries must focus on structural transformation that generates decent jobs to absorb the growing labour force, particularly young people. A recent study on growth and poverty in developing economies shows that changes in productivity and employment intensity across sectors had a major impact on the extent to which growth contributed to reducing poverty between 1990 and 2013.[335] Countries that underwent structural transformation, particularly toward high value-added sectors such as manufacturing, trade, and transport and communications made a major dent on poverty.

The large mining and utilities sectors account for only 2 per cent of employment in the Arab region.[336] A more diversified economic structure is needed to spread growth benefits more equitably across society. Environmental considerations, particularly with regard to the production and use of energy and water, must be addressed so that development does not harm future generations. More must be done to favour the formal over the informal economic sector.

The State must play a central role in allocating resources to promote human development and social justice. The three critical expenditure shares that influence human development are: the public expenditure ratio, defined as the proportion of income spent by the various levels of Government; the social allocation ratio, or the proportion of total government expenditure on human development; and the priority ratio, which is the proportion of total human development sector expenditure allocated to priorities. Even if the public expenditure ratio is the same between two countries, a higher social allocation ratio and, in particular, a higher priority ratio to human development sectors will boost human development.[337]

Policies for the fair allocation of resources should take into account the concerns of disadvantaged population groups and those who face discrimination and social exclusion, such as persons with disabilities, young people, older persons, migrant workers and refugees.[338] Public services in growing urban areas need to be scaled up, but policies must also be put into place to prevent the deterioration of service quality in rural areas.[339]

Measuring connections between governance and human development is complex.[340] Figures 5.25a and b, which plot a control of corruption index and a rule of law index against the 2014 HDI for Arab countries and the average of high-income OECD countries, show a positive association between HDI and control of corruption and rule of law. The OECD average represents high human development, greater control of corruption and better rule of law. The countries scoring low on control of corruption and rule of law, such as Djibouti, Iraq, the Syrian Arab Republic and Yemen, also have low HDI scores. Therefore, a key aspect of governance reforms in the region is to ensure economic growth with equity.

2. Modernizing statistics and monitoring tools

Monitoring progress is an important aspect of policymaking. Development indicators must capture short-term impacts and reflect human development priorities and principles, and reveal disparities in terms of gender, geography, ethnicity, income, and multidimensional poverty. For example, assessment of the short-term performance of health and education policies could draw on several indicators, including the teacher-pupil ratio, years of schooling among those aged 15-24, technical education among those aged 15-24, nutritional status and out-of-pocket expenditure on health. Fukuda-Parr and others[341] developed the following framework for such assessments, known as the "three perspectives" that can be applied to any policymaking exercise (table 5.2):

- Average perspective, showing overall progress in a country;
- Deprivation perspective, showing progress by the most deprived group;
- Inequality perspective, showing progress in narrowing inequalities.

Applying this framework also helps to generate disaggregated data to ensure that policy is based on accurate evidence. Data must be broken down into subgroups, across space or population groups, in order to inform effective policymaking. However, monitoring will only be efficient if it is backed by rule of law, thus requiring reporting of all wealth and income and open access to all data on household expenditure and living conditions.

Figure 5.25 Relationship between governance indicators and HDI

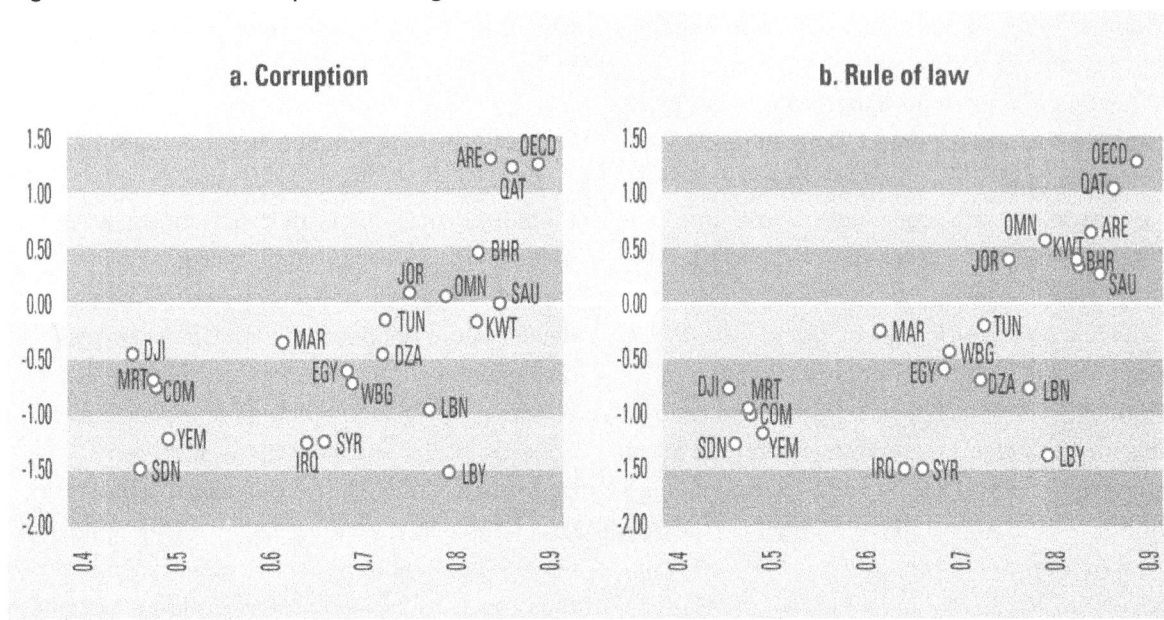

a. Corruption

b. Rule of law

Source: Based on data from World Bank, 2015e; and the United Nations Anti-Corruption for Development database, available from http://www.anti-corruption.org/index.php/en/ (accessed 30 November 2014).

Note: Countries are designated by their ISO codes.

Table 5.2 Three perspectives for assessing performance using national and subnational development indicators for policy planning

Time frame	Average perspective	Deprivation perspective	Inequality perspective
One period	What is the national average?	Who are the most deprived by the following:	What is the disparity between the following:
		• Income quintile • Multidimensional poverty • Gender • Region/province • Rural or urban • Ethnic group • Educational level	• Bottom and top quintile • Females and males • Worst-off and best-off regions/provinces (by income/multidimensional poverty) • Rural and urban • Worst-off and best-off ethnic groups (by income/multidimensional poverty) • No education and higher education
Over time	Has the national average changed?	How have the most deprived population group progressed?	How have disparities between population groups changed – have they widened or narrowed?

Source: Authors, based on Fukuda-Parr and Shivakumar, 2003.

Under the SDGs, the assessment of human well-being will focus on quality rather than just quantitative progress. Although the HDI takes into account health and education, in addition to income, it fails to consider other important qualitative dimensions of human development, such as freedom, human security and the environment. Such assessments are rendered more complex in times of crisis. Falling income caused by conflict would be noted, but the difficulties people face during transition or resettlement in terms of education and medical care, would not.

There is a clear need for a data revolution in the region. Household surveys need to combine income and non-income aspects of well-being, such as health, education, employment and social protection. A pan-Arab multipurpose survey (PAMPS) could be effective for harmonizing household surveys and methodologies.[342]

Effective monitoring of human development indicators and the SDGs requires better statistics. Statistics bodies need new survey tools and techniques, training on new concepts and measures, modern tools of analysis and access to technology for greater data outreach. National surveys need to take into consideration new demands of data and social accountability. Deeper involvement by citizens can lead to more effective monitoring of government performance. Social accountability is particularly relevant for Arab countries undergoing democratic transitions.

3. Ensuring quality health care

Access to quality health-care services, including for reproductive health, is essential for reducing child and maternal mortality rates. Wealthier people can pay for care, but the poor depend on the State. This explains the high child and maternal mortality rates in Arab LDCs and among low-income households. Skilled care for mothers during pregnancy, and during and after delivery, improves the survival chances of mothers and children. Moreover, when mothers are educated, child mortality declines.

Bangladesh and Thailand demonstrate how the commitment to provide public health care for all in developing countries has significantly reduced under-5 and maternal mortality, as shown in table 5.3. Increased vaccination coverage is key to reducing diseases that are major causes of death among children; preventing infectious and chronic diseases is cheaper than treating them.[343]

Malnutrition and obesity are problems. Egypt, Iraq and the Syrian Arab Republic have high rates of adult obesity and child stunting. Countries must develop nutrition support programmes and health awareness initiatives to tackle those issues.

Quality health care entails stronger service monitoring and regulation, such as accrediting health-care facilities and professionals. Some high-income countries are establishing regulatory bodies, such as the National Health Regulatory Authority of Bahrain, and the Health Authority of Abu Dhabi and Dubai Health Authority in the United Arab Emirates.[344]

4. Advancing education for a knowledge society

The Arab region needs to ensure equal education opportunities for all, so that girls and boys, especially from poor families, can complete primary and secondary school. Although the region has done well in primary education, many children do not reach secondary school because of the high cost of education.

Technical and higher education are essential for developing a skilled labour force whose members can respond to the labour market and contribute to innovations throughout their lives. Countries should focus on reforming curricula and investing in education for all and skills training programmes for young people, the elderly and persons with disabilities. Increasing access to higher education related to ICT, entrepreneurship, and research and development is vital for creating a knowledge society and economy.

The State should aim policy at promoting respect for freedom of thought, opinion and belief; equality in rights and duties; and a healthy family atmosphere to form balanced personalities. Such enablers will be the cornerstone for sustainable development, and Arab societies thus need to generate dialogue on how to create efficient knowledge societies. Institutional reforms should be undertaken to assess the performance of students and teachers, and implement quality assurance systems, on-the-job training and skills enhancement.

Table 5.3 Policy instruments that helped improving health standards in other developing countries

Health policy instruments: Thailand	Achievements
Over several decades, Thailand has gradually developed its public health system, focusing on delivering primary health care through the 1971 Social Security Act of 1971. The 2002 Universal Health Coverage Policy reaches the whole population through three health insurance schemes: the Civil Servant Medical Benefit Scheme, the Social Security Scheme and the Universal Coverage Scheme.[a]	Under-five mortality rate 37.1 per 1,000 (1990) 22.5 per 1,000 (2000) 13.5 per 1,000 (2012)[b] Maternal mortality ratio 42.0 per 100,000 (1990) 40.0 per 100,000 (2000) 26.0 per 100,000 (2013)[c]
Health policy instruments: Bangladesh	Achievements
Fifth goal of the 2011 national health policy: undertake programmes to reduce child and maternal mortality rates to an acceptable level within the next five years.[d] Gradual improvement of basic health and nutrition services have generated a sharp fall in under-five mortality.[e] Progress in reproductive health and maternal mortality outcomes has been achieved through antenatal care, skilled birth attendance, and postnatal care.[f]	Under-five mortality rate 143.7 per 1,000 (1990) 88.1 per 1,000 (2000) 41.1 per 1,000 (2013)[g] Maternal mortality ratio 550 per 100,000 (1990) 340 per 100,000 (2000) 170 per 100,000 (2013)[h]

[a] Thailand, Ministry of Public Health, 2006.
[b] United Nations, Department of Economic and Social Affairs, n.d.a.
[c] Ibid.
[d] See http://bdhealth.com/App_pages/Main/NationalHPB.aspx.
[e] El-Saharty, Zunaid-Ahsan and May, 2014.
[f] Ibid.
[g] United Nations, Department of Economic and Social Affairs, n.d.a.
[h] Ibid.

5. Poverty and social exclusion

Regional income and multidimensional poverty indicators are needed in order to measure poverty and inequality more precisely. Standard global extreme poverty measures on money-metric and multidimensional poverty fail to reflect the extent of the problem in the Arab region. Developing consistent household surveys and other measurement methodologies across countries is essential in order to produce comparable national poverty assessments.[345] Better information on money-metric poverty can be arrived at by assigning different poverty lines to country groupings on the basis of their standard of living, such as level of expenditure per capita.[346] A new multidimensional poverty index (MPI) used to provide more accurate information on multidimensional poverty in Iraq, Jordan and Morocco, can be applied equally to other middle-income countries.[347]

Policy should address the concerns of persons with disabilities, young people, older persons, migrant workers and refugees. A universal, rights-based approach to social policy is key to achieving social justice.[348] Comprehensive social protection systems[349] are essential to safeguarding poor and vulnerable groups against natural and human-induced shocks, disaster risks and economic insecurities (box 5.6). ILO Recommendation No. 202 could guide national efforts.

6. Agricultural productivity and food security

Investing in rural areas and agriculture, including through scientific research and innovation, is essential to boosting agricultural production and rural non-farm activities.

Increasing agricultural productivity in several Arab countries could be done with no, or little, environmental cost. Environmentally friendly technologies need to be explored, especially those that maximize water-use efficiency. Effective water management would improve water-use efficiency in agriculture by 15-30 per cent, which could boost agricultural production, increase farmers' income and conserve non-renewable groundwater for future generations.[350] Investment in wastewater facilities would increase reuse, and subsidies and loans would expand water-saving technologies.

Policies are needed to stabilize food prices and respond to food emergencies. Immediate options may include the direct provision of food, food vouchers and subsidies. Food aid is essential for responding to sudden declines in availability and market failures; it also plays a key role in conflict-affected countries and LDCs in keeping food prices low and increasing access, even for those outside the aid distribution system, to avoid displacement.

Combating food insecurity in the Arab region requires more inter-Arab cooperation, as highlighted in the 2008 Riyadh Declaration. The ambitious Arab Food Security Emergency Programme 2011-2031, launched by the Arab Organization for Agricultural Development, is designed to provide relief during food shortages and emergencies, reduce hunger and malnutrition, and boost productivity.[351] Estimated investment commitments by Governments are $14.3 billion until 2016, rising to around $28.5 billion until 2021, and $31.5 billion by 2031. The programme is expected to receive $12 billion in private-sector funding too.

Box 5.6 Benefits of social protection programmes

Over the past 10 years, social protection and cash transfer programmes have flourished, mainly in Latin America. Their popularity stems in part from their relatively cheap cost, around 1-2 per cent of GDP.

Evaluations consistently show that cash transfers have a positive impact on education and health. Brazil's *Bolsa Família* and Mexico's *Oportunidades* programmes have led to increased school enrolment and attendance rates, and reduced child labour. Both achieved successes in education owing to additional cash incentives for enrolment, and have been associated with a 2.7 per cent decline in income inequality.

In Bangladesh, monetary incentives for female students, under the Female Secondary School Stipend Programme, have increased enrolment rates by 23 per cent. The Malawian Social Cash Transfer Programme, targeting households with children, boosted school enrolment by 5 per cent among children aged between 6 and 17.

With regard to health, *Bolsa Família* has brought about an increase in the number of visits to health clinics by beneficiary households. *Red de Oportunidades*, the cash transfer programme of Panama, provides cash to female household heads provided that they use health and education services; the State, in turn, has committed itself to delivering those services. Access to primary care and vaccinations is free for children under five, as are birth control and care for pregnant women. The Colombian *Famílias en Acción* programme has reduced illness and improved childhood growth rates by supplying nutritional supplements to children.

The Zambian social cash transfer programme in the district of Kalomo has helped to increase food and non-food consumption by the poor, reduce illness, increase asset ownership, and boost business investment. In Ghana, the School Feeding Programme, which covers more than half a million pupils, and the Livelihoods Empowerment Against Poverty targeted cash transfer programme have reduced poverty levels, food insecurity and malnutrition. The latter benefits over 35,000 households across 54 districts, mostly farmers who have suffered from droughts and floods.

Source: UNDP, 2010b.

7. Promoting gender equality

Commitment at the national, local and individual levels is needed to end violence against women and girls; prevent early marriage of girls; ensure that women have equal opportunities to develop their capabilities and access resources; and increase their participation in decision-making processes.

Countries should develop programmes to provide basic services and offer new opportunities to women. More concerted efforts are needed to strengthen integrated sexual and reproductive health and HIV services. Laws should be passed to address past gender injustices and advance women's rights, including through quotas for political participation.[352] Discriminatory legislation should be repealed.

Development policies based on existing statistics are mostly "gender blind" because of a lack of data disaggregated by gender.[353] For instance, statistics capture women in paid work, but do not offer a complete picture of their economic contribution, especially unpaid household work. Countries must therefore strengthen the capacities of the statistics offices.

8. Fiscal space for human development

Given high fiscal deficits, high public debt, and low ODA and FDI flows to the region, options for raising development finance from public sources are limited, particularly in non-oil-rich countries. These countries need to prioritize human development expenditures to make the most of limited resources.

In 2011, it was estimated that a basic social protection floor package[354] for selected Arab countries[355] would require 1.4-2.5 per cent of GDP for child benefits, 0.2-0.7 per cent of GDP for unemployment benefits and 0.9-2 per cent of GDP for pensions and disability. The total costs would range from 3.1 per cent of GDP in Saudi Arabia to 4 per cent of GDP in Tunisia.[356] Adding essential health care, based on previous costing exercises, would amount to 1.5-5.5 per cent of annual GDP,[357] making the cost of the total package for Arab countries 4.6-9.5 per cent of GDP. The total cost of financing a basic package between 2015 and 2030 would be $2.2-4.5 trillion.[358] However, the predicted rise in dependent elderly populations may further strain social services and increase the ratio of GDP for social protection.

Average government social expenditure in Arab countries was 8 per cent of GDP in 2011, although part of this may have been spent on social expenditures other than those integral to the social protection floor. Assuming that all social expenditures currently spent on health

and education and other social services will be allocated to the basic social protection floor, the average Arab country would only need to add around 1.5 per cent of GDP to finance the most basic social protection floor unassisted, excluding education and other non-basic services. However, there are large variations in financing gaps across Arab countries. Some are already spending enough on various social services, while others are off the mark by as much as 7 per cent of GDP.

In terms of affordability in the short term, countries can be grouped into the following three categories: those with a reasonable fiscal situation, in particular oil-rich countries, which should mainly focus on the role and efficiency of social policy; countries with severe fiscal constraints in the short term, coupled with high social protection costs owing to demographic pressures, such as Egypt, the Syrian Arab Republic and Yemen, which might need external financial assistance; and countries such as Lebanon, Morocco and Tunisia, which can afford a basic social protection package and should review current expenditures and initiate reforms to increase domestic resources.

Many Arab countries must reform subsidy policies for food and fuel, which are a large drain on Government expenditure and generally benefit wealthier groups more than the poor. Energy subsidy rates, for example, range between 50 per cent and 85 per cent, representing 3-14 per cent of GDP. In Egypt, energy subsidies are 9 per cent of GDP, equivalent to 27 per cent of Government expenditure, or more than $20 billion. The richest groups in Egypt capture 46 per cent of energy subsidies, compared with only 9 per cent for the poorest groups.[359] Iraq spends 13.3 per cent of its GDP, or $11.3 billion, on energy subsidies, which is much higher than the amount spent on health or education.

Reforming tax systems is another mechanism for increasing social protection resources. Tax mixes should focus on redistributive effects, taking into account equity concerns.[360]

The Arab region should also reduce military spending, which at 3.7 per cent of GDP in 2013 was among the highest in the world, in favour of greater expenditure on economic diversification and social protection policies.

E. Conclusion

The first Arab Human Development Report, published in 2002, identified the following three priorities to overcome the human development crisis in the Arab region: full respect for human rights and human freedoms; complete empowerment of Arab women by building their capabilities; and knowledge acquisition and its effective use.[361] Over a decade later, these shortcomings still persist and several new concerns have emerged. Development objectives are severely impeded by longstanding armed conflicts and crises, and poverty, hunger and health concerns are pressing challenges in many countries. Large-scale displacement, internally

and internationally, has spread hunger and undernourishment at alarming rates. Across the region, lack of quality education and opportunities for skill development are strong barriers to the labour market. Young people and women suffer most from lost opportunities because of a lack of industrial diversification; both groups generally hold poor quality service jobs. Many Arab countries, especially those in political transition, face high and rising fiscal deficits and public debts.

The gaps between the business-as-usual and vision scenarios on selected human development indicators are remarkable, thus emphasizing the need for transformative policy intervention. A developmental State that promotes socially inclusive and economically just policies and programmes is a prerequisite for achieving the Vision 2030. Malaysia, the Republic of Korea and Thailand, among other countries, provide examples of State policies and actions that the Arab region should consider.

Advancing quality education is critical for driving countries towards a knowledge society and building productive economic capacity that can lead to a virtuous cycle of growth and human development. Other key development priorities include: guaranteeing quality health care, reducing poverty and social exclusion, boosting agricultural productivity and food security, promoting gender equality, and mobilizing fiscal space for human development.

6. Regional Integration

A. Introduction

At a time when the Arab region is caught up in unprecedented turmoil, it is worth re-examining regional integration as one of the few options it has to confront its myriad security and development conundrums. That premise prompted ESCWA to release its 2014 flagship report, *Arab Integration: A 21st Century Imperative.*

The establishment of an Arab Citizens Common Economic Security Space (ACCESS) could consolidate the visions outlined in the preceding chapters and the ideal of Arab unity. By combining efforts at the regional level, Arab developmental States could set off a virtuous developmental cycle.

This chapter examines the potentially beneficial effects of regional integration on development, challenges to current regionalization and Arab integration initiatives and the way forward to 2030. Thereafter, the conceptual framework for a regional integration initiative (ACCESS) is presented. It rests on the idea of developmental regionalism, or the extrapolation of actions taken by developmental States in pursuit of their national agendas to the regional level. Ultimately, ACCESS provides a possible pathway to fulfil the aims of Arab developmental regionalism and ultimately the ideal Arab Unity.

B. The case for deeper regional integration

The fragile security situation in the region (see chapter 2), which has long been wracked by civil conflict, foreign intervention, occupation and forced migration, appears to undermine chances of deepening integration. However, conflict resolution has been a central motive for the conclusion of regional trade arrangements around the world.[362] The recognition that instability in certain countries may threaten an entire region can galvanize it to strive for greater integration. It has been asserted by some that membership of regional trade arrangements can reduce the likelihood of disputes between members by 15 per cent and of military conflict by 50 per cent.[363] Others consider that evidence for such claims is inconclusive.[364] Nevertheless, the literature generally supports the view that regional integration leads to measurable decreases in the number of conflicts.[365]

By abandoning plans for an Arab defence and economic union in the 1950s, the region is seen by some as having aggravated insecurity. The headlong rush to establish the Arab Customs Union in 2015 demonstrates that the issue of regional integration, especially in the context of the security situation, remains of key concern, even as Arab States sign up to mutually exclusive extraregional arrangements for a variety of political, security, socioeconomic and even cultural reasons.

Regional integration also influences the quality of governance (chapter 3) and provokes institutional transformation at the national level.[366] Similarly, high-quality institutions at the national level can stimulate intraregional trade. Countries are more likely to experience institutional improvements when the institutions of their trading partners and neighbours are of high quality.[367] The EU experience highlights the endogenous relation between regional integration and changes in governance structures, as successive expansions in EU membership have been associated, albeit with the help of pre-accession financial support, with improvements in the governance performance of some new members.

Conversely, without good governance at the regional level, the fruits of integration may not materialize.[368] The developmental State model argued for in chapter 1 acquires new dimensions when viewed through the broader prism of regional integration. Measuring governance from a regional integration perspective is conceivably a game changer, especially when the balance and mix of governance components function under a transposed *modus operandi* operated by supranational institutions. Countries that endorse uniform regulatory frameworks and upgrade institutional quality tend to witness increased trade flows with the effects becoming self-reinforcing.

Structural transformation has been advanced as a prime accelerator of development (chapter 4). However, most, if not all, of the measures that fueled transformational growth in East Asia are now regulated, or have been prohibited, by the World Trade Organization (WTO).[369] The rationale behind industrial policy may still be valid; what changed is how its tools are framed and what is admissible. Achieving transformational growth is not all about "pushing the technology frontier, but rather changing the production towards higher productivity".[370] That is where regional integration comes in, providing options for the pooling, transfer and diffusion of technology and, as a result, potential to improve productivity and growth.[371]

Technological change is essential for tapping the transformational potential of regional integration. The contemporary model of technology transfer capitalizes on the various industrial cumulation schemes that operate within regional trade arrangements. It benefits from the fragmentation of production processes under global value chains (GVCs) as well as developing regional ones. Multilateral and regional initiatives to liberalize services, information technology and environmental goods, along with the technological spillovers of FDI, provide new avenues to induce technological change. The transfer of technology along traditionally overregulated channels, such as the compulsory licensing of intellectual property, may still be necessary to make transfer of technology a reality.

It is not possible merely to latch on to GVCs without factoring in intra-Arab and extraregional trade arrangements or the international obligations of member States of WTO. Multilateral trade rules and preferential trade arrangements can limit the traditional drivers of structural transformation. Matters are complicated by regional trade arrangements, with their liberalizing goals and rules of origin, concluded over the past two decades between some Arab States and non-Arab trading partners.

If the developmental State model includes the private sector, civil society and quasi-public authorities in the State's efforts to plan, finance, implement and evaluate national development and social justice policies (chapter 5), developmental regionalism involves the State sharing or ceding aspects of its development policy to intergovernmental or supranational institutions in order to implement a region-wide strategy. Such a strategy can be set against the SDGs, which would be adapted to the realities and priorities of the region.

The Arab High-Level Forum on Sustainable Development recognized that achievement of the SDGs requires deeper forms of integration in the Arab region. It also reiterated the positive impact of the ACU on the three main dimensions of sustainable development. Trade features prominently among the 169 proposed SDG targets.[372] Developmental regionalism can resemble other forms of development cooperation expressed in terms of specific goals, including health, education, water, environment, and infrastructure, which have positive effects on human development.

Much research has been devoted to quantifying the potential effects of intra-Arab regional trade liberalization, but few attempts have been made to assess its socioeconomic impact, the interplay between trade, regional integration and developmental regionalism, or the overall potential benefits of Arab proposals for deeper regional integration. Such research would need to factor in global, regional and national socioeconomic conditions, and the multilateral disciplines governing trade (goods and services) investment, environment and labour standards operating under dynamic global monetary, banking and fiscal governance. Those factors heavily influence how regional integration evolves and trade arrangements are negotiated and enforced. However, quantitative tools and the assumptions upon which they rest can undermine their precision.

C. Where the Arab region stands today

1. The state of trade integration

The degree to which the Arab region has thus far succeeded in integrating trade is a bone of contention. Some observers consider the level of integration disappointing, although by some accounts intra-Arab trade is 10-15 per cent higher than recorded by official statistics.[373] Others suggest that establishment of the Greater Arab Free Trade Area (GAFTA) has resulted in trade growth of 26 per cent.[374] ESCWA gravity analysis has found that the region is already trading close to its potential.[375] The sheer disparity of the results on intra-Arab trade casts doubt over the adequacy of the tools, assumptions and data employed to assess intraregional trade arrangements.[376] Nonetheless, the following five observations provide insight on intra-Arab trade and the potential for deepening regional integration:

(a) Although oil continues to dominate intra-Arab trade, ESCWA has found that, by 2012, intra-Arab non-oil trade was growing 25 per cent faster than the region's total exports to the rest of the world, running counter to the view that the Arab region barely trades with itself.[377] Non-oil exports shares in intra-Arab trade appear comparable to those in the Association of South-East Asian Nations (ASEAN) and MERCOSUR in Latin America, although smaller in absolute terms;

(b) A study in 2010 found that, in 13 Arab countries, intra-Arab trade had a greater impact on per capita growth than extraregional trade, including Arab-EU trade, by almost 9 per cent. This could be because intra-Arab trade is more diversified than trade between the region and the rest of the world, which remains dominated by oil;

(c) Many observers suggest that intra-Arab trade has grown at a much slower pace than that of trade blocs such as the EU. Care should be taken, however, when making such comparisons, bearing in mind statistical and trade balance distortions, and structural considerations associated with the "Rotterdam-Antwerp effect".[378] EU internal trade figures tend to be artificially inflated, as large portions of EU imports arriving through ports (namely Rotterdam and Antwerp) are recorded as intra-EU exports when moving to their final destination in the EU.[379] Such comparisons also overlook the substantial negative balances that States register in their intra-EU trade;

(d) High transport costs adversely affect trade in the Arab region, but the fact that it is cheaper to send a 20-foot container from Egypt to the EU than from the Maghreb indicates that transport problems reflect poor logistics rather than mere distance.[380] Improving the Logistics Performance Index scores of five Arab Mediterranean countries to average levels recorded by middle-income countries would bring about significant export returns, higher than those rendered by eliminating non-tariff measures, running from as much as 40 per cent in Egypt to 70 per cent in Algeria.[381] The situation in Palestine is especially striking. The cost of shipping a container 75 km from Ramallah to Ashdod is $1,200, the same amount as it costs to ship a container from Ashdod to Japan.[382] More perplexing, when transporting goods to and from Gaza, Palestinian operators are directed to one entry and exit point at the Israeli-controlled Karni crossing, where they face illicit charges of $2,000-$6,000 per truck;[383]

(e) In the Arab region, the average share of services value added to GDP rose by 10 percentage points between 1990 and 2013. That is significantly lower than the world average, but there are considerable disparities between Arab countries; high performers include Egypt, Jordan and Morocco. Studies on service trade restrictiveness indices (STRI) indicate that the GCC countries are the most restrictive in the region in terms of services trade. Liberalizing services in the Arab region could generate three times the gains made from liberalizing merchandise trade alone.[384]

2. Intra and extraregional trade arrangements

At the Third Economic and Social Summit in Riyadh in 2013, Arab leaders renewed their resolve to establish the Arab Customs Union (ACU) by 2015, which would effectively supersede GAFTA. Customs unions can be formed as a logical next step from free trade areas, out of security concerns, as a springboard for deeper regional integration or to address specific economic weaknesses. All of those motives would justify creating the ACU. However, Arab States have continued to engage in unilateral and mutually exclusive forms of extraregional integration, enforced through arrangements that take precedence over Arab integration. That issue requires scrutiny. It is argued by some that deeper integration with the EU or even the United States will dampen incentives for closer regional integration. Moreover, in spite of the declared intention to create an Arab single market by 2020, some Arab States intend to join other single markets, such as the African Common Market.

The Deauville Partnership with Arab Countries in Transition, launched by the Group of Eight (G8) in May 2011 and inspired largely by security concerns, contained provisions for fostering greater economic integration of the countries concerned (Egypt, Jordan, Libya, Morocco and Tunisia) between one another and with G8 countries. Under the partnership, the United States would continue to develop bilateral economic accords with those countries in transition, the EU would undertake negotiations on deep and comprehensive free trade area (DCFTA) agreements, and Canada, Russia and Japan would pursue their own free trade objectives with Arab countries. Many Arab LDCs also have preferential trade deals with non-Arab trade partners. This comes on top of a raft of arrangements concluded by Arab States over the past two decades, including the Euro-Mediterranean Association Agreements and the free trade agreements with the United States, the European Free Trade Area (EFTA), MERCOSUR, Turkey, Singapore, the Common Market for Eastern and Southern Africa

(COMESA) and the Continental Free Trade Area sponsored by the African Union. Arab LDCs benefit from an array of generalized systems of preference (GSP) with the EU, China, India, Norway and others.

Most of those integration schemes preclude involvement of the League of Arab States and have led Arab States to vie with one another for trade deals.

A substantial share of the region's commodities is traded under preferential conditions. The terms of extra-preferential trade, however, pose potential obstacles to the creation of the ACU and its capacity to pursue a developmental regionalism and structural transformation agenda.

3. The political context

Lip service has been paid to the idea of Arab unity since the 1950s but the idea has largely failed because of the lack of political will to see it through. A case in point is the protocol annexed to the 1957 Arab Economic Unity Agreement, which, contrary to the terms of any conventional economic union, allowed Arab States to "unilaterally conclude economic agreements for special political and defense purposes" with non-Arab contracting parties.

At the national level, "political capture", of the use of public institutions, regulations and resources to serve the private interests of the ruling elite and private-sector cronies is deeply embedded.[385] Policies can be manipulated in any number of ways, such as by favouring monopolies and subsidizing private-sector cronies. Political capture largely influenced the ownership structures of State-owned companies privatized in the late 1990s[386] and the decision to establish qualified industrial zones (QIZ).

4. Regulatory confusion and governance

Today, deep extraregional trade agreements impose beyond-the-border commitments that require developing countries to converge their regulatory frameworks with those applied by their developed-country counterparts. The failure of the Arab region to articulate its own regulatory framework only made it more susceptible to taking on asymmetric regulatory frameworks tailored by other trading partners. An oft heard plea is for the trading partners of the Arab region to treat it as a strategic equal, rather than simply trying to foist technical regulations and rules on countries in transition.[387]

Migrating heterogeneous regulatory frameworks involving technical standards and sanitary measures has been found to have trade-diverting effects for developing countries.[388] They can also adversely influence the enforcement of extraregional trade arrangements. The conclusion of regional trade agreements that impose rules affecting policy areas not regulated multilaterally increases the risks of inconsistencies between these agreements and gives rise to regulatory confusion, distortion of markets and implementation problems, especially where agreements overlap.[389]

The World Trade Report 2013 found that export competitiveness for goods and services has been adversely affected by regulatory heterogeneities. Extra-Arab preferential agreements thus pose challenges that go beyond the negative effects of each agreement. The EU, for instance, tends to select certain modes of external governance because they replicate norms of internal governance.[390] As Arab States compete to enter into and expand trade agreements with non-Arab partners, they effectively surrender their right to regulate (at a supranational level) by making concessions required of them in order to seal such deals. Indeed, the adoption of varying forms of economic governance has forced Arab States to take conflicting positions over international economic issues.

5. Non-tariff measures

The Arab region is plagued by non-tariff measures (NTMs), which have replaced traditional tariff protection. NTMs are maintained for a variety of legitimate purposes, such as environmental, health and safety reasons, as well as for protectionist ends. Their incidence is therefore difficult to quantify or assess in terms of type and impact. The study of NTMs in the Arab region extends beyond measurement of their trade restrictiveness to the broader realm of their effects on regulatory governance, productivity, poverty, income distribution and social welfare. According to the World Bank, "NTMs cover an average of 40 per cent of the products imported by the Arab region and ... these frequencies are quite similar to what is observed in other regions of the world".[391]

More problematic than NTMs themselves are the procedural obstacles arising from adherence to sanitary, phytosanitary and technical regulations, conformity assessment requirements, rules of origin, testing, and certification, all of which increase compliance costs. The International Trade Center estimates that the removal of NTMs could increase intra-Arab trade by 10 per cent, create more than two million jobs, including 80,000 skilled jobs, and boost welfare levels by at least 2 per cent by 2025.[392] Others predict 35 per cent growth in intraregional exports by 2030 if NTMs are removed in the southern Mediterranean.[393]

6. Rules of origin and global value chains

Global value chains can open new pathways to structural transformation by segmenting the production process and relocating stages of production. Firms can link to international production networks and draw on the technological prowess of leading firms in these chains while not making the effort themselves.[394] Indeed, "globalization and the splitting up of the production chain do not allow the luxury of establishing naturally integrated production structures within countries".[395]

However, intra- and extra-Arab trade has been adversely affected by asymmetric rules governing cumulation of origin. Under the Pan-Euro-Mediterranean system, the EU employs two types of industrial cumulation, driving a wedge between Maghreb countries, which receive "full cumulation" of manufacturing processing among themselves and diagonal cumulation with other Euro-Med partners, and countries in the Mashreq, which have been granted only diagonal cumulation. The Agadir Agreement failed to remedy that situation.

According to the WTO, outward processing schemes promote low value-added output in "spoke countries", while permitting the "hub" (the United States, EU and others) to specialize in higher value-added activities.[396] Preferential rules of origin have been tailored to the industrial landscape of developed partners and are applied, with little margin for derogations, across the board, thereby failing to consider the level of industrial sophistication in the Arab region and how industries source intermediate inputs.[397]

These considerations go some way to explaining the low intra-industry trade among the more diversified Arab economies,[398] and slow or non-existent structural transformation in some Arab States.[399] In some cases, the cost of compliance with rules of origin has exceeded benefits offered by the relevant preferential agreements.[400] The costs are further compounded in situations where different cumulation of origin schemes are simultaneously applied.[401] Such situations encourage industries to change sourcing patterns in order to acquire originating status and exploit available preferences, irrespective of the impact on competitiveness and Arab integration. Examples are seen from the minimum content requirements and outward processing schemes employed by the US-sponsored QIZs and from the EU prohibition on drawbacks.

D. The road to 2030 – business as usual

Should current trends continue, several Arab countries that initially supported the establishment of the ACU are likely to have pursued membership of other customs or economic unions, creating legal and operational uncertainties and, in all probability, eroding the potential benefits of the Union or any other deep form of regional integration. In essence, by 2030, accommodating competing extraregional integration schemes will have all but buried prospects for deep Arab integration.

1. The European Neighbourhood Policy

By 2030, several Arab States will have undergone a process of regulatory harmonization with the EU. Under the European Neighbourhood Policy (ENP), they will acquire a share in the European single market. The extent of that share will depend on the pace of democratic reform and regulatory harmonization, which is the basis of the "more for more" principle underlying the ENP strategy.

EU-tailored DCFTAs will provide reciprocal concessions for the free trade of industrial goods. Agricultural exports will be granted market access to the extent that they do not disrupt the EU Common Agricultural Policy. Services will be traded under surgical conditions, whereby market access would depend on observing EU regulations. Cross-border cooperation and mobility packages would provide regulated channels of migration, including managed movement for some categories of persons, and closer partnerships in strategic sectors such as energy and telecommunications. There will be opportunities to participate in EU programmes and agencies.

Participating Arab States, however, would lose policy space in international norm-setting bodies. The mandates of Arab agencies to harmonize regional economic regulations would be eroded.

By 2030, some participating Arab States would, with EU financial support, seek "advanced status". The ENP, which was advanced as a strategic policy applying Europe's soft power for system change or government transformation, would evolve as a tool to balance between soft, hard and human security in response to mounting insecurity and conflict in the EU neighbourhood and to address the sources of pressure in Arab States.[402]

2. The Middle East Free Trade Area

More Arab States will also join Bahrain, Jordan, Morocco and Oman in signing free trade agreements with the United States, bringing the idea of a US-led Middle East Free Trade Area (MEFTA) closer to fruition. In so doing, the region will endorse yet another set of reciprocal liberalization commitments extending beyond goods to include services, intellectual property, procurement, labour and environmental standards enforceable through litigation, backed by the possibility of suspending concessions and/or obligations for compensatory payments.[403]

Arab States that do not sign free trade agreements will maintain trade and investment framework agreements (TIFAs), giving US operators favourable trade conditions and market access for certain sectors, such as logistics and other trade-related services.

Bilateral investment treaties (BITs) will safeguard national treatment and other additional investment guarantees to ensure the free transfer of funds, compensation in the event of expropriation, and both State-State and investor-State dispute settlement. As in earlier trade agreements, the United States would push for tough intellectual property rights to back the aggressive pricing practices of pharmaceutical companies unnecessarily extending copyright and patent protection.[404] Those agreements would also eventually incorporate aspects of US anti-trust law, which may run contrary to State-aid and EU-DCFTA provisions on competition or future regional or plurilateral competition agreements.

Given the region's economic vulnerabilities, national and regional investment reforms would be enacted to provide generous concessions and guarantees for FDI, as is clear from amendments to the Arab Unified Agreement on Investment and Capital made in 2014. Attracting FDI will still depend on issues relating to enforcement and other variables, including: tariff openness, infrastructure, tax havens, exchange rate policy, technological progress, labour costs and factor productivity. Those variables are affected by security, governance, and macroeconomic and institutional conditions at the national and regional levels.

3. The rest of the world

The situation will be further complicated by a raft of free trade agreements with regional blocs such as the African Unions, Organization of Islamic States, European Free Trade Association (EFTA) and Mercosur. Following the lead of the Gulf Cooperation Council (GCC), various Arab countries will negotiate similar agreements with partners such as Australia, Canada, China and Japan.

By 2030, the Arab region could host trade preferences from five continents covering at

least 110 countries. Most, if not all, of the region's commodity and services imports will enjoy duty free conditions or be traded under preferential conditions that would not necessarily obey identical or harmonious economic and trade regulations and systems. That is in addition to trade schemes available to developing countries under the Global System of Trade Preferences.

4. The Arab Customs Union

Establishment of the ACU gives Arab States a chance to rationalize existing integration schemes and to foster structural transformation and sustainable development. However, according to a plan drafted in 2014, responsibility for developing the Union would rest with an intergovernmental committee from the moment 6 member States of the League of Arab States declared their intention to join it and until 15 (two thirds) of member States joined. Only then would responsibility be assumed by the League and its Economic and Social Council. It would appear that an opportunity to give the League real supranational powers has thus been wasted. Indeed, what has been proposed appears to be little more than an enlargement of the GCC Customs Union.

Although there is as yet no agreement on the common external tariff (CET) of the ACU, a resolution passed at the March 2015 Summit of the League of Arab States called on Arab States to converge their tariff structures to serve the "CET of the ACU". However, this decision does not necessarily imply the de-facto convergence to the GCC Common Custom Tariff levels unless a prior understanding is reached for Arab States to abandon flexibility and waive their rights to raise national tariffs.

The GCC Customs Union was tailored to avoid the use of high tariffs to protect domestic industries following the advice of international institutions.[405] Pareto-efficient unions require members to share authority over the choice of CET.[406] Customs unions with poorly crafted CETs lead to operational deficiencies and tensions.

(a) Beyond the commodity trade

Trade gains from the creation of the ACU or enlargement of the GCC Customs Union would come mainly through the elimination of non-tariff barriers, regulatory harmonization and the liberalization of services. This would require an overhaul of Arab domestic regulations and the removal of asymmetries in terms of qualification requirements, technical standards, licensing procedures and government procurement.

It would be equally important to review how services are supplied, including the right of establishment and the free movement of natural service providers, and to remove most-favoured-nation and national treatment exemptions.[407] Sooner or later, negotiations would have to move beyond reciprocal market access to the regulation of services trade along the four modes of service supply under the General Agreement on Trade in Services (GATS). Ideally, services would fall under a common external trade policy, but this appears to be a long way off.

Maximizing benefits of the liberalization of services within the ACU, and more broadly

ACCESS, will require addressing other challenges, including distorted supply chains, high transport costs, modest factor productivity and mobility, and discriminatory procurement practices.[408]

(b) The outlier effect

Proposals for the ACU make no reference to the treatment of preferential trade arrangements between Arab and non-Arab States, or to a common external trade policy. They also ignore country or region-specific problems, such as the terms of the State of Palestine's ACU accession under current limitations imposed by the Paris Protocol, or whether Gulf States would accede as a block following the 2002 Unified GCC Commercial Policy.

The potential difficulties are already evident in the GCC Customs Union, which has been upset by the conclusion of free trade agreements between two member States, Bahrain and Oman, with the United States, in contravention of the 2001 GCC Economic Agreement.[409]

The hazards pertaining to this "outlier effect" prompted the governing body of the GCC at one point to suspend free trade negotiations with other trading partners, including Australia, India, Japan and New Zealand, until an appropriate resolution to inconsistencies could be found.[410] A situation also arose in which the CET was applied to US goods passing through other GCC States before arriving in Bahrain or Oman. Operators in those two countries claimed that they were unable to reclaim those duties and charges as per the terms of their free trade agreement with the United States. Other internal controls were imposed to prevent the re-exportation or release of those goods into free circulation within the GCC Customs Union. In a unconventional move, GCC member States dealt with the problem by deciding that any new preferential agreement concluded by any GCC State would apply equally to all members.[411] The decision not only has trade implications for States that are not parties to such agreements, but poses legal and operational conundrums, not least for the non-Arab parties to such agreements. Such position would also cause problems for the ACU, especially if such a position were maintained after GCC members acceded, collectively or individually, to the Union.

Were the outlier effect to prevail under the ACU, preferences granted by Bahrain, Jordan, Morocco and Oman to US exports under their respective free trade agreements could extend to other ACU members. Arab States not bound by free trade agreements with the US could transship their exports via those States, making use of the preferential access granted to them, in violation of those agreements and the premise that goods may be placed in free circulation only if accompanied by a certificate of origin.

The kinds of problems experienced by merchants in Bahrain and Oman within the GCC Customs Union would multiply in the ACU. Similar predicaments would arise in the context of preferential trade agreements with other States and blocs. Such a situation would undermine the premise of free circulation of goods and services within the ACU and, however unpalatable a result, is not unlikely as a business-as-usual outcome. In effect, the ACU would be reduced to little more than a free zone. In addition, Arab States would be vulnerable to litigation for violating the terms of the various bilateral arrangements and/or WTO regulations on transparency.

5. The ACU and Israel

Moves to deepen Arab regional integration that explicitly exclude Israel could meet with opposition from the United States and Europe.[412]

Arab States continue, formally, to boycott Israel. However, in addition to reported clandestine trade,[413] some Arab States maintain business and commercial contacts with Israel.[414] Others have normalized economic relations via free trade agreements or quasi-preferential trade and industrial schemes, renounced some tiers of the boycott under influence as part of their accession to the WTO[415] or simply do not enforce the boycott.[416] The State of Palestine continues, however, to be bound by the terms of an irregular economic/customs union that it was brought to maintain with Israel, albeit recognizing that the West Bank, Gaza Strip and East Jerusalem are part of a separate Palestinian customs territory.

Such asymmetries are incompatible with the idea of the ACU, which would need to adopt an unequivocal position regarding preferential trade with and/or the boycott of Israel, in order not to undermine the principle of goods in free circulation. In order to maintain the boycott of Israel as a security exception, the ACU would have to make such a declaration upon its establishment and notify the WTO.

Although no Arab State has invoked the right of non-application of its WTO rights and obligations with respect to Israel, that does not mean that the boycott could not be maintained under the ACU. Israel and the United States have sought to use WTO accession negotiations by Arab countries to pressure them into normalizing relations with Israel or, at least, renouncing the boycott or reducing the severity of its application.[417]

The resolution of such issues will depend on the terms of a future Arab-Israeli settlement, economic relations between Israel and the State of Palestine, the terms of the latter's accession to the ACU, and how State succession is approached, especially with respect to treaties. Arab obligations under the multilateral trading system would also influence the outcome of conflict arising from the application of asymmetric trade relations with Israel.

Under a one-State solution, transitional measures would be required to integrate such a State into the ACU. Any extraregional trade arrangements with non-Arab partners concluded prior to or accompanying the creation of the one-State settlement would need to be adapted to the ACU charter. The same would go for other extant extraregional trade arrangements, such as MEFTA and EU association agreements. The ACU would need to be involved in negotiations leading to a one-State solution. However, a single State would have little incentive to join the ACU if it became little more than a free zone as postulated above.

Under a two-State solution, the State of Palestine would probably continue to depend economically on Israel in a business-as-usual scenario. Its options for regional integration would be limited. Transitional arrangements

under the Paris Protocol could become permanent, wherein Israel would continue to dictate the terms of its customs union with the State of Palestine, or an amended form thereof, and would maintain its exclusive and highly irregular control over it.[418] It could continue to impose import quotas and export restrictions on Palestinian products, control the collection of taxes and customs proceeds "on behalf" of the Palestinians, and maintain internal barriers and other restrictions hindering the movement of Palestinian goods, services and people.

Palestinian membership of the ACU, and thus effectively of two distinct customs unions at the same time, would give rise to conundrums under international law and multilateral trade rules. The State of Palestine would be challenged as it attempts to adopt asymmetric external tariff structures, trade policies and other regulations of commerce. ACU members would not necessarily feel bound by the current system of entry, exit and checkpoints or restrictions on the movement of goods, services, labour and capital into and from the State of Palestine. The latter's membership of the ACU would make revision of the Paris Protocol unavoidable.

ACU members maintaining preferential trade arrangements with Israel prior to accession to the Union would have to review those arrangements. ACU members not bound by them would be reluctant to allow duty-free access to the Union for Israeli goods. Jordan, for instance, might seek compensation in those circumstances, although the ACU would be free to terminate its preferential concessions even in the absence of a settlement. Israel might reciprocate and move to withdraw equivalent preferential and non-preferential concessions, but Israel would have to demonstrate how its official trade flows, if any, had been adversely affected by the formation of the ACU and accession to it by Jordan.

Maintaining QIZ schemes in their current form after the formation of the ACU would require treating such zones as enclaves or pockets within the ACU. Internal controls would be needed to ensure that imported duty-free Israeli components and the final products are shipped directly outside of the ACU to avert another case of outlier effect. Failure to set up control and verification mechanisms prior to the establishment of the ACU would effectively open up unfettered access for Israeli goods to ACU members that otherwise would not grant such access. Israeli products would not require proofs of origin once placed in free circulation or within the ACU.

Such quasi-preferential trade and industrial schemes could be abrogated as they would fall within the ambit of non-reciprocal preferences, although not notified as such to the WTO. They derive their preferences and legality from an entirely separate free trade agreement between the United States and Israel.[419] Egypt might seek compensation for loss of preferences to the United States market.[420] However, that could be resolved through an ACU-United States free trade agreement.

The establishment of the ACU under the business-as-usual scenario, with numerous free trade and other preferential agreements with States outside the union still in place, would provoke serious problems, not the least of which could be litigation arising from violations of those agreements and WTO rules. The likelihood of litigation would increase if Arab States succumbed to pressure to relinquish the flexibility to establish their own regional trade arrangements. In any event, free trade arrangements between ACU members and other States would have to be reviewed prior to the establishment of the ACU, and some Arab States might therefore opt to postpone accession. In short, the failure to put an end to the independent, asymmetric and indiscriminant use of trade policy and trade remedies by individual States and to enforce a common external trade policy would call into question the very reason for even setting up the ACU in the first place.

E. Vision 2030

The League of Arab States adopted a broad conceptual approach to collective Arab security at its 2015 summit, held in Sharm el-Sheikh, Egypt. In the same spirit, this report proposes the creation of ACCESS. Under this ambitious scheme, borders drawn up by colonial powers would lose meaning as a single Arab economic identity and territory evolved.

Making ACCESS a reality will require political resolve and could enable the region to become an autonomous power bloc free of the geopolitical shackles in which it has languished for most of the twentieth century and up to the present day. Drawing on international experience and conceived in the light of contemporary multilateral trade and investment rules, governance and jurisprudence, ACCESS takes into account key issues in order to achieve deep regional integration:

- The political considerations that lead countries to pursue extraregional trade agreements rather than intraregional integration, and the need to reconcile those two processes;
- The need for deeper integration within the region and in the global economy in order to reap the benefits of global value chains and reverse patterns that have made the region a net exporter of capital and remittances;
- The need to respect trade rules in a way that maintains open trading systems, ensures that any process of Arab regional integration is not subject to disputes or demands for compensation, and that Arab developmental rights are respected;
- The supranational governance needed to rationalize collective Arab economic action and ensure a level playing field for all economic actors;
- The legal aspects arising from the Vienna Conventions on the Law of Treaties and on the Succession of States.

1. ACCESS in detail

The nature of the Arab region precludes the simple application of existing models of regional integration. However, existing structures can provide guidance on steps to take. The acronym of this vision proposal for 2030 provides clues to the way forward and the underlying philosophy of ACCESS. It is intended to serve as a basis for discussion and doubtless would require fine-tuning.

Arab. This regional vision encapsulates a single Arab identity and provides a framework in which extraregional strategies would serve Arab developmental regionalism rather than

undermine it. ACCESS would rise above the subregional demarcations that typically ignore the ideal of Arab unity (such as Mashreq, Maghreb, Levant, South Mediterranean, Middle East).

Citizens. The idea of Arab citizenship embodies the socioeconomic rights and obligations of all legal persons and their equal treatment within a single regional market. This would include the freedom to compete in goods, services and procurement markets, and invest in and guarantee private and public capital. It would also entail the regulated circulation of persons, whereby the rights of migrant workers and their families would be upheld; the protection of intellectual property; and equitable sustainable development policies. Implicit in the idea of citizenship is fulfillment of the aspirations of all social classes and addressing problems such as welfare erosion, inequality, poverty and unemployment. ACCESS would provide a regulatory framework transcending national boundaries and safeguarding equal and harmonized access to socioeconomic rights across the region.

Common area of the rule of law. One aim of ACCESS is to foster a just Arab society through the pursuit of freedom, the absence of discrimination and the equitable distribution of material well-being in terms of access to economic growth, health care, education, water and sanitation, social protection and decent housing, and fairness in terms of taxation, poverty reduction expenditure, social cohesion and efforts to combat corruption. Under ACCESS, a pan-Arab system for the protection of human rights and fundamental freedoms would be created. This would involve the review and development of several legal instruments, including the Arab Human Rights Charter, the Arab Charter on Cultural and Heritage Unity, the Cairo Declaration on Human Rights in Islam and the proposals on region-wide civil and criminal codes. The system would be enforced by institutions including a regional court of justice, human rights courts, an ombudsman, and a regional anti-corruption agency. Added force would come through empowerment of the Arab Parliament.

Economic. ACCESS would, until the ultimate goal of Arab unity can be achieved, function as a single common market. Commodities and services exported from the region would bear an "ACCESS" mark of origin. The Arab economic space would be a sufficiently broad framework allowing all Arab States, regardless of their development status or membership of the ACU, to benefit from liberalization and economic policy harmonization, including regional flanking policies. The economic capacity of the region would be boosted by an Arab common industrial space and a regional research and innovation framework. The obligations of the single market would take precedence over extraregional trade arrangements. The ACU would simply be a step on the road to establishing the economic space and contribute to ending extra-Arab economic unilateralism. An Arab economic commission would be financed through, for example, common customs duties, common charges on goods and services imports and a uniform levy on harmonized taxes and charges. Supranational institutions would review all intraregional and extraregional agreements to ensure their consistency with ACCESS plans for socioeconomic development and structural

transformation. A common external trade policy and common external tariff would be introduced, mechanisms for tariff revenue distribution and compensation would be set up, and intra-Arab non-tariff barriers would be swept aside as uniform trade regulations are adopted. Talks that have dragged on for more than a decade on specific rules of origin could be abandoned as the principle of free circulation of goods takes effect. In short, the Arab economic space would take up ideas contained in key documents such as the 1953 Convention for Facilitating Trade Exchange and the Regulation of Transit Trade between States of the Arab League; 1980 Strategy for Joint Arab Economic Action; 1980 Arab Charter of National Economic Action; 1980 Unified Agreement for the Investment of Arab Capital in the Arab States; 2000 Beirut Agreement on Services Liberalization; and a series of agreements on labour mobility (1967, 1975 and 1976).

Security Space. The ACCESS single market would be the motor of socioeconomic convergence and contribute to achievement of the SDGs. A common sustainable development area would require a pan-Arab renewable energy platform, mandated to achieve the Pan-Arab Renewable Energy Strategy 2030, Desert Power 2050, the Solar Heating Arab Mark and Certification Initiative (SHAMCI), and Arab nuclear power strategies. Other missions include completion of the Arab Emergency Food Security strategy to meet an expected increase in the region's food bill to $71 billion by 2030, and research and development programmes adopted by the Arab Organization for Agricultural Development, in particular the 2030 Arab emergency food security strategy. The role of regional specialized agencies, such as the Arab Atomic Energy Agency, would need to be developed. The security space would moderate rentier and consumption tendencies and mitigate climate risks through economic diversification and the use of low-carbon technologies. The development of broadband networks and technological infrastructure will encourage an Arab electronic market fostering openness, security, diversity, access and critical Internet resources, and by extension regional "ICT 4 Development" solutions, which itself will contribute to achievement of the SDGs and potentially the generation of millions of jobs.[421]

The development of transport networks (road, rail, maritime and air) would render the single market more secure and effective. The Integrated Transport System in the Arab Mashreq (ITSAM) and the Arab Roads and Railways Network within the League of Arab States (extension of ESCWA agreements) would pave the way for the establishment of an integrated trans-Arab transport system. Almost 60 per cent of transport time and costs along international road corridors in the region are incurred waiting at border crossings.[422]

The removal of border controls will slash the cost of transportation and facilitate the development of regional supply chains. A multimodal transport system, with its own advisory board and comprising all stakeholders (including ESCWA, GCC, the League of Arab States, and regional development banks and funds) would be created as an extension to ITSAM. It would set contingency plans to mitigate the impact of crisis and conflicts on transport, and to rebuild the war-damaged infrastructure. The World Bank estimates that the region needs to invest $100 billion a year on infrastructure to meet domestic demand for its fast growing population.[423]

2. Structural transformation under ACCESS

(a) Multilateral and extraregional constraints

Replicating the growth model of the East Asian countries in the latter half of the twentieth century will be impossible at a time of increasingly fragmented production networks within regional and global value chains. Under current multilateral trade regulations and given the plethora of extra-Arab preferential trade arrangements, under which trade is carried out at near duty-free and quota-free levels, the reintroduction of tariffs or the application of subsidies to protect infant industries and foster structural transformation would require renegotiation of the terms of those agreements. Nevertheless, ACCESS can exploit the limited leeway available to stimulate structural transformation.

(b) Subsidy, rules of origin, tariffs and services-led structural transformation

One approach to the subsidy-led transformation advanced under ACCESS entails "green structural transformation", whereby non-specific region-wide industrial subsidies would be channeled to subsidize research and technological innovation and promote environmentally friendly industries.

An Arab research and innovation framework would promote innovation[424] and monitor compliance with WTO rules. It would encourage scientific production and innovation, enhance industrial sophistication, localize technologies, pool intellectual property and exploit joint opportunities for the licensing of patents and industrial designs. That would reinforce the Arab common industrial space, which in turn would help to sweep away dividing lines between national industries and develop regional supply chains. A regional form of cumulation system of origin would be employed under ACCESS when exporting goods to non-Arab trading partners in order to exploit extraregional trade preferences.

Rules of origin now enforced in intra-Arab trade would cease under ACCESS, once members adopted a common external tariff and the goods in free circulation principle was enforced. Alternatively, rules of origin that once caused uncertainty in intra-Arab preferential trade[425] would be tailored to the region's structural transformation needs.

A region-wide set of industrial codes, building on the 2005 Arab Industrial Development Strategy, would be drafted to promote industrial activity.[426] The proposed Arab Economic Commission would oversee enforcement of those codes, on matters such as competition, mergers and acquisitions, industrial safety, health and the environment. Common rules on accreditation and conformity would be adopted, and a regionally accredited patent authority would protect intellectual property. Arab States would adopt common positions vis-à-vis non-Arab trading partners and in multilateral forums on industrial development and cooperation.

A single regional industrial space would help to promote small and medium enterprises (SMEs).

Clustering and specialization would be propelled by an Arab SME network cluster observatory,[427] building on regional initiatives such as the proposed SME Development Fund. Industrial mapping could be used to spur diversification in SMEs, and information on industries and suppliers of intermediate products would be gathered to consolidate regional value chains, through which businesses could then tap into GVCs.

Under ACCESS, national treatment exemptions and service subsidies could also help to develop services infrastructure, given that GATS does not restrict the provision of subsidies for services provided in the exercise of Governmental authority. "Security exceptions", allowing the application of protectionist policies in times of "emergency in international relations",[428] could also be invoked.

The adoption of the relatively low GCC weighted average common external tariff of 4.5 per cent would not necessarily induce structural change for non-oil producing countries or Arab LDCs.[429] Policymakers who heavily weight future growth will want high tariffs in skill-intensive industries.[430]

Renegotiating WTO schedules of commitments would be an option. Nonetheless, invoking the Enabling Clause to create the ACU would open pathways for further flexibility.

Tariff-induced structural transformation under ACCESS could be fostered by raising current applied tariffs and capitalizing on tariff overhangs to induce skills-biased protection. In the case of most Arab WTO members, in particular non-oil producers, considerable overhangs are available to raise tariff protection (42.4 per cent in Tunisia, 30.1 per cent in Morocco and 18.4 per cent in Egypt). With the exception of Bahrain, GCC States do not fall into that category.[431]

(c) Financing

There is a plethora of proposals on how to finance Arab integration efforts, including new structures such as an Arab bank for reconstruction and development, Arab development agency, Inter-Arab development bank, Arab regional integration fund, multi-donor trust funds, Arab regional integration sovereign funds and more. These come on top of the many existing bilateral and multilateral Islamic and Arab development and investment funds, institutions and agencies.[432] It is not so much that new institutions are needed, but rather a newly defined manner by which financing and investment decisions are taken to address regional priorities and their timing, especially at a time when the geopolitical and security situation is deteriorating.

International and regional aid has thus far been insufficient to overcome the multiple crises facing the region, exacerbated by the record numbers of refugees and displaced people in the region. The cost of reconstruction in conflict-affected countries is running as high as $650 billion,[433] which should be mobilized through an internationally backed Arab reconstruction and recovery plan.

The Arab Monetary Fund reports that, by 2012, the cumulative aggregate of intraregional ODA had reached $76.6 billion,[434] in addition to $253.9 billion in ODA received from external development partners.[435] On a per capita basis, the region received $60 in 2013, more than any other region and three times the global average.

ESCWA has found that the Arab region had enough resources to fill a finance gap of $54.5 billion (associated with achieving 7 per cent growth rates) and finance the reduction of unemployment by half, for which an estimated $54.9 billion would be required. However, total remittances, FDI and extraregional ODA leaving the region amounted to $78.1 billion, representing approximately 1.4 times the finance gap.[436]

By 2013, Arab development institutions had allocated only 59 per cent of their cumulative financing to intraregional operations.[437]

The Global Financial Integrity report (2014) found that illicit outflows from the region between 2003 and 2012 amounted to $740 billion as a result of corruption, trade misinvoicing, leakages or omissions from balance of payments.

A swift remedy to this malaise is crucial in order to rationalize the necessary finance to support regional integration. Other avenues to explore include public-private partnerships; expanded debt and equity markets; and an enhanced capital market, including pension fund investments. Innovative financing sources can be tapped, including green bonds. Arab remittances can be leveraged to raise an additional $225 billion in development financing in 2030 by reducing remittance costs and mobilizing diaspora savings.[438]

F. Conclusion

Much ink has been spilled on the subject of Arab regional integration since the end of the Second World War. It has been perceived as an aspiration, a material goal, a panacea and a malaise all in one. In spite of the many declarations of intent and agreements signed, joint action by the Arab States has been largely hamstrung by their desire to maintain sovereignty and defend their national economic interests and pursue economic rapprochement with major external trading partners.

The rising tide of extraregional agreements, mostly confined to trade in goods, has pushed Arab countries away from regional integration and instead led them to compete with one another. The potential of integration to spur growth and socioeconomic development through services liberalization and labour mobility has remained largely untapped. Efforts are needed to reconcile the twin objectives of sustainable development and integration throughout the region.

By reworking the objectives, scope and instruments of integration, the benefits of developmental regionalism can be harnessed. This is ultimately the intent of ACCESS. It rests on the notion of an Arab economic security space (for extraregional purposes) encapsulating a single market configuration (for trade in goods, services, investments, labour, industrial development, research and innovation) and customs union operating as one within a single Arab space with uniform regulations, including full cumulation of origin and duty drawback, enforced by regional bodies.

By 2030, the region would have consolidated its infrastructure, energy and renewable energy networks; developed new trade routes to enhance regional supply chains; and become more open to production fragmentation and to technological advancement through GVCs. It would also witness increasing diversity in its commodities and services trade and in the direction of trade itself. The region would be guided by a policy of economic alignment based on its own integration strategies and be in a position to have real influence on the terms of its extraregional economic cooperation.

Annex I

Sustainable Development Goals

Goal 1	End poverty in all its forms everywhere
Goal 2	End hunger, achieve food security and improved nutrition and promote sustainable agriculture
Goal 3	Ensure healthy lives and promote well-being for all at all ages
Goal 4	Ensure inclusive and equitable quality education and promote lifelong learning opportunities for all
Goal 5	Achieve gender equality and empower all women and girls
Goal 6	Ensure availability and sustainable management of water and sanitation for all
Goal 7	Ensure access to affordable, reliable, sustainable and modern energy for all
Goal 8	Promote sustained, inclusive and sustainable economic growth, full and productive employment and decent work for all
Goal 9	Build resilient infrastructure, promote inclusive and sustainable industrialization and foster innovation
Goal 10	Reduce inequality within and among countries
Goal 11	Make cities and human settlements inclusive, safe, resilient and sustainable
Goal 12	Ensure sustainable consumption and production patterns
Goal 13	Take urgent action to combat climate change and its impacts
Goal 14	Conserve and sustainably use the oceans, seas and marine resources for sustainable development
Goal 15	Protect, restore and promote sustainable use of terrestrial ecosystems, sustainably manage forests, combat desertification, and halt and reverse land degradation and halt biodiversity loss
Goal 16	Promote peaceful and inclusive societies for sustainable development, provide access to justice for all and build effective, accountable and inclusive institutions at all levels
Goal 17	Strengthen the means of implementation and revitalize the global partnership for sustainable development

Source: A/RES/70/1

Annex II
Structure of the macroeconomic model

Introduction

Hereafter we suggest a standard model for economic growth in the Arab region, by looking at the level of growth in physical capital, the total factor productivity and growth in human capital. This model enables us to foresee the movements of those three factors up to 2025.

The original model

This model is based on the classic growth model proposed by Solow (1960). The $GDP(i,t)$ for a particular country is composed of three main factors: capital $K(i,t)$, labour $L(i,t)$ and exogenous technical progress $A(i,t)$:

$$GDP(i,t) = A(i,t)K(i,t)^\mu L(i,t)^{1-\mu}$$

The investment rate over the past period identifies the level of capital accumulation. The increase in the labour force is the result of International Labour Organization (ILO) projections, taking into account demographic factors and growth in total factor productivity. However, productivity growth can be modelled through mechanisms of convergence or indicators of accumulation in human capital. For ease of analysis, we used simple mechanisms to prepare uncomplicated scenarios.

The estimation of capital appreciation

Physical capital is calculated according to the method adopted by Klino Rodriguez and Clark in 1997, and the amount of investment required is calculated using the following equation: $K(i,t)$

$$K_i(t) = \sum_{j=0}^{t}(1-\delta)^{t-j}\bar{I}_{i,j} + (1-\delta)^t K_i(1960)$$

$\bar{I}_{i,j}$ is the average of investment divided by GDP for the period covered by the study, while $\bar{I} = \dfrac{INV}{GDP}$ represents the decrease rate of capital δ, which is equal to 5 per cent. The estimation of the size of initial investment is calculated according to the following equation:

$$K(1960) = \left(\frac{\bar{I}}{g+\delta+n}\right)GDP(1960)$$

where n represents the rate of population growth and g the average rate of economic growth for the period studied. The data used was extracted from the World Bank database. GDP has been calculated (at constant United States dollar prices of 2005). The investment is the continuous formation of fixed assets from 2005 and the period of analysis stretches from 1960 to 2025.

The capital formation is calculated, according to the standard formula, which is based on the level of investment I_t and the level of capital depreciation δ:

$$K_{t+1} = I_t - (1 - \delta)K_t$$

The estimation of the active labour force

Estimations of population growth until 2100 carried out by the United Nations have been adopted, but data for the economically active population have been taken from ILO, which estimated its according to age groups for the period 1970-2025. This allows us to take into account economic participation rates and estimations regarding school attendance by age group. We took the 15-64 age group, and calculated the proportion of the economically active population using the equation that multiplies the participation rate in the labour market (by age groups), by the adult population according to the following equation:

The economically active population (15-64 years) = $\sum_{tg} \sigma_{tg} \times pop_{tg}$

tg being the studied age group.

Since the ILO estimations only went up to the year 2020, we had to complete them up until 2025 using the same calculation methodology and indicators. The data indicate ongoing high levels of growth in the proportion of economically active population in all Arab countries but Libya and Tunisia, where the pace of growth is slower.

Total factor productivity

Total factor productivity is estimated by reversing the equation of production. The following equation has been adopted for the calculation process with $\alpha = 0.33$

$$A_i = GDP_i / K_i^{\alpha} L_i^{1-\alpha}$$

Growth forecasts were based on three components:

Total factor productivity growth is calculated on the basis of factors such as institutional and external convergence mechanisms;

Capital growth is driven by investment growth;

The growth of labour is driven by the growth of the economically active population related to human capital.

Scenarios

The model is designed to simulate the growth potential of the Arab economies. We must not ignore adverse incidents experienced by some Arab countries during democratic transition. Those incidents, although transitory, could have a long-term impact. Therefore, we proposed transition scenarios for some Arab countries built on the political and economic reality and changes that occurred since the Arab Spring.

Future scenarios are simulated through the evolution of the three variables associated in the equation below: A, L and K

$$g_{GDP} = \alpha g_K + (1 - \alpha)g_L + g_A$$

g_{GDP} Growth rate of the gross domestic product

g_K Growth rate of capital reserves

g_L Growth rate of labour

g_A Growth rate of total factor productivity

Bibliography

Abdmoulah, W. (2011). Arab trade integration evidence from zero-inflated negative binomial model. *Journal of Economic Cooperation and Development*, vol. 32, No. 2, pp. 39-65.

Abdmoulah, W., and B. Laabas (2010). Assessment of Arab export competitiveness in international markets using trade indicators. API/WPS 1010. Kuwait: The Arab Planning Institute.

Abedini, J., and N. Péridy (2008). The Greater Arab Free Trade Area (GAFTA): an estimation of its trade effects. *Journal of Economic Integration*, vol. 23, No. 4 (December), pp. 848-872.

Abu-Ismail, K., G. Abou Taleb, and R. Ramadan (2012). Rethinking global poverty measurement. International Policy Centre for Inclusive Growth Working Paper, No. 93. Brasilia: United Nations Development Programme.

Abu-Ismail, K., and N. Sarangi (2013). A new approach to measuring the middle class: Egypt. Economic and Social Commission for Western Asia (ESCWA) Working Paper Series. E/ESCWA/EDGD/2013/WP.2.

_____ (2015). Rethinking the measurement of the middle class: evidence from Egypt. World Institute for Development Economics Research (WIDER) Working Paper, No. 2015/023. Helsinki: WIDER, United Nations University.

Abu-Ismail, K., and others (2011a). The ADCR 2011 – Arab human development and deprivation: phenomenal progress or mixed results? Arab Development Challenges Background Paper, No. 2011/01. Cairo: United Nations Development Programme.

_____ (2011b). The ADCR 2011: employment, vulnerability, social protection and the crisis of Arab economic reforms. Arab Development Challenges Background Paper, No. 2011/05. Cairo: United Nations Development Programme.

_____ (2014). An Arab perspective on the post-2015 agenda: national targets, regional priorities and global goals. ESCWA Working Paper Series. E/ESCWA/EDGD/2014/WP.1.

_____ (2015). Multidimensional poverty index for middle-income countries: Findings from Jordan, Iraq, and Morocco. ESCWA Working Paper Series. E/ESCWA/EDID/2015/WP.2.

Acemoglu, D., S. Johnson, and J. Robinson (2001). The colonial origins of comparative development: an empirical investigation. *American Economic Review*, vol. 91, No. 5 (December), pp. 1369-1401.

Acemoglu, D., and J. Robinson (2006). *Economic Origins of Dictatorship and Democracy*. Cambridge: Cambridge University Press.

_____ (2012). *Why Nations Fail: The Origins of Power, Prosperity, and Poverty*. New York: Crown Publishers.

Acemoglu, D., and others (2008). Income and democracy. *American Economic Review*, vol. 98, No. 3, pp. 808-842.

Ahmad, A. (2014). The customs union & Israel's no-State solution, 26 November. Available from http://al-shabaka.org/briefs/the-customs-union-and-israels-no-state-solution.

Adalah – The Legal Center for Arab Minority Rights in Israel (2012). The Discriminatory Laws Database. Available from www.adalah.org/en/content/view/7771. Accessed 30 January 2015.

Ahmari-Moghaddam, A. (2012). *Towards International Islamic Human Rights: A Comparative Study of Islamic Law, Shari'ah, with Universal Human Rights as Defined in the International Bill of Human Rights*. Available from https://tspace.library.utoronto.ca/bitstream/1807/32513/5/AhmariMoghaddam_Ali_20126_LLM_thesis.pdf.

Al-Ali, Z., and M. Dafel (2013). Egyptian constitutional reform and the fight against corruption. Working Paper, No. 1 (June). Stockholm and New York: International Institute for Democracy and Electoral Assistance and the Center for Constitutional Transitions at NYU Law. Available from http://constitutionaltransitions.org/wp-content/uploads/2013/06/1_Al-Ali_Dafel_Egypt_Corruption.pdf.

Al-Atrash, H., and T. Yousef (2000). Intra-Arab trade: is it too little? Working Paper, WP/00/10. Washington, D.C.: International Monetary Fund. Available from http://www.imf.org/external/pubs/ft/wp/2000/wp0010.pdf.

Al-Barghouti, Tamim (2008). *The Umma and the Dawla; the Nation State and the Arab Middle East*. London: Pluto Press.

Al-Dardari, A., and H. Bchir (2014). Assessing the impact of the conflict on Syrian economy and looking beyond. ESCWA Working Paper Series. E/ESCWA/EDGD/2014/WP.2.

Al-Darwish, A, and others (2015). *Saudi Arabia: Tackling Emerging Economic Challenges to Sustain Growth*. Washington, D.C.: International Monetary Fund.

Al-Najjar, Sabika (2002). Women migrant domestic workers in Bahrain. International Migration Papers, No. 47. Geneva: International Labour Organization.

Al-Zadjali, Tariq (2010). The role of the Arab Organization for Agricultural Development (AOAD) in Arab food security. Available from http://www.fao.org/fileadmin/templates/cfs/Docs0910/CFS36Docs/CFS36_Session_Presentations/CFS36_Agenda_Item_V_AOAD.pdf.

Al-Zubari, W. K. (2003). Alternative water policies for the Gulf Cooperation Council countries. In *Water Resources Perspectives: Evaluation, Management, and Policy*, A.S. Al-Sharhan and W.W. Wood, eds. Amsterdam: Elsevier Science.

Ali, A. A. G. (2009). The political economy of inequality in the Arab region and relevant development policies. Working Paper, No. 502. Cairo: Economic Research Forum. Available from http://www.erf.org.eg/CMS/uploads/pdf/1251636223_502.pdf.

Ali, O., and I. Elbadawi (2012). The political economy of public sector employment in resource dependent countries. Working Paper, No. 673. Cairo: Economic Research Forum. Available from http://www.erf.org.eg/CMS/uploads/pdf/673.pdf.

Alkire, S., and S. Deneulin (n.d.). A normative framework for development. Available from http://css.escwa.org.lb/sd/1382/chapters1-3.pdf.

Alkire S., and M. E. Santos (2010). Acute multidimensional poverty: a new index for developing countries. Working Paper, No. 38. Oxford: Oxford Poverty and Human Development Initiative. Available from http://www.ophi.org.uk/acute-multidimensional-poverty-a-new-index-for-developing-countries.

Alon, G., and A. Benn (2003). Netanyahu: Israel's Arabs are the real demographic threat. *Haaretz*, 19 December. Available from www.haaretz.com/print-edition/news/netanyahu-israel-s-arabs-are-the-real-demographic-threat-1.109045.

Alvaredo F., and T. Piketty (2014). Measuring top incomes and inequality in the Middle East: data limitations and illustration with the case of Egypt. Working Paper, No. 832. Cairo: Economic Research Forum. Available from http://www.erf.org.eg/CMS/uploads/pdf/832.pdf.

Amnesty International (2013). *The Dark Side of Migration: Spotlight on Qatar's Construction Sector ahead of the World Cup*. London: Amnesty International Publications.

Amsden, A. (2001). *The Rise of 'the Rest': Challenges to the West from Late-industrializing Economies*. New York: Oxford University Press.

Arab Center for Research and Policy Studies (2014). *The 2014 Arab Opinion Index.* Doha. Available from http://english.dohainstitute.org/file/get/00ba3989-ec1e-49ba-9f33-56b8e1861ce4.pdf.

Arab Water Council (AWC) (2011). *Second Arab Water Forum: Synthesis Report, Cairo, Egypt, 20-23 November 2011*.

Arab World for Research and Development (2010). Results of an opinion poll, 9 November. Available from www.awrad.org/pdfs/English_tables-Ocotober2010.pdf.

Arndt, C., and C. Oman (2006). *Uses and Abuses of Governance Indicators*. Paris: Organisation for Economic Co-operation and Development.

Artadi, E., and X. Sala-i-Martin (2003). The economic tragedy of the XXth century: growth in Africa. Working Paper, No. 9865. Cambridge, MA: National Bureau of Economic Research.

Assaad, R. (2014). Making sense of Arab labor markets: the enduring legacy of dualism. *IZA Journal of Labor and Development*, vol. 3, No. 6 (April).

A.T. Kearney (2014). *The 2014 A.T. Kearney Global Services Location Index. A Wealth of Choices: From Anywhere on Earth to No Location at All*. Available from https://www.atkearney.com/documents/10192/5082922/A+Wealth+of+Choices.pdf/61c80111-41b2-4411-ad1e-db4a3d6d5f0d.

Augier, P., and others (2012). Non-tariff measures in the MNA region: improving governance for competitiveness. Working Paper Series, No. 56. Washington, D.C.: World Bank.

Avery, G. (2012). The European Economic Area revisited. European Policy Centre Policy Brief. Available from http://www.epc.eu/documents/uploads/pub_1428_the_european_economic_area_revisited.pdf.

Aziz, Sahar (2014). Egypt's judiciary, coopted, 20 August. Available from http://carnegieendowment.org/sada/?fa=56426.

Azour, J. (2014). Social justice in the Arab world. E/ESCWA/SDD/2014/Background Paper.1. Beirut: Economic and Social Commission for Western Asia.

Balabanova, D., M. McKee, and A. Mills, eds. (2011). *'Good Health at Low cost' 25 years on. What Makes a Successful Health System*. London: London School of hygiene and Tropical Medicine.

Barro, R. J. (1997). *Determinants of Economic Growth: A Cross-Country Empirical Study*. Cambridge, Mass.: Massachusetts Institute of Technology (MIT) Press.

Bchir, M. H., and others (2002). MIRAGE, a computable general equilibrium model for trade policy analysis. CEPII Working Paper, No. 2002-17. Available from http://www.cepii.fr/%5C/anglaisgraph/workpap/pdf/2002/wp02-17.pdf.

Bchir, M. H., M.A. Chemingui and T. Rajhi (forthcoming). Arab economic outlook: the technical approach. ESCWA Technical Paper.

Beaumont, P. (2014). Netanyahu pushes to define Israel as nation-State of Jewish people only. *The Guardian*, 4 May. Available from www.theguardian.com/world/2014/may/04/binyamin-netanyahu-israel-jewish-state.

Beblawi, H. A. (1987). The rentier state in the Arab world. In *The Rentier State*, H. A. Beblawi and G. Luciani, eds. London and New York: Croom Helm and Methuen.

Beeson, M., and I. Islam (2005). Neoliberalism and East Asia: resisting the Washington Consensus. *Journal of Development Studies*, vol. 41, No. 2, pp. 197-219.

Behr, T. (2010). Regional integration in the Mediterranean: moving out of the deadlock? Studies and Research Report, No. 77. Notre Europe. Available from http://www.institutdelors.eu/media/etud77-mediterraneanintegration-tbehr-en.pdf?pdf=ok.

Behrman, J. R. (1990a). The action of human resources and poverty on one another: what we have yet to learn. Living Standards Measurement Study (LSMS) Working Paper, No. 74. Washington, D.C.: World Bank.

_____ (1990b). Human Resource Led Development? Review of Issues and Evidence. New Delhi: Asian Regional Team for Employment Promotion and International Labour Organization.

_____ (1993). The economic rationale for investing in nutrition in developing countries. *World Development*, vol. 21, No. 11 (November), pp. 1749-1771.

_____ (1996). The impact of health and nutrition on education. *The World Bank Research Observer*, vol. 11, No. 1 (February), pp. 23-37.

Ben Hammouda, H. and P. N. Osakwe (2006). Global trade models and economic policy analyses: relevance, risks, and repercussions for Africa. Report No. 47. United Nations Economic Commission for Africa, African Trade Policy Centre.

Bhagwati, J. (1995). US trade policy: the infatuation with FTAs. Discussion Paper Series, No. 726. Columbia University. Available from http://storage.globalcitizen.net/data/topic/knowledge/uploads/20090222131937814.pdf.

Bhaduri, A., and S. Marglin (1990). Unemployment and the real wage: the economic basis for contesting political ideologies. *Cambridge Journal of Economics*, vol. 14, pp. 375-393.

Bhattachargay, B. N., and P. De (2005). Promotion of trade and investment between People's Republic of China and India: toward a regional perspective. *Asia Development Review*, vol. 22, No. 1, pp. 45-70.

Bhattacharyya, S., and R. Hodler (2010). Natural resources, democracy and corruption. *European Economic Review*, vol. 54, No. 4 (May), pp. 608-621.

_____ (2014). Do natural resource revenues hinder financial development? The role of political institutions. OXCarre Research Paper, No. 53. Oxford: University of Oxford.

Blaydes, L. (2008). Authoritarian elections and elite management: theory and evidence from Egypt. Paper presented at the Conference on Dictatorships. Princeton, N.J., April. Available from https://www.princeton.edu/~piirs/Dictatorships042508/Blaydes.pdf.

Bora, B., P. J. Lloyd, and M. Pangestu (1999). Industrial policy and the WTO. Paper presented at the World Trade Organization/World Bank Conference on Developing Countries' Interests in a Millennium Round. Geneva, September.

Bourguignon, F. (2003). The growth elasticity of poverty reduction: explaining heterogeneity across countries and time periods. In T. S. Eicher and S. J. Turnovsky (eds.), *Inequality and Growth: Theory and Policy Implications*. Cambridge, Mass.: MIT Press.

Brady, H. E., S. Verba, and K. L. Schlozman (1995). Beyond SES: a resource model of political participation. *The American Political Science Review*, vol. 89, No. 2 (June), pp. 271-294.

Brenton, P. (2011). Preferential Rules of Origin. In *Preferential Trade Agreement Policies for Development: A Handbook*, J.P. Chauffour and J.C. Maur, eds. Washington, D.C.: International Bank for Reconstruction and Development/World Bank.

Brenton, P., F. Flatters, and P. Kalenga (2005). Rules of origin and SADC: the case for change in the mid term review of the Trade Protocol. Africa Region Working Paper Series, No. 83. Washington, D.C.: World Bank.

Brenton, P., and M. Manchin (2002). Making EU trade agreements work: the role of rules of origin. Working Document, No. 183. Brussels: Centre for European Policy Studies.

Brenton, P., and C. Özden (2009). Trade preferences for apparel and the role of rules of origin – the case of Africa. In *Trade Preference Erosion: Measurement and Policy Response*, Hoekman, B., W. Martin and C. A. Braga, eds. Washington, D.C.: World Bank.

British Petroleum (2015). *Energy Outlook 2035*. Available from http://www.bp.com/content/dam/bp/pdf/energy-economics/energy-outlook-2015/bp-energy-outlook-2035-booklet.pdf.

Bruder, R. (2015). How to encourage more women into MENA's workforce, 21 May. Available from https://agenda.weforum.org/2015/05/how-to-encourage-more-women-into-menas-workforce.

Brumberg, D. (2002). Democratization in the Arab world? The trap of liberalized autocracy. *Journal of Democracy*, vol. 13, No. 4, pp. 57-67.

Bruno, M., M. Ravallion, and L. Squire (1998). Equity and growth in developing countries: old and new perspectives on the policy issues. In *Income Distribution and High-quality Growth*, V. Tanzi and K. Chu, eds. Cambridge, Mass.: MIT Press.

Bulgaria, National Statistics Institute (n.d.). Foreign Trade Database. Available from http://www.nsi.bg/en/content/12726/%D0%BC%D0%B5%D1%82%D0%B0%D0%B4%D0%B0%D0%BD%D0%BD%D0%B8/foreign-trade. Accessed 30 November 2014.

Busse, M., and others, eds. (2007). *Institutions, Governance and Trade: An Empirical Investigation of the Linkages in View of the Proposed ACP/EU Economic Partnership Agreements*. Bonn: Friedrich-Ebert-Stiftung.

Cabral, A. (1974). National liberation and culture. *Transition*, No. 45, pp. 12-17. Available from https://racismandnationalconsciousnessresources.files.wordpress.com/2008/11/amilcar-cabral-national-liberation-and-culture.pdf.

Callahan, K. (2007). Citizen participation: models and methods. *International Journal of Public Administration*, vol. 30, No. 11, pp. 1179-1196.

Cammett, M. (2014). *Compassionate Communalism: Welfare and Sectarianism in Lebanon*. Ithaca and London: Cornell University Press.

Cattaneo, O., and others (2013). Joining, upgrading and being competitive in global value chains: a strategic framework. Policy Research Working Paper, No. 6406. Washington, D.C.: World Bank.

Central Intelligence Agency (CIA) (n.d.a). The World Factbook: Iran. Available from www.cia.gov/library/publications/resources/the-world-factbook/geos/ir.html. Accessed 30 November 2014.

_____ (n.d.b). The World Factbook: Turkey. Available from www.cia.gov/library/publications/resources/the-world-factbook/geos/tu.html. Accessed 30 November 2014.

Centre for International Private Enterprise (CIPE) (2015). Libya or Tunisia: who needs the other more? 17 April. Available from http://www.cipe.org/blog/2015/04/17/libya-or-tunisia-who-needs-the-other-more/#.VVx-A_mqpHw.

Center for Systemic Peace (CSP) (n.d.). The Polity Project: Polity IV. Available from http://www.systemicpeace.org/polityproject.html. Accessed 30 November 2014.

Chandra, A. (2009). *The Pursuit of Sustainable Development through Regional Economic Integration: ASEAN and its Potential as a Development-oriented Organization*. Winnipeg, Manitoba: International Institute for Sustainable Development.

Chang, H.J. (2003). Kicking away the ladder: the "real" history of free trade, 30 December. Available from http://fpif.org/kicking_away_the_ladder_the_real_history_of_free_trade/.

Chang, H.J., and P. Evans (2005). The role of institutions in economic change. In *Reimagining Growth: Institutions, Development, and Society*, S. de Paula and G. Dymski, eds. London: Zed Books.

Chenery, H., and T. Srinivasan, eds. (1988). *Handbook of Development Economics – Volume 1*. Amsterdam: Elsevier.

Cingranelli, David L., David L. Richards, and K. Chad Clay (2014). The CIRI Human Rights Dataset. Version 2014.04.14, 1.8.2015, Available from http://www.humanrightsdata.com/p/data-documentation.html. Accessed 30 November 2014.

CIRI Human Rights Data Project (n.d.). Data and Documentation. Available from http://www.humanrightsdata.com/p/data-documentation.html. Accessed 30 November 2014.

Collier, P. (2010). *Wars, Guns, and Votes: Democracy in Dangerous Places*. London: Vintage Books.

Collier, P., and A. Hoeffler (2007). Testing the neocon agenda: democracy in resource-rich societies, November. Available from http://users.ox.ac.uk/~econpco/research/pdfs/TestingTheNeocon Agenda.pdf.

Commission of the European Communities (2003). Green paper on the future of rules of origin in preferential trade arrangements. COM/2003/787/FINAL. Brussels. Available from http://eur-lex.europa.eu/procedure/EN/187770.

_____ (2006). Communication from the Commission to the Council and to the European Parliament on the general approach to enable ENP partner countries to participate in Community agencies and Community programmes. COM(2006) 724 final. Available from http://eur-lex.europa.eu/legal-content/EN/TXT/?uri=CELEX:52006DC0724.

Committee on the Rights of the Child (2013). Concluding observations on the second to fourth periodic reports of Israel, adopted by the Committee at its sixty-third session (27 May – 14 June 2013).

Common Market for Eastern and Southern Africa (COMESA) (2009). *Official Gazette of the Common Market for Eastern and Southern Africa*, vol. 15, No. 4 (June).

Credit Suisse (2014). *Global Wealth Report 2014*. Zurich. Available from https://publications.credit-suisse.com/tasks/render/file/?fileID=60931FDE-A2D2-F568-B041B58C5EA591A4.

Dadush, U., and L. Falcao (2009). Regional arrangements in the Arabian Gulf. Carnegie Endowment for International Peace Policy Outlook. Available from http://carnegieendowment.org/files/gcc1.pdf.

Dagdeviran, H., R. Van der Hoeven, and J. Weeks (2001). Redistribution and growth for poverty reduction. Working Paper Series, No. 118. International Labour Organization and SOAS. Available from https://www.soas.ac.uk/economics/research/workingpapers/file28860.pdf.

Dalacoura, K. (2007). *Islam, Liberalism and Human Rights*. Third Edition. London: I. B. Tauris.

De Lombaerde, P., and others (2008). Quantitative monitoring and comparison of regional integration processes: steps towards good practice. UNU-CRIS Working Paper, W-2008/9. Available from http://www.cris.unu.edu/fileadmin/workingpapers/W-2008-9.pdf.

Deaton, A. (2003). How to monitor poverty for the Millennium Development Goals. *Journal of Human Development*, vol. 4, No. 3 (November).

_____ (2008). Price trends in India and their implications for measuring poverty. *Economic and Political Weekly*, vol. 43, No. 6 (February), pp. 43-49.

_____ (2013). *The Great Escape: Health, Wealth, and the Origins of Inequality*. Princeton, N.J.: Princeton University Press.

Dennis, A. (2006). The impact of regional trade agreements and trade facilitation in the Middle East and North Africa region. Policy Research Working Paper, No. 3837. Washington, D.C.: World Bank.

Dent, C. M. (2008). The Asian Development Bank and developmental regionalism in East Asia. *Third World Quarterly*, vol. 29, No. 4, pp. 767-786.

Dervi , K., Bocock, P., and Devlin, J. (1998). Intraregional trade among Arab countries. Paper presented at the Middle East Institute 52nd Annual Conference. Washington, D.C., October.

Deutsche Gesellschaft für Internationale Zusammenarbeit (GIZ), Federal Ministry for Economic Cooperation and Development (BMZ), and League of Arab States (2012). *Climate Change and Water in the Arab Region: Mapping of Knowledge and Institutions*. Cairo: GIZ.

Devarajan, S., V. Swaroop, and H-F Zou (1996). The composition of public expenditure and economic growth. *Journal of Monetary Economics*, vol. 37, No. 2, pp. 313-344.

Dewhirst, P., and A. Kapur (2015). *The Disappeared and Invisible: Revealing the Enduring Impact of Enforced Disappearance on Women*. New York: International Center for Transitional Justice.

DiCaprio, A., and K. P. Gallagher (2006). The WTO and the shrinking of development space: how big is the bite? *The Journal of World Investment and Trade*, vol. 7, No. 5 (October), pp. 781-804.

Dion D.-P. (2004). Regional integration and economic development: an empirical approach. Discussion Paper, No. 21. Governance and the Efficiency of Economic Systems. Available from http://www.sfbtr15.de/uploads/media/21.pdf.

Diop, N. (2010). Knowledge and innovation for growth and job creation in Tunisia. Background Note for the High-level Conference on Beyond Recovery: Tunisia's Knowledge Approach to Long-term Growth and Job Creation. Washington, D.C., October.

Diwan, I. (2012). Understanding revolution in the Middle East: the central role of the middle class. Working Paper, No. 726. Cairo: Economic Research Forum.

Dollar, D., and A. Kraay (2002). Growth is good for the poor. *Journal of Economic Growth*, vol. 7, No. 3, pp. 195-225.

Donner Abreu, M. (2013). Preferential rules of origin in regional trade agreements. Staff Working Paper, No. 05. Geneva: Economic Research and Statistics Division, World Trade Organization.

Drazen, A. (2000). *Political Economy in Macroeconomics*. Princeton, N.J.: Princeton University Press.

Drukker, D., P. Gomis-Porqueras, and P. Hernandez-Verme (2005). Threshold effects in the relationship between inflation and growth: a new panel-data approach. Working Paper, No. 38225. Munchen: Munich Personal RePEc Archive (MPRA).

Dyke J., and A. Mojalli (2015). Shipping ban deepens Yemen's fuel crisis, 16 April. Available from http://www.irinnews.org/report/101371/shipping-ban-deepens-yemen-s-fuel-crisis.

Easterly, W., and R. Levine (2001). It's not factor accumulation: stylized facts and growth models. *The World Bank Economic Review*, vol. 15, No. 2, pp. 177-219.

_____ (2003). Tropics, germs, and crops: how endowments influence economic development. *Journal of Monetary Economics*, vol. 50, No. 1 (January), pp. 3-39.

The Economic Agreement between the GCC States (2001). Adopted by the GCC Supreme Council at its twenty-second session in Muscat on 31 December. Available from http://sites.gcc-sg.org/DLibrary/download.php?B=168.

The Economic Policy Research Foundation of Turkey (TEPAV) (2011). High-quality governance requires a new constitution, 16 December. Available from http://www.tepav.org.tr/en/kose-yazisi-tepav/s/2965.

The Economist (2009). Bourgeoning bourgeoisie, 12 February. Available from http://www.economist.com/node/13063298.

Economist Intelligence Unit (2014). The Economist Intelligence Unit Database. Available from http://www.eiu.com. Accessed 30 November 2014.

El-Affendi, A. (2011). Political culture and the crisis of democracy in the Arab world. In *Democracy in the Arab World: Explaining the Deficit*, Elbadawi and Makdisi, eds. New York and Ottawa: Routledge and International Development Research Centre.

El-Ashry, M., N. Saab, and B. Zeitoon, eds. (2010). Arab Environment: Water – Sustainable Management of a Scarce Resource. Beirut: Arab Forum for Environment and Development.

El-Hwany, N. (2005). *Integration and Enlargement of the European Union: Lessons to be Drawn for the Arab Region*. Cairo: Konrad-Adenauer Foundation.

El-Jourchi, S. (2014). Social protection in the Arab world: the other side of the crisis in society and the State. Arab NGO Network for Development. Available from http://www.annd.org/cd/aw2014/pdf/english/one4.pdf.

El-Saharty, S., K. Zunaid-Ahsan., and J. F. May (2014). Population, family planning and reproductive health policy harmonization in Bangladesh. Discussion Paper, No. 92650. Washington, D.C.: International Bank for Reconstruction and Development/World Bank.

Elasrag, H. (2012). The developmental role of SMEs in the Arab countries. Paper No. 40608. MPRA. Available from http://mpra.ub.uni-muenchen.de/40608/1/MPRA_paper_40608.pdf.

Elbadawi, I. (2004). The politics of sustaining growth in the Arab world: getting democracy right. Lecture and Working Papers Series, No. 2. Beirut: Institute of Financial Economics, American University of Beirut.

Elbadawi, I., and S. Makdisi (2013). Understanding democratic transitions in the Arab world. Working Paper Series, No. 765. Giza: Economic Research Forum.

Elbadawi, I., S. Makdisi, and G. Milante (2011). Explaining the Arab democracy deficit: the role of oil and conflicts. In *Democracy in the Arab World: Explaining the Deficit*, I. Elbadawi and S. Makdisi, eds. New York and Ottawa: Routledge and International Development Research Centre.

Elbadawi, I., and E. Refaat (2015). Competitive real exchange rates are good for the poor: evidence from Egyptian household surveys. Paper presented at the Economic Research Forum 21st Annual Conference. Gammarth, March.

Elbadawi, I., and R. Soto (2012). Resource rents, political institutions and economic growth. Working Paper, No. 678. Giza: Economic Research Forum.

Engdahl, F. W. (2012). The new Mediterranean gas and oil bonanza, 3 March. Available from www.globalresearch.ca/the-new-mediterranean-oil-and-gas-bonanza.

Erdogan, A. M. (2014). Foreign direct investment and environmental regulations: a survey. *Journal of Economic Surveys*, vol. 28, No. 5 (December), pp. 943-955.

Esarey, J., and L. Schwindt-Bayer (2015). Women's representation, accountability, and corruption in democracies, 17 March. Available from http://jee3.web.rice.edu/gender-corruption-accountability.pdf.

Estevadeordal, A., and K. Suominen (2008). Sequencing regional trade integration and cooperation agreements. *The World Economy*, vol. 31, No. 1, pp. 112-140.

European Commission (n.d.a). *A User's Handbook to the Rules of Preferential Origin Used in Trade between the European Community, other European Countries and the Countries Participating to the Euro-Mediterranean Partnership*. Available from http://ec.europa.eu/taxation_customs/resources/documents/handbook_en.pdf.

_____ (n.d.b). Intra-EU trade in goods – recent trends. Eurostat Statistics Explained. Accessed 15 December 2014. Available from http://ec.europa.eu/eurostat/statistics-explained/index.php/Intra-EU_trade_in_goods_-_recent_trends.

_____ (n.d.c). Joint Research Centre. Available from https://ec.europa.eu/jrc.

_____ (n.d.d). Research and innovation: bioeconomy. Available from http://ec.europa.eu/research/bioeconomy/policy/coordination/jpi/index_en.htm.

_____ (n.d.e). Research and innovation: FP7. Available from http://ec.europa.eu/research/fp7/index_en.cfm.

_____ (2008). Compliance with statistics under single authorization for simplified procedures and centralised clearance. Paper presented at the Customs Seminar on Single Authorisation for Simplified Procedures/Centralised Clearance. Budapest, October. Available from http://ec.europa.eu/taxation_customs/resources/documents/customs/policy_issues/conference_events/budapest2008/speech1.pdf.

_____ (2011a). A new response to a changing neighbourhood. Joint Communication to the European Parliament, the Council, the European Economic and Social Committee and the Committee of the Regions. COM(2011) 303 final. Available from http://eur-lex.europa.eu/legal-content/EN/TXT/PDF/?uri=CELEX:52011DC0303&from=EN.

_____ (2011b). A partnership for democracy and shared prosperity with the Southern Mediterranean. Joint Communication to the European Council, the European Parliament, the Council, the European Economic and Social Committee and the Committee of the Regions. COM(2011) 200 final. Available from http://eur-lex.europa.eu/legal-content/EN/TXT/PDF/?uri=CELEX:52011DC0200&from=EN.

_____ (2013). Implementation of the European neighbourhood policy in 2012 regional report: a partnership for democracy and shared prosperity with the Southern Mediterranean. Joint Staff

Working Document, SWD(2013) 86 final. Brussels. Available from http://eeas.europa.eu/enp/pdf/docs/2013_enp_pack/2013_southern_mediterranean_en.pdf.

European Union Institute for Security Studies (2012). *Global Trends 2030- Citizens in an Interconnected and Polycentric World.* Paris.

Evans, P. (1995). *Embedded Autonomy: States and Industrial Transformation.* Princeton: Princeton University Press.

The Executive Bureau for the Acceleration of Aid Absorption and Support for Policy Reforms (TEBAASPR) (n.d.). Yemen's status update (as of June 28, 2015). Available from http://www.ebyemen.org/en.

Fanon, F. (1961). *The Wretched of the Earth.* Translated from French by Richard Philcox. New York: Grove Press.

_____ (1967). *Black Skin, White Masks.* Translated from French by Richard Philcox. New York: Grove Press.

FARS News Agency (2015). Iran renews support for political solution to Syrian crisis, 4 September. Available from http://english.farsnews.com/newstext.aspx?nn=13940613000325.

Farsakh, Leila (2002). Palestinian labor flows to the Israeli economy: a finished story? *Journal of Palestine Studies*, vol. 32, No. 1. Available from www.palestine-studies.org/jps/fulltext/41127.

Fattouh, B., and L. El-Katiri (2012). Energy subsidies in the Arab world. Arab Human Development Report Research Paper Series. New York: United Nations Development Programme (UNDP) Regional Bureau for Arab States.

Fattouh, B., and R. Mallinson (2013). Refining dynamics in the GCC and implications for trade flows. Oxford Institute for Energy Studies. Available from http://www.oxfordenergy.org/wpcms/wp-content/uploads/2013/12/Refining-Dynamics-in-the-GCC-and-Implications-for-Product-Trade-Flows.pdf.

Ferrero-Waldner, B. (2005). Quo vadis Europa? Statement to EPP "Paneuropa" Group. Strasbourg, 14 December. Available from http://europa.eu/rapid/press-release_SPEECH-05-797_en.htm?locale=en.

Financial Times (2013). Israel bypasses diplomatic freeze with Gulf 'virtual embassy', 23 July. Available from http://www.ft.com/intl/cms/s/0/4495b17c-f3a7-11e2-942f-00144feabdc0.html#axzz3eREefIQ4.

_____ (2014). New trade routes: Arab world, 29 June. Available from http://www.ft.com/intl/reports/arab-trade.

Fischer, S. (1993). The role of macroeconomic factors in growth. Working Paper, No. 4565. Cambridge, MA: National Bureau of Economic Research.

Fjeldstad, O.-H., and A. Zagha (2002). Between Oslo and al-Aqsa: taxation and State formation in Palestine 1994-2000. Report No. 2002: 13. Bergen: Chr. Michelsen Institute.

Food and Agriculture Organization of the United Nations (FAO) (2015a). AQUASTAT Database. Available from http://www.fao.org/nr/water/aquastat/main/index.stm. Accessed 15 November 2014.

_____ (2015b). Food Security Indicators, Available from http://www.fao.org/economic/ess/ess-fs/ess-fadata/en/#.VjHYsiurKmF. Accessed on 12 October 2015.

Food and Agriculture Organization of the United Nations (FAO), International Fund for Agricultural Development (IFAD), and World Food Programme (WFP) (2014). *The State of Food Insecurity in the World 2014: Strengthening the Enabling Environment for Food Security and Nutrition*. Available from http://www.fao.org/3/a-i4030e.pdf.

Fosu, A. K. (2010). Growth, inequality and poverty reduction in developing countries: recent global evidence. Working Paper, No. 2011/01. United Nations University – World Institute for Development Economics Research.

Frankel, J., and D. Romer (1999). Does trade cause growth? *American Economic Review*, vol. 89, No. 3 (June), pp. 379-399.

Freund, C., and M. Jaud (2013). Growth and political change: transition duration is critical, 24 January. Available from http://www.voxeu.org/article/growth-effects-democratisation-new-evidence.

Fritz, V., and A. R. Menocal (2007). Developmental States in the new millennium: concepts and challenges for a new aid agenda. *Development Policy Review*, vol. 25, No. 5, pp. 531-552.

Fukuda-Parr, S. and A. K. Shivakumar, eds. (2003). *Readings in Human Development.* Oxford: Oxford University Press.

Galal, A., and B. Hoekman, eds. (2003). *Arab Economic Integration: Between Hope and Reality*. Cairo and Washington, D.C.: Egyptian Center for Economic Studies and Brookings Institution Press.

Gallagher, J., and R. Robinson (1953). The imperialism of free trade. *The Economic History Review*, vol. 6, No. 1, pp. 1-15.

Gallegos-Paniagua, D., and J. G. Vargas-Hernández (2011). Securitization as a factor of economic integration. *Journal of Knowledge Management, Economics and Information Technology*, Issue 4 (June).

Galor, O., and S. Michalopoulos (2006). The evolution of entrepreneurial spirit and the process of development. Working Paper, No. 111. The Carlo Alberto Notebooks.

Gandhi, J., and E. Lust-Okar (2009). Elections under authoritarianism. *Annual Review of Political Science*, vol. 12 (June), pp. 403-422.

Ganoulis, J., A. Aureli, and J. Fried, eds. (2011). *Transboundary Water Resources Management: A Multidisciplinary Approach*. Weinheim: Wiley-VCH Verlag & Co. KGaA.General Agreement on Trade in Services (GATS) (1994). Adopted on 15 April in Marrakesh. Available from https://www.wto.org/english/tratop_e/serv_e/gatsintr_e.htm.

Geradin, D. (2004). Competition law and regional economic integration: an analysis of the Southern Mediterranean countries. Working Paper, No. 35. Washington, D.C.: World Bank.

German Aerospace Center (DLR) (2007). *Concentrating Solar Power for Seawater Desalination*. Stuttgart. Available from http://www.dlr.de/tt/desktopdefault.aspx/tabid-2885/4422_read-10813/.

Ghoneim, A. (2010). Challenges of services liberalization in the multilateral and regional contexts: the case of Arab countries. In *The Services Sector, Trade Policy, and the Challenges of Development in the Arab Region (Part I)*, K. Mohamadieh and A. Ghoneim, eds. Beirut: Arab NGO Network for Development.

Ghoneim, A., and others (2012). Shallow vs. deep integration in the Southern Mediterranean: scenarios for the region up to 2030. Mediterranean Prospects (MEDPRO) Technical Report, No. 13. Available from http://www.ceps.eu/system/files/MEDPRO%20TR%2013%20Ghoneim%20et%20al%20Shallow%20vs%20Deep%20Integration.pdf.

Gibney, M., L. Cornett, and R. Wood (2015). Political Terror Scale 1976-2014. 1.8.2015, from the Political Terror Scale. Available from http://www.politicalterrorscale.org/.

Ginsburg, T. (2013). The Tunisian judicial sector: analysis and recommendations. Consolidating the Arab Spring: Constitutional Transition in Egypt and Tunisia Working Paper Series, No. 5. Stockholm and New York: International IDEA and The Center for Constitutional Transitions at NYU Law.

Gottfredson, M., and T. Hirshi (1990). *General Theory of Crime*. Stanford: Stanford University Press.

Greider, W. (2015). It's official: the Pentagon finally admitted that Israel has nuclear weapons, too, 26 February. Available from http://arabnyheter.info/sv/2015/03/23/its-official-the-pentagon-finally-admitted-that-israel-has-nuclear-weapons-too/.

Groll, E. (2014). You can't understand how beleaguered Kobani is until you see these maps, 7 October. Available from http://blog.foreignpolicy.com/posts/2014/10/07/you_can_t_understand_how_beleaguered_kobani_is_until_you_see_these_maps?utm_content=buffer06427&utm_medium=social&utm_source=twitter.com&utm_campaign=buffer.

Gros, D., and C. Alcidi, eds. (2013). *The Global Economy in 2030: Trends and Strategies for Europe*. Center for European Policy Studies. Available from http://europa.eu/espas/pdf/espas-report-economy.pdf.

Grossmann, H., and others (2007). Growth potential for maritime trade and ports in Europe. *Intereconomics: Review of European Economic Policy*, vol. 42, No. 4, pp. 226-232.

Gupta, S., H. Davoodi, and E. Tiongson (2000). Corruption and the provision of health care and education services. Working Paper, WP/00/116. Washington, D.C.: International Monetary Fund.

Haaretz (2014). Netanyahu's Cabinet Approves Controversial Bill Enshrining Israel as "Jewish Nation-state". *Haaretz*, 23 November 2014. Available from http://www.haaretz.com/israel-news/1.628001.

Hall, K., and M. Chuck-A-Sang, eds. (2012). *Regional Integration: Key to Caribbean Survival and Prosperity*. Kingston: Ian Randle Publishers.

Hall, R., and C. Jones (1999). Why do some countries produce so much more output per worker than others? *The Quarterly Journal of Economics*, vol. 114, No. 1 (February), pp. 83-116.

Hall, P. A., and D. Soskice (2001). An introduction to the varieties of capitalism. In *Varieties of Capitalism*, Peter A. Hall and David Soskice, eds., Oxford: Oxford University Press.

Hanafi, S., and R. Arvanitis (2012). *The Broken Cycle: Universities, Research and Society in the Arab Region. Proposals for Change*. Beirut: National Council for Scientific Research, ESCWA and Institut de recherche pour le développement.

Haque, I. (2007). Rethinking industrial policy. Discussion Papers, No. 183. Geneva: United Nations Conference on Trade and Development. Available from http://unctad.org/en/docs/osgdp20072_en.pdf.

Hassine, N. B. (2014). Economic inequality in the Arab region. Policy Research Working Paper, No. 6911. Washington, D.C.: World Bank.

Heilbroner, R., and W. Milberg (1995). *The Crisis of Vision in Modern Economic Thought*. Cambridge, MA: Cambridge University Press.

Hemming, R., M. Kell, and S. Mahfouz (2002). The effectiveness of fiscal policy in stimulating economic activity: a review of the literature. Working Paper, No. 02/208. Washington, D.C.: International Monetary Fund.

Hodler, R. (2013). The political economics of the Arab spring. OxCarre Working Papers, No. 101. Oxford: University of Oxford, Centre for Analysis of Resource Rich Economies.

Hoekman, B., A. Mattoo, and P. English, eds. (2002). *Development, Trade and the WTO: A Handbook*. Washington, D.C.: International Bank for Reconstruction and Development/World Bank.

Hoekman, B., and P. Messerlin (2002). Harnessing trade for development in the Middle East. New York: Council on Foreign Relations, Inc.

_____ (2003). Initial conditions and incentives for Arab economic integration: a comparison with the European Community. In *Arab Economic Integration: Between Hope and Reality*, A. Galal and B. Hoekman, eds. Cairo and Washington, D.C.: Egyptian Center for Economic Studies and Brookings Institution Press.

Hoekman, B., and K. Sakkat (2009). Deeper integration of goods, services, capital and labor markets: a policy research agenda for the MENA region. Policy Research Paper, No. 32. Giza: Economic Research Forum.

_____ (2010). Arab economic integration: the missing links. Working Paper. Paris: Groupe d'Economie Mondiale. Available from http://www.ecipe.org/app/uploads/2014/12/Hoekman_arab_economic_integration.pdf.

Horovitz, D. (2014). Netanyahu finally speaks his mind. *The Times of Israel*, 13 July. Available from www.timesofisrael.com/netanyahu-finally-speaks-his-mind.

Hossain, N., C. Nyamu Musembi, and J. Hughes (2010). *Corruption, Accountability and Gender: Understanding the Connections*. United Nations Development Programme and Fonds de développement des Nations Unies pour la femme.

Human Rights Watch (n.d.). Israel/Palestine. Available from https://www.hrw.org/middle-east/n-africa/israel/palestine.

_____ (2015). *World Report 2015: Events of 2014*. New York.

Huntington, S. (1996). Democracy for the long haul. *Journal of Democracy*, vol. 7, No. 2, pp. 3-13.

Indrawati, S. M. (2013). Op-ed: No end to poverty without better governance, 16 May. Available from http://www.worldbank.org/en/news/opinion/2013/05/16/op-ed-no-end-to-poverty-without-better-governance.

Inter-American Development Bank (1999). MERCOSUR report No. 5: 1998-1999. Buenos Aires. Available from http://ctrc.sice.oas.org/geograph/south/intal5.pdf.

International Center for Trade and Sustainable Development (ICTSD) (2004). US, Egypt, Israel sign 3-way trade pact; may fall foul of WTO. *Bridges*, vol. 8, No. 43 (December). Available from http://www.ictsd.org/bridges-news/bridges/news/us-egypt-israel-sign-3-way-trade-pact-may-fall-foul-of-wto.

International Center for Trade and Sustainable Development (ICTSD), and World Economic Forum (WEF) (2013). *The E15 Initiative: Strengthening the Multilateral Trading System – The functioning of the WTO group: Proposals and Analysis*. Geneva: ICTSD. Available from http://e15initiative.org/wp-content/uploads/2014/11/Functioning_WTO_Proposals_Analysis.pdf.

International Committee of the Red Cross (ICRC) (2012). Internal conflicts or other situations of violence – what is the difference for victims? Available from https://www.icrc.org/eng/resources/documents/interview/2012/12-10-niac-non-international-armed-conflict.htm.

International Court of Justice (ICJ) (2004). Reports of judgments, advisory opinions and orders: legal consequences of the construction of a wall in the Occupied Palestinian Territory. Advisory opinion 9 July. Available from http://www.icj-cij.org/docket/files/131/1671.pdf (in French).

International Crisis Group (ICG) (2010). Squaring the circle: Palestinian security reform under occupation. Middle East Report, No. 98. Available from www.crisisgroup.org/~/media/Files/Middle%20East%20North%20Africa/Israel%20Palestine/98%20Squaring%20the%20Circle%20--%20Palestinian%20Security%20Reform%20under%20Occupation.ashx.

International Energy Agency (IEA) (2013). *World Energy Outlook 2013*. London.

International Fund for Agricultural Fund (IFAD) (2009). *Fighting Water Scarcity in the Arab Countries*. Rome.

International Labour Organization (ILO) (2004). *Gender & Migration in Arab States: The Case of Domestic Workers*. Beirut: ILO Regional Office for Arab States.

_____ (2008). Can low-income countries afford basic social security? Social Security Policy Briefings, No. 3. Geneva.

_____ (2012a). *Global Employment Trends 2012: Preventing a Deeper Jobs Crisis*. Geneva.

_____ (2012b). Text of the Recommendation Concerning National Floors of Social Protection. Presented at the 101st Session of the International Labour Conference. Geneva.

_____ (2013). *Global Employment Trends for Youth 2013: A Generation at Risk*. Geneva.

_____ (2015). Realizing a fair migration agenda: labour flows between Asia and Arab States, Summary Report of the Interregional Experts' Meeting, 3-4 December 2014 Annapurna Hotel, Kathmandu, Nepal.

International Labour Organization, and United Nations Development Programme (2012). *Rethinking Economic Growth: Towards Productive and Inclusive Arab Societies*. Beirut: ILO.

International Monetary Fund (IMF) (2005a). Review of the IMF's Trade Restrictiveness Index. Background Paper to the Review of Fund Work on Trade, 14 February. Available from https://www.imf.org/external/np/pp/eng/2005/021405r.pdf.

_____ (2005b). *World Economic Outlook: Building Institutions*. Washington, D.C.

_____ (2012). *World Economic Outlook: Coping with High Debt and Sluggish Growth*. Washington, D.C.

_____ (2014a). Energy subsidies in the Middle East and North Africa: lessons for reform. Available from https://www.imf.org/external/np/fad/subsidies/pdf/menanote.pdf.

_____ (2014b). Lebanon: selected issues. IMF Country Report, No. 14/238. Available from http://www.imf.org/external/pubs/ft/scr/2014/cr14238.pdf.

_____ (2015). World Economic Outlook Database, October 2015. Available from http://www.imf.org/external/ns/cs.aspx?id=28. Accessed on 8 November 2015.

International Relations and Security Network (2013). Gas finds complicate Eastern Mediterranean security, 26 June. Available from www.isn.ethz.ch/Digital-Library/Articles/Detail/?id=165423.

International Trade Center (ITC) (2012). Free trade agreements: necessary but not sufficient – Lessons from the Arab region. Available from www.intracen.org/fta-lessons-from-arab-region.

Islam, R. (2004). The nexus of economic growth, employment and poverty reduction: an empirical analysis. Discussion Paper, No. 14. Geneva: International Labour Office.

Jalilian, H., C. Kirkpatrick, and D. Parker (2007). The impact of regulation on economic growth in developing countries: a cross-country analysis. *World Development*, vol. 35, No. 1, pp. 87-103.

The Jerusalem Post (2014). Desmond Tutu: Israel guilty of apartheid in treatment of Palestinians, 3 October. Available from http://www.jpost.com/Diplomacy-and-Politics/Desmond-Tutu-Israel-guilty-of-apartheid-in-treatment-of-Palestinians-344874.

Johnson, A. (2014). Mecca under threat: outrage at plan to destroy the 'birthplace' of the Prophet Mohamed and replace it with a new palace and luxury malls. *The Independent*, 12 November.

Johnson, S. (2015). Saudi Arabia destroyed 98% of its cultural heritage, 1 January. Available from http://uscar.usc.edu/?p=1123.

Jaraisy, R. and T. Feldman (n. d.). The status of the right to demonstrate in the occupied territories. The Association for Civil Rights in Israel, Position Paper. Available from www.acri.org.il/en/wp-content/uploads/2014/12/Right-to-Demonstrate-in-the-OPT-FINAL.pdf.

Kakwani, N. (1993). Poverty and economic growth with application to Côte d'Ivoire. *Review of Income and Wealth*, vol. 39, No. 2, pp. 121-139.

Kakwani, N., and others (2005). Growth and investment requirements for halving poverty by 2015 in Yemen. United Nations Development Programme.

Kaldor, N. (1963). Will underdeveloped countries learn to tax? *Foreign Affairs*, vol. 41, No. 2 (January).

Kaufman, D., A. Kraay, and M. Mastruzzi (2014). The Worldwide Governance Indicators (WGI) Project. World Bank. Available from info.worldbank.org/governance/wgi/index.aspx#home.

Keane, J., and C. Melamed (2014). Trade and the post-2015 agenda: from Millennium Development Goals to Sustainable Development Goals. Briefing, No. 89. London: Overseas Development Institute.

Keating, J. (2015). Why was Tunisia the only Arab Spring country that turned out well? 28 January. Available from www.slate.com/blogs/the_slatest/2015/01/28/why_was_tunisia_the_only_arab_spring_country_that_turned_out_well.html.

Kehoe, K. (2013). Factbox: women's rights in the Arab world, 11 November. Available from http://www.reuters.com/article/2013/11/12/us-arab-women-factbox-idUSBRE9AB00I20131112.

Kemp, M. C., and H. Jr. Wan (1976). An elementary proposition concerning the formation of customs unions. *Journal of International Economics*, vol. 6, No. 1 (February), pp. 95-97.

Khalidi, R., and S. Taghdisi-Rad (2009). *The Economic Dimensions of Prolonged Occupation: Continuity and Change in Israeli Policy towards the Palestinian Economy*. New York and Geneva: United Nations Conference on Trade and Development. Available from http://unctad.org/en/Docs/gds20092_en.pdf.

Khan, M., and A. Senhadji (2000). Threshold effects in the relationship between inflation and growth. Working Paper, WP/00/110. Washington, D.C.: International Monetary Fund.

Khatib, L. (2013). Political participation and democratic transition in the Arab world. *University of Pennsylvania Journal of International Law*, vol. 34, No. 2 (April), pp. 315-340.

Kheir-el-Din, H. (2005). Issues paper on the assessment of implementation of regional trade agreements in the Arab countries and the economic and regulatory policy implications of their overlapping: the case of Egypt, Jordan, Morocco, Tunisia. Research Report Series, No. 0424. Giza and Ottawa: Economic Research Forum and International Development Research Centre.

King, S. J. (2003). *Liberalization against Democracy: The Local Politics of Economic Reform in Tunisia*. Bloomington and Indianapolis: Indiana University Press.

King, R., and R. Levine (1993). Finance, entrepreneurship, and growth: theory and evidence. *Journal of Monetary Economics,* vol. 32, No. 3, pp. 513-542.

Kleiman, E. (1998). Is there a secret Arab-Israeli trade? *The Middle East Quarterly,* vol. 5, No. 2 (June), pp. 11-18. Available from http://www.meforum.org/393/is-there-a-secret-arab-israeli-trade.

Kohler-Koch, B. (2005). European governance and system integration. European Governance Papers, No. C-05-01. Available from http://edoc.vifapol.de/opus/volltexte/2011/2453/pdf/egp_connex_C_05_01.pdf.

Kommerskollegium (2012). *The Impact of Rules of Origin on Trade: A Comparison of the EU's and the US's Rules for the Textile and Clothing Sector*. Stockholm.

Konan, D. E., and K. Kim (2004). Beyond border barriers: the liberalisation of services trade in Tunisia and Egypt. *The World Economy*, vol. 27, No. 9 (September), pp. 1429-1447.

Kremer, S., A. Bick, and D. Nautz (2009). Inflation and growth: new evidence from a dynamic panel threshold analysis. *Empirical Economics*, vol. 44, No. 2, pp. 861-878.

Krueger, A. O. (1993). Free trade agreements as protectionist devices: rules of origin. Working Paper, No. 4352. Cambridge, MA: National Bureau of Economic Research.

_____ (2004). Expanding trade and unleashing growth: the prospects for lasting poverty reduction. Remarks at the International Monetary Fund Seminar on Trade and Regional Integration. Dakar, 6 December. Available from https://www.imf.org/external/np/speeches/2004/120604.htm.

Krugman, P. (2013). The new growth fizzle, 18 August. Available from http://krugman.blogs.nytimes.com/2013/08/18/the-new-growth-fizzle.

Kuhn R. (2011). On the role of human development in the Arab spring. *Population and Development Review*, vol. 38, No. 4, pp. 649-683.

Kun i , A. (2014). Institutional quality dataset. *Journal of Institutional Economics*, vol. 10, No. 1 (March), pp. 135-161.

Kun i , A., and J. Šušterši (2012). Political economy of Central Europe. In *Regional and International Relations of Central Europe*, Z. Šabi and P. Drulák, eds. Hampshire: Palgrave Macmillan.

Lahn, G., and P. Stevens (2011). *Burning Oil to Keep Cool: The Hidden Energy Crisis in Saudi Arabia*. London: Chatham House.

Lakshman, N. (2003). The political economy of good governance for poverty alleviation policies. ERD Working Paper Series, No. 39. Manila: Asian Development Bank. Available from http://www.adb.org/sites/default/files/publication/28331/wp039.pdf.

Lamy, P. (2013). Statement to the OECD Policy Dialogue on Aid for Trade. Paris, 16 January. Available from https://www.wto.org/english/news_e/sppl_e/sppl262_e.htm.

Lawrence, R. Z. (2006). Recent US free trade initiatives in the Middle East: opportunities but no guarantees. Harvard Kennedy School Working Paper, No. RWP06-050. Available from http://ssrn.com/abstract=939656.

Lea, R., and B. Binley (2012). *Britain and Europe: A New Relationship*. London: Global Vision. Available from http://www.europarl.org.uk/resource/static/files/global-vision-paper-lr.pdf.

League of Arab States, International Renewable Energy Agency (IRENA), and Regional Center for Renewable Energy and Energy Efficiency (RCREEE) (2014). *Pan-Arab Renewable Energy Strategy 2030: Roadmap of Actions for Implementation*. Abu Dhabi.

Lele, U. (1986). Women and structural transformation. *Economic Development and Cultural Change*, vol. 34, No. 2 (January), pp. 195-221.

Leslie, J. (2015). New Zealand Trade Strategy and Evolving Asian-Pacific Regional Economic Architecture. Report One. Asia New Zealand Foundation. Available from http://asianz.org.nz/reports/wp-content/uploads/2015/01/ANZF1034-Trade-Strategy-Report-_-FA.pdf.

Levi-Faur, D., ed. (2011). *Handbook on the Politics of Regulation*. London: Edward Elgar Publishing Limited.

Levine, R., N. Loayza, and T. Beck (2000). Financial intermediation and growth: causality and causes. *Journal of Monetary Economics*, vol. 46, pp. 31-77.

Levine, R., and D. Renelt (1991). A sensitivity analysis of cross-country growth regressions. Working Paper Series, No. 609. Washington, D.C.: World Bank.

Lewis, B. (1994). *Islam and the West*. New York: Oxford University Press (2nd edition).

Limam, I., and A. Abdalla (n.d.). Inter-Arab trade and the potential success of AFTA. Working Paper Series, No. 9806. Kuwait: Arab Planning Institute.

Lings, M. (1991). *Symbol and Archetype: A Study of the Meaning of Existence*. Cambridge: Quinta Essentia.

Lust-Okar, E. (2004). Divided they rule: the management and manipulation of political opposition. *Comparative Politics*, vol. 36, No. 2, pp. 159-179.

Machowski, M. (2011). Qatar-Israeli relations: a historical overview. *MidEastJournal*, 19 May. Available from http://www.matthewmachowski.com/2011/05/qatar-israel-relations.html.

Malecki, E. (1997). *Technology and Economic Development: The Dynamics of Local, Regional, and National Competitiveness*. London: Longman (2nd edition).

Malik, A., and B. Awadallah (2011). The economics of the Arab Spring. Working Paper Series, No. 23. Oxford: Center for the Study of African Economies, University of Oxford. Available from http://www.csae.ox.ac.uk/workingpapers/pdfs/csae-wps-2011-23.pdf.

Mansfield, E. D., and J. C. Pevehouse (2000). Trade blocs, trade flows, and international conflict. *International Organization*, vol. 54, No. 4, pp. 775-808.

Marouani, M. A., and L. Munro (2009). Assessing barriers to trade in services in the MENA region. OECD Trade Policy Papers, No. 84. Paris: OECD Publishing.

Masaki, T., and N. Van de Walle (forthcoming). The impact of democracy on economic growth in sub-Saharan Africa, 1982-2012. In *The Oxford Handbook of Africa and Economics: Context and Concepts*, C. Monga and J. Yifu Lin, eds. Oxford: Oxford University Press.

Mauro, P. (1996). The effects of corruption on growth, investment, and government expenditure. Working Paper, WP/96/98-EA. Washington, D.C.: International Monetary Fund.

McCarthy, R. (2007). Israel risks apartheid-like struggle if two-State solution fails, says Olmert. *The Guardian*, 30 November. Available from http://www.theguardian.com/world/2007/nov/30/israel.

McKinley, T. (2003). The macroeconomics of poverty reduction, initial findings of the UNDP Asia-Pacific Regional Programme. Available from http://siteresources.worldbank.org/INTCAMBODIA/Resources/macroeconomics.pdf.

Meeus, R. (n.d.). *Road Transport: Developing a Trade and Road Transport Facilitation Strategy for the Arab World*. Islamic Development Bank, Arab Union of Land Transport, and International

Road Transport Union. Available from http://www.iru.org/cms-filesystem-action/mix-publications/IDB-booklet-Road_Transport-EN-web.pdf.

Melatos, M., and A. Woodland (2009). Common external tariff choice in core customs unions. *Review of International Economics*, vol. 17, No. 2, pp. 292-303.

Melton, J. (2013). Do constitutional rights matter? The relationship between de jure and de facto human rights protection. Working Paper. Available from http://citeseerx.ist.psu.edu/viewdoc/download?doi=10.1.1.375.9784&rep=rep1&type=pdf.

Miniesy, R.S., and J. B. Nugent (2006). Are there shortfalls in MENA trade? If so, to what extent are they due to the rise in EU-EE Trade and to other factors? Paper presented at the CNR-ISSM Conference on Bridging the Gap: The Role of Trade and FDI in the Mediterranean. Naples, June.

Miniesy, R., J. Nugent, and T. Yousef (2004). Intra-regional trade integration in the Middle East: past performance and future potential. In H. Hakimian and J. Nugent, eds., *Trade Policy and Economic Integration in the Middle East and North Africa: Economic Boundaries in Flux*. London: Routledge Curzon.

Mirumachi, N. (2015). Cooperation is not enough: why we need to think differently about water, 19 May. Available from http://www.newsecuritybeat.org/2015/05/cooperation-enough-differently-water.

Mitchell, T. (1991). *Colonising Egypt*. Berkeley: University of California Press.

Mohammed bin Rashid Al Maktoum Foundation, and United Nations Development Programme (2009). *Arab Knowledge Report 2009: Towards Productive Intercommunication for Knowledge*. Available from http://www.arab-hdr.org/akr/AKR2009/English/AKR2009-Eng-Full-Report.pdf.

_____ (2011). *Arab Knowledge Report 2010/2011: Preparing Future Generations for the Knowledge Society*. Available from http://www.undp.org/content/dam/rbas/report/AKR2010-2011-Eng-Full-Report.pdf.

Moore, M. (2007). How does taxation affect the quality of governance? *Tax Notes International*, vol. 47, No. 1 (July).

Moore, P. (2004). *Doing Business in the Middle East: Politics and Economic Crisis in Jordan and Kuwait*. London: Cambridge University Press.

Nabli, M. K., and H. Ben Hammouda (forthcoming). The potential economic dividends of North African revolutions. In *The Oxford Handbook of Africa and Economics: Context and Concepts*, C. Monga and J. Yifu Lin, eds. Oxford: Oxford University Press.

Nabli, M. K., and C. Silva-Jáuregui (2006). Democracy for better governance and higher economic growth in the Arab region? In *Proceedings of the International Economic Association World Congress 2006,* Marrakesh, Morocco. Palgrave/Macmillan.

Nasrawi, S. (2007). Mecca's ancient heritage is under attack. *Los Angeles Times*, 16 September. Available from http://articles.latimes.com/2007/sep/16/news/adfg-mecca16.

Nell, E., ed. (1998). *Transformational Growth and the Business Cycle*. London: Routledge.

Nordås, H. K., and H. Kox (2009). Quantifying regulatory barriers to services trade. OECD Trade Policy Papers, No. 85. Paris: OECD Publishing.

North, D. (2005). Institutions and the performance of economies over time. In *Handbook of New Institutional Economics*, C. Ménard and M. M. Shirley, eds. Dordrecht: Springer.

Norton, A., ed. (1995). *Civil Society in the Middle East* – Volume 1. Leiden: Brill.

Nunn, N., and D. Trefler (2006). Putting the lid on lobbying: tariff structure and long-term growth when protection is for sale. Working Paper, No. 12164. Cambridge, MA: National Bureau of Economic Research.

Ocampo, J., C. Rada, and L. Taylor (2009). *Growth and Policy in Developing Countries: A Structuralist Approach*. New York: Columbia University Press.

Ojalo, J. (2013). The effects of regional integration on the prevalence of conflicts. Masters thesis, Leiden University. Available from https://openaccess.leidenuniv.nl/handle/1887/25838.

Olaya, J., and K. Hussmann (2013). Preventing and combatting corruption: good governance and constitutional law in Tunisia. Consolidating the Arab Spring: Constitutional Transition in Egypt and Tunisia Working Paper Series, No. 6. Stockholm and New York: International IDEA and The Center for Constitutional Transitions at NYU Law.

Omran, M. (2001). Detecting the performance consequences of privatizing Egyptian State-owned enterprises: does ownership structure really matter? Available from http://citeseerx.ist.psu.edu/viewdoc/download?doi=10.1.1.456.516&rep=rep1&type=pdf.

Onaran, O. (2015). Europe needs a wage-led recovery. Policy Viewpoint, No. 3. Foundation for European Progressive Studies. Available from http://www.feps-europe.eu/assets/fe43d974-3668-4648-bbb4-3ad8b6c86659/pv-3-2015-oov1pdf.pdf.

Organisation for Economic Co-operation and Development (OECD) (n.d.a). Aid Statistics. Available from http://www.oecd.org/dac/stats. Accessed 30 November 2014.

_____ (n.d.b). OECD Better Life Index. Available from http://www.oecdbetterlifeindex.org. Accessed 30 November 2014.

_____ (n.d.c). Policy coherence for inclusive and sustainable development. OECD and Post-2015 Reflections. Element 8, Paper 1. Available from http://www.oecd.org/pcd/POST-2015%20PCD.pdf.

_____ (2007). *International Investment Perspectives: Freedom of Investment in a Changing World* – 2007 Edition. Paris.

Orr, S. (n.d.). The normative theory of social exclusion: perspectives from political philosophy. Available from http://www.ucl.ac.uk/~ucesswo/IJSSP%20ms.doc.

Ostry, J. D., A. Berg, and C. G. Tsangarides (2014). Redistribution, inequality and growth. IMF staff discussion note, SDN/14/02. Washington, D.C.

Palestinian Central Bureau of Statistics (PCBS) (2014a). On the eve of the International Day of Refugees, 20 June. Available from www.pcbs.gov.ps/portals/_pcbs/PressRelease/Press_En_IntRefDy2014E.pdf.

_____ (2014b). Palestinians at the end of 2014. Available from www.pcbs.gov.ps/portals/_pcbs/PressRelease/Press_En_PalnE2014E.pdf.

Palestinian Central Bureau of Statistics, Palestine Monetary Authority (PMA), and Palestine Economic Policy Research Institute (MAS) (2013). Economic and Social Monitor: Annual Volume 2012, No. 32 (May).

Partrick, N. (2011). The GCC: Gulf state integration or leadership cooperation? Kuwait Programme on Development, Governance and Globalisation in the Gulf States Research Paper, No. 19. London: The London School of Economics and Political Science.

Patel, S. J., P. Roffe, and A. Yusef, eds. (2001). *International Technology Transfer: The Origins and Aftermath of the United Nations Negotiations on a Draft Code of Conduct.* The Hague: Kluwer Law International.

Paternoster, R., and S. Simpson (1996). Sanction threats and appeals to morality: testing a rational choice model of corporate crime. *Law & Society Review*, vol. 30, No. 3, pp. 549-584.

Pedrosa-Garcia, J. A. (2013). Access to finance by small and medium enterprises in the Arab region: policy considerations. ESCWA Working Paper. E/ESCWA/EDGD/2013/WP.1.

Péridy, N., and Ghoneim, A. (2008). *The Greater Arab Free Trade Area: An Ex-post Appraisal within an Imperfect Competition Framework.* Femise Research Project No. FEM32-03. Available from http://www.femise.org/PDF/ci2007/FEM32-03.pdf.

Philippopoulos-Mihalopoulos, A. (2010). Spatial justice: law and the geography of withdrawal. *International Journal of Law in Context*, vol. 6, No. 3, pp. 201-216.

Piketty, T. (2014). *Capital in the Twenty-First Century.* Translated by A. Goldhammer. Cambridge, MA: Harvard University Press.

Powers, K. L. (2003). Regional trade agreements as security institutions: managing international conflict through integration in security and natural resources. Paper presented at the European Consortium for Political Research Joint Session of Workshops. Edinburgh, March.

The PRS Group (n.d.). International Country Risk Guide methodology. Available from http://www.prsgroup.com/wp-content/uploads/2012/11/icrgmethodology.pdf.

Qatar, National Human Rights Committee (2013). Report of the National Human Rights Committee of Qatar on the Human Rights Situation in the State and the Outcomes of the Committee's Work during 2013. Doha. Available from http://www.nhrc-qa.org/wp-content/uploads/2014/01/2013.pdf.

Rabi, A. (2012). *Integrating a System of Child Benefits into Egypt's Fiscal Space: Poverty Impact, Costing, and Fiscal Space.* United Nations Children's Fund. Available from http://www.socialprotectionfloor-gateway.org/files/Egypt.Costing_Tool_application.pdf.

Ranaweera, T. (2003). Alternative paths to structural adjustment in Uzbekistan in a three-gap framework. Policy Research Working Paper, No. 3145. Washington, D.C.: World Bank.

Ranis, G., and F. Stewart (2005.) Dynamic links between the economy and human development. United Nations Department of Economic and Social Affairs Working Paper, No. 8. ST/ESA/2005/DWP/8.

Ranis, G., F. Stewart, and A. Ramirez (2000). Economic growth and human development. *World Development,* vol. 28, No. 2, pp. 197-219.

Ravallion, M. (1998). Poverty lines in theory and practice. Living Standards Measurement Study Paper, No. 133. Washington, D.C.: World Bank.

Ravallion, M., and S. Chen (1997). What can new survey data tell us about recent changes in distribution and poverty? *The World Bank Economic Review*, vol. 11, No. 2, pp. 357-382.

Ravallion, M., and G. Datt (1991). Growth and redistribution components of changes in poverty measures: a decomposition with applications to Brazil and India in the 1980s. Living Standards Measurement Study Working Paper, No. 83. Washington, D. C.: International Bank for Reconstruction and Development/World Bank.

Ravid, B. (2015). Netanyahu: If I'm elected, there will be no Palestinian State. *Haaretz*, 16 March. Available from www.haaretz.com/news/israel-election-2015/1.647212.

Reddy, S. (2009). The emperor's new suit: global poverty estimates reappraised, United Nations Department of Economic and Social Affairs Working Paper, No. 79. ST/ESA/2009/DWP/79.

Reed, J. (2013). The Palestinian economy's hard road out of isolation. *Financial Times*, 6 November. Available from http://www.ft.com/intl/cms/s/2/7d436d30-3fdc-11e3-a890-00144feabdc0.html#slide0.

Reuters (2015). Turkey's Erdogan says will "never allow" Kurdish State – media, 27 June. Available from http://uk.reuters.com/article/2015/06/27/uk-mideast-crisis-turkey-kurds-idUKKBN0P70QA20150627.

Rigobon, R., and D. Rodrik (2005). Rule of law, democracy, openness, and income: estimating the interrelationships. *Economics of Transition*, vol. 13, No. 3, pp. 533-564.

Rijkers, B., C. Freund, and A. Nucifora (2014). All in the family: State capture in Tunisia. Policy Research Working Paper, No. 6810. Washington, D.C.: World Bank.

Rishmawi, M. (2009). The revised Arab Charter on Human Rights. In *International Protection of Human Rights: A Text Book*, C. Krause and M. Scheinin (eds.), Second revised edition. Turku: Åbo Akademi University Institute for Human Rights.

Risse, M. (2012). *On Global Justice*. Princeton: Princeton University Press.

Rivera-Batiz, F. (2002). Democracy, governance and economic growth: theory and evidence. *Review of Development Economics*, vol. 6, No. 2 (June), pp. 225-247.

Roach, K. (2013). Security forces reform for Tunisia. Consolidating the Arab Spring: Constitutional Transition in Egypt and Tunisia Working Paper Series, No. 7. Stockholm and New York: International IDEA and The Center for Constitutional Transitions at NYU Law. Available from http://constitutionaltransitions.org/working-paper-no7.

Rodrik, D. (1997). Democracy and economic performance. Paper presented at the Conference on Democratization and Economic Reform in South Africa. Cape Town, January. Available from https://www.sss.ias.edu/files/pdfs/Rodrik/Research/democracy-economic-performance.PDF.

_____ (1999). Institutions for high-quality growth: what they are and how to acquire them. Paper prepared for the International Monetary Fund Conference on Second-Generation Reforms.

Washington, D.C., November. Available from https://www.imf.org/external/pubs/ft/seminar/1999/reforms/rodrik.htm#P9_78.

_____ (2004). Industrial policy for the twenty-first century. Discussion Paper, No. 4767. London: Centre for Economic Policy Research.

_____ (2007). *One Economics, Many Recipes: Globalization, Institutions, and Economic Growth*. Princeton: Princeton University Press.

Rodrik, D., A. Subramanian, and F. Trebbi (2004). Institutions rule: the primacy of institutions over geography and integration in economic development. *Journal of Economic Growth*, vol. 9, No. 2, pp. 131-165.

Rodrik, D., and R. Wacziarg (2005). Do democratic transitions produce bad economic outcomes? *The American Economic Review*, vol. 95, pp. 50-56.

Romer, P. (1990). Endogenous technological change. *Journal of Political Economy*, vol. 98, No. 5, pp. S71-S102.

Roshdi, R. (2008). The Arab nation and indigenous acquisition of scientific knowledge. *Contemporary Arab Affairs*, vol. 1, No. 4, pp 519-538.

Rouis, M., and S. Tabor (2013). *Regional Economic Integration in the Middle East and North Africa: Beyond Trade Reform*. Washington, D.C.: International Bank for Reconstruction and Development/World Bank.

Roy, R., A. Heuty, and E. Letouzé (2007). Fiscal space for what? Analytical issues from a human development perspective. Paper presented at the G-20 Workshop on Fiscal Policy. Istanbul, June.

Roy, R., and J. Weeks (2004). *Making Fiscal Policy Work for the Poor*. New York: United Nations Development Programme. Available from http://www.undp.org/content/dam/aplaws/publication/en/publications/poverty-reduction/poverty-website/making-fiscal-policy-work-for-the-poor/MakingFiscalPolicyWorkforthePoor.pdf.

Roy, J., and J. Zarrouk (2002). Completing the GCC Customs Union, 6 June. Available from http://siteresources.worldbank.org/INTMNAREGTOPTRADE/Resources/Roy-Zarrouk.pdf.

Ruggeri Laderchi, C., Saith, R., and Stewart, F. (2003). Does it matter that we don't agree on the definition of poverty? A comparison of four approaches. QEH Working Paper Series, No. 107. Oxford: Queen Elizabeth House.

Rush, C. R. (2000). Brazil is the target of Chile-U.S. trade accord. *Executive Intelligence Review*, vol. 27, No. 50 (December), pp. 4-5.

Sab, R. (2014). Economic impact of selected conflicts in the Middle East: what can we learn from the past? Working Paper, WP/14/100. Washington, D.C.: International Monetary Fund.

Sabbagh, A. (2005). The Arab States: enhancing women's political participation. In *Women in Parliament: Beyond Numbers. A Revised Edition*, J. Ballington and A. Karam (eds.). Stockhom: International Institute for Democracy and Electoral Assistance.

Sachs, J., and others (2004). Ending Africa's poverty trap. Brookings Papers on Economic Activity, No. 1. Available from http://www.unmillenniumproject.org/documents/ BPEAEndingAfricasPovertyTrapFINAL.pdf.

Sachs, J. (2015). The Boston Globe. TPP is too flawed for a simple 'yes' vote. Available from http://www.bostonglobe.com/opinion/2015/11/08/jeffrey-sachs-tpp-too-flawed-for-simple-yes-vote/sZd0nInCr18RurX1n549Gl/story.html

Said, E. W. (1978). *Orientalism: Western Conceptions of the Orient*. London: Routledge and Kegan Paul PLC.

_____ (1993).*Culture and Imperialism*. New York: Vintage.

Sarangi, N. (forthcoming). Economic growth, employment and poverty in Arab countries. ESCWA Working Paper.

Sarangi, N., and K. Abu-Ismail (2015). Economic growth, inequality and poverty in the Arab region. Issues Brief for the Arab Sustainability Development Report. Available from http://css.escwa.org.lb/SDPD/3572/Goal1.pdf.

Sarangi, N., and others (2015). Towards better measurement of poverty and inequality in Arab countries: a proposed pan-Arab multipurpose survey. ESCWA Working Paper. E/ESCWA/SD/2014/WP.1.

Schulz, M., F. Söderbaum, and J. Öjendal, eds. (2001). *Regionalization in a Globalizing World: A Comparative Perspective on Forms, Actors, and Processes*. London: Zed Books.

Sen, A. K. (1983). Development: which way now? *The Economic Journal*, vol. 93, No. 372 (December), pp. 745-762.

_____ (1985). *Commodities and Capabilities*. Oxford: Elsevier Science Publishers.

_____ (1999). *Development as Freedom*. Oxford: Oxford University Press.

_____ (2003). Development as capability expansion. In *Readings in Human Development*, S. Fukuda-Parr and A. K. Shivakumar, eds. Oxford: Oxford University Press.

Shahid, S. (2011). Does the nature of regional trade agreements matter in promoting trade? Centre for Trade and Economic Integration Working Paper, CETI-2011-11. Geneva: The Graduate Institute.

Sharma, D., and U. P. Gielen, eds. (2014). *The Global Obama: Crossroads of Leadership in the 21st Century*. New York: Routledge.

Shehabi, S. (2008). Destruction of Islamic architectural heritage in Saudi Arabia: a wake-up call, 8 February. Available from http://theamericanmuslim.org/tam.php/features/articles/ destruction_of_islamic_architectural_heritage_in_saudi_arabia_a_wake_up_cal.

Soja, E. W. (2008). Seeking spatial justice. Paper prepared for the Conference on Spatial Justice. Nanterre, March. Available from http://www.jssj.org/wp-content/uploads/2012/12/JSSJ1-1en4.pdf.

Son, H., and N. Kakwani (2004). Economic growth and poverty reduction: initial conditions matter. Working Paper, No. 2. Brasilia: International Poverty Centre, United Nations Development Programme.

Squire, L. (1993). Fighting poverty. *The American Economic Review*, vol. 83, No. 2 (May), pp. 377-382.

Stiglitz, J. (1998). The private uses of public interests: incentives and institutions. *Journal of Economic Perspectives*, vol. 12, No. 2 (Spring), pp. 3-22.

_____ (2013). The global crisis, social protection and jobs. *International Labour Review*, vol. 148, No. 1-2 (June), pp. 1-13.

Stiglitz, J., A. Sen, and J.-P. Fitoussi (2008). Report by the Commission on the Measurement of Economic Performance and Social Progress. Available from http://www.stiglitz-sen-fitoussi.fr/documents/rapport_anglais.pdf.

Stockhammer, E. (2015). Wage-led growth. Report No. 5 (April). London: Social Europe. Available from http://www.socialeurope.eu/wp-content/uploads/2015/04/RE5-Stockhammer.pdf.

Strauss, J., and D. Thomas (1995). Human resources: empirical modeling of household and family decisions. In *Handbook of Development Economics*, Volume III, J. R. Behrman and T. N. Srinivasan, eds. Amsterdam: North Holland.

Swamy, A., and others (2000). Gender and corruption. Working Paper, No. 2000-10. Department of Economics: Williams College.

Syrian Centre for Policy Research (SCPR) (2015). Syria – Alienation and Violence: Impact of Syria Crisis Report 2014. Damascus. Available from http://www.unrwa.org/sites/default/files/alienation_and_violence_impact_of_the_syria_crisis_in_2014_eng.pdf.

Taub, Gadi (2010). Beware apartheid discourse. *Ynet news.com*, 2 February. Available from www.ynetnews.com/articles/0,7340,L-3842192,00.html.

Tavares, J., and R. Wacziarg (1996). How democracy fosters growth. Harvard University. Taylor, L. (1988). *Varieties of Stabilization Experience: Towards Sensible Macroeconomics in the Third World*. Oxford: Clarendon Press.

_____ (1991). *Income Distribution, Inflation, and Growth: Lectures on Structuralist Macroeconomic Theory*. Cambridge, MA: MIT Press.

Tessler, M., A. Jamal, and C. G. d. Miguel (2008). Determinants of political participation and electoral behavior in the Arab world: findings and insights from the Arab Barometer. Paper presented at the American Political Science Association Conference. Boston, August. Available from http://www.princeton.edu/~ajamal/Tessler.Jamal.DeMiguel.pdf.

Testas, A. (1998). The significance of trade integration among developing countries: a comparison between ASEAN and AMU. *Journal of Economic Development*, vol. 23, No. 1 (June), pp. 117-130.

_____ (2002). The advantages of an intra-Maghreb free trade area: quantitative estimates of the static and dynamic output and welfare effects. *The Journal of North African Studies*, vol. 7, No. 1 (Spring), pp. 99-108.

Thailand, Ministry of Public Health (2006). *Health Policy in Thailand 2006.* Available from http://bps.ops.moph.go.th/webenglish/Policy.htm.

Thakur R., and L. Van Langenhove (2006). Enhancing global governance through regional integration. *Global Governance*, vol. 12, No. 3 (July/September), pp. 233-240.

The Daily Star (2014). Al-Azhar condemns ISIS as corrupt and a danger to Islam, 13 August. Available from http://www.dailystar.com.lb/ArticlePrint.aspx?id=267022&mode=print.

Tisdall, S. (2011). The failure of governance in the Arab world. *The Guardian*, 11 January. Available from http://www.theguardian.com/world/2011/jan/11/tunisia-algeria-riots-failure-arab-governance.

Tocci, N. (2005). Europeanization in Turkey: trigger or anchor for reform? *South European Society and Politics*, vol. 10, No. 1 (April), pp. 73-83.

Tonutti, A. (2013). Feasting on the occupation: illegality of settlement produce and the responsibility of EU Member States under international law. Position Paper. Ramallah: Al-Haq.

Transparency International (2014). Corruption Perceptions Index 2014: Results. Available from http://www.transparency.org/cpi2014/results. Accessed 30 March 2015.

Tzannatos, Z. (2011). Labour demand and social dialogue: two binding constraints for creating decent employment and ensuring effective utilization of human resources in the Arab region. Paper presented at the Islamic Development Bank Meeting on Addressing Unemployment and Underemployment in the Islamic Development Bank Member Countries in the Post-Crisis World. Jeddah, May.

_____ (2014). The Arab youth in the labor market: mismeasured, misunderstood and mistreated. Presentation made at the Economic Research Forum 20th Annual Conference on Social Justice and Economic Development. Cairo, March.

United Arab Emirates, Department of Economic Development (n.d.). Free trade agreements. Briefing Note. Dubai. Available from http://www.dubaided.gov.ae/en/Documents/Free%20Trade%20Agreements%20Briefing%20Paper-%20Ver%201%20(2).docx.

United Nations (n.d.a). Macroeconomic policy questions (including international trade, international financial system and external debt sustainability). TST Issues Brief. Available from https://sustainabledevelopment.un.org/content/documents/2076TST%20Issues%20Brief%20-%20Macro%20policy%20questions_Final_11_Oct.pdf.

_____ (n.d.b). Urban shelter: women's property rights. Available from http://www.un.org/ga/Istanbul+5/34.pdf.

_____ (1948). The Universal Declaration of Human Rights. Available from http://www.un.org/en/documents/udhr.

_____ (2013). A new global partnership: eradicate poverty and transform economies through sustainable development. The Report of the High-level Panel of Eminent Persons on the post-2015 Development Agenda. New York.

United Nations, Committee on the Elimination of Racial Discrimination (2012). Considerations of reports submitted by States parties under article 9 of the Convention. 9 March. CERD/C/ISR/CO/14-16.

United Nations, Department of Economic and Social Affairs (n.d.a). Millennium Development Goals Indicators. Available from http://mdgs.un.org/unsd/mdg/Default.aspx. Accessed 5 February 2015.

_____ (n.d.b). National Accounts Main Aggregates Database. Available from http://unstats.un.org/unsd/snaama/Introduction.asp. Accessed 20 June 2014.

_____ (2006). Social Justice in an Open World: The Role of the United Nations. ST/ESA/305.

_____ (2013). *World Population Prospects: The 2012 Revision*. New York.

_____ (2014). *World Urbanization Prospects.* New York.

United Nations, Economic and Social Council (2014). World Economic and Social Survey 2014: reducing inequality for sustainable development. Overview. E/2014/50*.

United Nations, General Assembly (2014a). Report of the Open Working Group of the General Assembly on Sustainable Development Goals. A/68/970.

_____ (2014b). The road to dignity by 2030: ending poverty, transforming all lives and protecting the planet. Synthesis report of the Secretary-General on the post-2015 sustainable development agenda. A/69/700.

_____ (2015). Economic and social repercussions of the Israeli occupation on the living conditions of the Palestinian people in the Occupied Palestinian Territory, including East Jerusalem, and the Arab population in the occupied Syrian Golan. Note by the Secretary-General. 8 May. A/70/82-E/2015/13.

United Nations, Human Rights Council (2007). Report of the Special Rapporteur on the situation of human rights in the Palestinian territories occupied since 1967, John Dugard. 29 January. A/HRC/4/17.

_____ (2014). Report of the Special Rapporteur on the situation of human rights in the Palestinian territories occupied since 1967, Richard Falk. 13 January. A/HRC/25/67.

_____ (2015). Report of the Special Rapporteur on the independence of judges and lawyers on her mission to Tunisia. 26 May. A/HRC/29/26/Add.3.

United Nations, Security Council (2004). The rule of law and transitional justice in conflict and post-conflict societies. Report of the Secretary-General. S/2004/616*.

_____ (2015). Letter dated 20 February 2015 from the Panel of Experts on Yemen established pursuant to Security Council resolution 2140 (2014) addressed to the President of the Security Council. S/2015/125.

United Nations, and League of Arab States (2013). *The Arab Millennium Development Goals Report: Facing Challenges and Looking beyond 2015*. E/ESCWA/EDGD/2013/1.

United Nations Children's Fund (UNICEF) (1999). Results of the 1999 Iraq child and maternal mortality surveys. Available from www.fas.org/news/iraq/1999/08/990812-unicef.htm.

_____ (2005). *Female Genital Mutilation/Cutting: A Statistical Exploration*. New York.

_____ (2013). *Children in Israeli Military Detention, Observations and Recommendations.* Available from http://www.unicef.org/oPt/UNICEF_oPt_Children_in_Israeli_Military_Detention_Observations_and_Recommendations_-_6_March_2013.pdf.

United Nations Conference on Trade and Development (UNCTAD) (2008). *Regional Trade Integrations: A Comparative Study – The Cases of GAFTA, COMESA, and SAPTA/SAFTA.* UNCTAD Virtual Institute. Available from http://vi.unctad.org/resources-mainmenu-64/digital-library?task=dl_doc&doc_name=252-rtiacs.

_____ (2009). *Least Developed Countries Report 2009: The State and Development Governance.* New York and Geneva. UNCTAD/LDC/2009.

_____ (2011). Economic cooperation and integration among developing countries. Briefing Notes, No. 1. Available from http://unctad.org/en/MigratedDocs/webecidc2011d1_en.pdf.

United Nations Development Programme (UNDP) (2002). *Arab Human Development Report 2002: Creating Opportunities for Future Generations.* New York.

_____ (2003). *Arab Human Development Report 2003: Building a Knowledge Society.* New York.

_____ (2007). *Human Development Report 2007/2008 – Fighting Climate Change: Human Solidarity in a Divided World.* New York.

_____ (2009a). *Arab Human Development Report 2009: Challenges to Human Security in the Arab Countries.* New York.

_____ (2009b). *Development Challenges in the Arab States: A Human Development Approach.* Cairo.

_____ (2010a). *Human Development Report 2010 – The Real Wealth of Nations: Pathways to Human Development.* New York.

_____ (2010b). *What Will It Take to Achieve the Millennium Development Goals? An International Assessment.* New York.

_____ (2010c). *Millennium Development Goals: Yemen Report 2010.* Available from http://www.arabstates.undp.org/content/rbas/en/home/library/MDGs/yemen---national-millennium-development-goals-report-.html.

_____ (2011). *Regional Integration and Human Development: A Pathway for Africa.* New York.

_____ (2012). *Arab Development Challenges Report 2011. Towards the Developmental State in the Arab Region.* Cairo: UNDP Regional Centre for Arab States.

_____ (2013). *Water Governance in the Arab Region: Managing Scarcity and Securing the Future.* New York.

United Nations Economic and Social Commission for Western Asia (ESCWA) (n.d.). Strengthening capacities to utilize workers' remittances for development. Available from http://www.escwa.un.org/sites/SCUWRD/index.asp.

_____ (2007). *Land Degradation Assessment and Prevention: Selected Case Studies from the ESCWA Region.* E/ESCWA/SDPD/2007/4.

188

_____ (2009). *ESCWA Water Development Report 3: Role of Desalination in Addressing Water Scarcity*. E/ESCWA/SDPD/2009/4.

_____ (2011a). *Progress in the Achievement of the Millennium Development Goals in the ESCWA Region: A Gender Lens*. E/ESCWA/ECW/2011/1.

_____ (2011b). Sustainable production and consumption patterns in energy and water sectors in the ESCWA region. SDPD Working Paper, No. 1. E/ESCWA/SDPD/2011/WP.1.

_____ (2012a). *Active Labour Market Policies in the Arab Countries*. E/ESCWA/SDD/2012/1.

_____ (2012b). *Addressing Barriers to Women's Economic Participation in the Arab Region*. E/ESCWA/ECW/2012/1.

_____ (2012c). *Economic Policy in the ESCWA Region and Its Impact on Employment*. E/ESCWA/SDD/2012/2.

_____ (2012d). Enhancing fiscal capacity to attain the Millennium Development Goals: financing social protection. EDGD Technical Paper, No. 1. E/ESCWA/EDGD/2012/Technical Paper.1.

_____ (2013a). The demographic profile of the Arab countries. SDD Technical Paper, No. 14. E/ESCWA/SDD/2013/Technical Paper.14.

_____ (2013b). *External Trade Bulletin of the Arab Region: Twenty-second Issue*. E/ESCWA/SD/2013/9.

_____ (2013c). Integrated social policy: towards a new welfare mix? Rethinking the role of the State, the market and civil society in the provision of social protection and social services. Report No. V. E/ESCWA/SDD/2013/1.

_____ (2013d). *Key Figures on Arab Trade*. E/ESCWA/EDGD/2013/Booklet.1.

_____ (2013e). Participation and transitional justice. Policy Brief, No. 1. E/ESCWA/SDD/2013/Technical Paper.5.

_____ (2013f). Women and political representation in the Arab region. Policy Brief. E/ESCWA/ECW/2013/Technical Paper.6.

_____ (2013g). Development policy implications of age-structural transitions in Arab countries. Population and Development Report, Issue No. 6. E/ESCWA/SDD/2013/2.

_____ (2013h). *Promises of Spring: Citizenship and Civic Engagement in Democratic Transitions*. E/ESCWA/SDD/2013/3.

_____ (2013i). *Public-Private Partnerships for Infrastructure Development in the Arab Region*. E/ESCWA/EDGD/2013/4.

_____ (2013j). *Institutional Development and Transition: Decentralization in the Course of Political Transformation*. E/ESCWA/ECRI/2013/3.

_____ (2014a). *Arab Governance Report: Governance Challenges in Countries Undergoing Transition*. E/ECRI/2013/4.

_____ (2014b). *Arab Integration: A 21st Century Development Imperative*. E/ESCWA/OES/2013/3.

_____ (2014c). *Arab Middle Class: Measurement and Role in Driving Change.* E/ESCWA/EDGD/2014/2.

_____ (2014d). Assessment of renewable energy projects through public-private partnerships: case studies in rural areas of Jordan. SDPD Technical Paper, No. 1. E/ESCWA/SDPD/2014/Technical Paper.1.

_____ (2014e). Conflict in the Syrian Arab Republic: macroeconomic implications and obstacles to achieving the Millennium Development Goals. EDGD Technical Paper, No. 5. E/ESCWA/EDGD/2014/Technical Paper.5.

_____ (2014f). *Country Profiles 2014: Key Energy Statistics.* E/ESCWA/SD/2014/Pamphlet.1.

_____ (2014g). *Institutional Frameworks for Managing Selected Energy Subsectors in Arab Countries: Fact Sheet.* E/ESCWA/SDPD/2014/Booklet.1.

_____ (2014h). *Projected Extreme Climate Indices for the Arab Region.* E/ESCWA/SDPD/2014/Fact Sheet.1.

_____ (2014i). The Libyan conflict and its impact on Egypt and Tunisia. Situation Brief, No. 1. E/ESCWA/EDGD/2014/Brief.1.

_____ (2014j). Social justice in the policies of Arab States. Discussion Paper. E/ESCWA/28/8.

_____ (2014k). *Survey of Economic and Social Developments in the Arab Region 2013-2014.* E/ESCWA/EDGD/2014/3.

_____ (2014l). Tax policy in Arab countries. SDD Technical Paper, No. 3. E/ESCWA/SDD/2014/Technical Paper.3.

_____ (2015a). A human rights approach to sustainable development in the Arab region. Background Paper for the Arab Sustainable Development Report. Available from http://css.escwa.org.lb/SDPD/3572/8-AzzamSD.pdf.

_____ (2015b). Energy in the Arab region. Issues Brief for the Arab Sustainable Development Report. Available from http://css.escwa.org.lb/SDPD/3572/Goal7.pdf.

_____ (2015c). *Summary of the Survey of Economic and Social Developments in the Arab Region 2014-2015.* E/ESCWA/EDID/2015/2/Summary.

_____ (2015d). Water and sanitation in the Arab region. Issues Brief for the Arab Sustainable Development Report. Available from http://css.escwa.org.lb/SDPD/3572/Goal6.pdf.

_____ (forthcoming a). *Arab Sustainable Development Report, 2015.*

_____ (forthcoming b). *Assessing Arab Economic Integration.*

United Nations Educational, Scientific and Cultural Organization (UNESCO) (2012). *EFA Global Monitoring Report 2012: Youth and Skills – Putting Education to Work.* Paris.

United Nations Entity for Gender Equality and the Empowerment of Women (UN Women) (2011). Violence against women prevalence data: surveys by country (as of March). Available from http://www.endvawnow.org/uploads/browser/files/vaw_prevalence_matrix_15april_2011.pdf. Accessed 6 July 2013.

United Nations Environment Programme (UNEP) (2011a). Annual Report 2010. Available from http://www.unep.org/annualreport/2010.

_____ (2011b). Assessment of Freshwater Resources Vulnerability to Environmental and Climate Change: Implication for Shared Water Resources in West Asia Region. Available from http://www.unep.org/dewa/westasia/documents/Vulnerability%20Report.pdf.

United Nations High Commissioner for Refugees (UNHCR) (n.d.). Syria Regional Refugee Response. Inter-agency Information Sharing Portal. Available from http://data.unhcr.org/syrianrefugees/regional.php. Accessed 30 November 2014.

_____ (2015a). Libya displaced, 16 January. Available from http://www.unmultimedia.org/tv/unifeed/2015/01/unhcr-libya-displaced.

_____ (2015b). *UNHCR Global Trends 2014 – Forced Displacement in 2014: World at War.* Available from http://www.unhcr.org/556725e69.html.

_____ (2015c). Update on Yemen situation, 14 April. Available from http://www.refworld.org/publisher,UNHCR,,,552d14e94,0.html.

United Nations Human Settlements Programme (UN-Habitat) (n.d.). Governance. Available from http://unhabitat.org/urban-themes/governance.

United Nations Industrial Development Organization (UNIDO) (2013). *Industrial Development Report 2013 – Sustaining Employment Growth: The Role of Manufacturing and Structural Change.* Vienna.

United Nations Millennium Project (UNMP) (2005). *Investing in Development: A Practical Plan to Achieve the Millennium Development Goals.* New York.

United Nations News Service (2015a). As Yemen crisis deepens, UN food relief agency calls on warring factions to allow supply restock, 16 April. Available from http://www.un.org/apps/news/story.asp?NewsID=50599#.VmqOIb9Wouc.

_____ (2015b). Millions of Yemenis face food insecurity amid escalating conflict, UN agency warns, 15 April. Available from http://www.un.org/apps/news/story.asp?NewsID=50584#.VmqO779Wouc.

United Nations Office for the Coordination of Humanitarian Affairs (UNOCHA) (n.d.). About the Crisis. Available from http://www.unocha.org/syrian-arab-republic/syria-country-profile/about-crisis.

United Nations Office on Drugs and Crime (UNODC) (2004). *United Nations Handbook on Practical Anti-corruption Measures for Prosecutors and Investigators.* Vienna.

United Nations Office of the High Commissioner for Human Rights (OHCHR) (n.d.). The core international human rights instruments and their monitoring bodies. Available from http://www.ohchr.org/EN/ProfessionalInterest/Pages/CoreInstruments.aspx.

_____ (1965). International Convention on the Elimination of All Forms of Racial Discrimination. Available from http://www.ohchr.org/Documents/ProfessionalInterest/cerd.pdf.

_____ (2012). Human rights violations and war crimes committed by both sides – the latest report on Libya. Available from http://www.ohchr.org/EN/NewsEvents/Pages/LibyaReport.aspx.

_____ (2014). Open wounds: torture and ill-treatment in the Syrian Arab Republic, 14 April. Available from http://www.ohchr.org/Documents/Countries/SY/PaperOnTorture.pdf.

_____ (2015a). 10th Report of the Independent International Commission of Inquiry on the Syrian Arab Republic. (A/HRC/30/48), 13 August 2015. Available from http://www.ohchr.org/EN/HRBodies/HRC/RegularSessions/Session30/Documents/A.HRC.30.48_AEV.pdf.

_____ (2015b). Human rights situation in the Occupied Palestinian Territory, including East Jerusalem, Report of the Secretary-General. A/HRC/28/45.

_____ (2015c). UN Commission of Inquiry on Syria: No end in sight for Syrian civilians. Available from http://www.ohchr.org/EN/NewsEvents/Pages/DisplayNews.aspx?NewsID=16377&LangID=E.

United Nations Population Fund (UNFPA) (2013). *Regional Strategy on Prevention and Response to Gender-Based Violence in the Arab States Region 2014-2017*. Available from http://arabstates.unfpa.org/public/pid/15888.

_____ (2014). *State of World Population 2014 – The Power of 1.8 Billion: Adolescents, Youth and the Transformation of the Future*. New York.

United Nations Relief and Works Agency for Palestine Refugees in the Near East (UNRWA) (2015). UNRWA in figures as of 1 January 2015. Available from www.unrwa.org/sites/default/files/unrwa_in_figures_2015.pdf.

United Nations System Task Team on the Post-2015 United Nations Development Agenda (UNSTT) (2012). Governance and development – Thematic Think Piece. Available from http://www.un.org/millenniumgoals/pdf/Think%20Pieces/7_governance.pdf.

United Nations World Water Assessment Programme (2015). *The United Nations World Water Development Report 2015: Water for a Sustainable World*. Paris: UNESCO.

Urdal, H. (2004). The devil in the demographics: the effect of youth bulges on domestic armed conflict, 1950-2000. Social Development Paper, No. 14. Washington, D.C.: World Bank. Available from http://www.eldis.org/vfile/upload/1/document/0708/DOC14714.pdf.

_____ (2011). A clash of generations? Youth bulges and political violence. Paper presented to the United Nations Expert Group Meeting on Adolescents, Youth and Development. New York, July. Available from http://www.un.org/esa/population/meetings/egm-adolescents/p10_urdal.pdf.

United States of America, National Intelligence Council (NIC) (2008). *Global Trends 2025: A Transformed World*. Washington, D.C.

_____ (2012). *Global Trends Report 2030: Alternative Worlds*. Washington, D.C.

United States Institute of Peace (USIP) (2010). *Governance, Corruption, and Conflict*. Washington, D.C. Available from http://www.usip.org/publications/governance-corruption-and-conflict.

Vandemoortele, J. (2014). Post-2015 agenda: mission impossible? *Development Studies Research*, vol. 1, No. 1, pp. 223-232. Available from http://www.tandfonline.com/doi/pdf/10.1080/21665095.2014.943415.

Vandemoortele, J., and R. Roy (2004). Making sense of MDG costing. Available from http://www.undp.org/content/dam/undp/library/Poverty%20Reduction/MDG%20Needs%20Assessment%20Tools/MakingsenseofMDGcosting.pdf.

VanGrasstek, C. (2013). *The History and Future of the World Trade Organization*. Geneva: World Trade Organization.

Van Marrewijk, C. (2008). Intra-industry trade. In *Princeton Encyclopedia of the World Economy*. Princeton: Princeton University Press.

Vaona, A., and S. Schiavo (2007). Nonparametric and semiparametric evidence on the long-run effects of inflation on growth. *Economics Letters*, vol. 94, No. 3, pp. 452-458.

Vatikiotis, P. J. (1987). *Islam and the State*. London: Croom Helm.

Venables, A. J. (2003). Winners and losers from regional integration agreements. *The Economic Journal*, vol. 113, No. 490 (October), pp. 747-761.

Vicard, V. (2008). Trade, conflicts, and political integration: explaining the heterogeneity of regional trade agreements. Centre d'Économie de la Sorbonne Working Paper, No. 22. Paris: Paris School of Economics.

_____ (2011). Determinants of successful regional trade agreements. *Economic Letters*, vol. 111, pp. 188-190. Available from http://www.parisschoolofeconomics.eu/docs/koenig-pamina/vicard_rta_econletters.pdf.

Von Arnim, R., and others (2011). The ADCR 2011 – Structural retardation of Arab economies: symptoms and sources. Arab Development Challenges Background Paper, No. 3. Available from http://www.arabstates.undp.org/content/dam/rbas/doc/poverty/BG_3%20Structural%20Transformation.pdf.

Wahbi, S. H. (2012). The Arab food security emergency programme: potential collaboration with UN agencies. Presentation made at the Coordination Meeting for the RCM Thematic Working Group on Food Security. Cairo, October.

Warwick, K. (2013). Beyond industrial policy: emerging issues and new trends. OECD Science, Technology and Industry Policy Papers, No. 2. Paris: Organisation of Economic Co-operation and Development Publishing.

Weber, M. (1978). *Economy and Society*. Berkeley, Cal.: University of California Press.

Weiss, J. (2005). Export growth and industrial policy: lessons from the East Asian miracle experience. Asian Development Bank Institute Discussion Paper, No. 26. Available from http://www.adb.org/sites/default/files/publication/156779/adbi-dp26.pdf.

Weiss, M. A. (2013). Arab League boycott of Israel. Congressional Research Service Paper. Available from http://fpc.state.gov/documents/organization/219630.pdf.

Wilkinson, R., and K. Pickett (2009). *The Spirit Level: Why Equality Is Better for Everyone*. London: Penguin Group.

Woo-Cumings, M., ed. (1999). *The Developmental State*. New York: Cornell University Press.

World Bank (n.d.a). Doing Business Data. Available from http://www.doingbusiness.org/data. Accessed 30 November 2014.

_____ (n.d.b). Libya Overview. Available from http://www.worldbank.org/en/country/libya/overview.

_____ (n.d.c). Governance and Public Sector Management. Available from http://web.worldbank.org/WBSITE/EXTERNAL/TOPICS/EXTPUBLICSECTORANDGOVERNANCE/0,,contentMDK:23352107~pagePK:148956~piPK:216618~theSitePK:286305,00.html.

_____ (2005). Regional trade and preferential trade agreements: a global perspective. In *Global Economic Prospects: Trade, Regionalism, and Development*. Washington, D.C.: International Bank for Reconstruction and Development/World Bank.

_____ (2007). Potential alternatives for Palestinian trade: developing the Rafah trade corridor. World Bank Technical Team Working Paper, No. 40446. Washington, D.C.: World Bank.

_____ (2008). *The Growth Report: Strategies for Sustained Growth and Inclusive Development*. Washington, D.C.

_____ (2010). Water sector brief. Available from http://siteresources.worldbank.org/INTMNAREGTOPWATRES/Resources/Water_Sector_Brief--Fall2010.pdf.

_____ (2012a). Conflict of interest restrictions and disclosure. A background primer prepared by the Public Accountability Mechanisms Initiative of the World Bank Public Sector and Governance Group. Available from https://agidata.org/Pam/Documents/COI%20Primer_30Sep2013.pdf.

_____ (2012b). From political to economic awakening in the Arab world: the path of economic integration. Deauville Partnership Report on Trade and Foreign Direct Investment, volume I, No. 68832-MNA. Washington, D.C. Available from https://openknowledge.worldbank.org/handle/10986/11886.

_____ (2015a). AGI Data Portal. Available from https://www.agidata.org/site. Accessed 28 February 2015.

_____ (2015b). *Global Monitoring Report*. Washington, D.C.

_____ (2015c). *Inequality, Uprisings, and Conflict in the Arab World*. Washington, D.C.

_____ (2015d). World Development Indicators Database. Available from http://databank.worldbank.org/data/views/variableselection/selectvariables.aspx?source=world-development-indicators. Accessed 2 December 2014.

_____ (2015e). Worldwide Governance Indicators Database. Available from http://info.worldbank.org/governance/wgi/index.aspx#home. Accessed 09 November 2015.

World Bank, Arab Water Council, and Islamic Development Bank (2011). *Water Reuse in the Arab World: From Principle to Practice. Voices from the Field*. Available from http://water.worldbank.org/sites/water.worldbank.org/files/publication/Water-Reuse-Arab-World-From-Principle%20-Practice.pdf.

World Bank, and the Development Research Center of the State Council (2013). *China 2030: Building a Modern, Harmonious, and Creative Society*. Washington, D.C.

World Bank, Food and Agriculture Organization of the United Nations, and International Fund for Agricultural Development (2009). *Improving Food Security in Arab Countries*. Washington, D.C.: World Bank.

World Food Programme (WFP) (2015). WFP calls for predictable pauses in fighting to deliver food to Yemen conflict zones. Available from http://www.wfp.org/news/news-release/wfp-calls-predictable-pauses-fighting-deliver-food-yemen-conflict-zones-0.

World Trade Organization (WTO) (1979). Differential and more favourable treatment: reciprocity and fuller participation of developing countries. Decision of 28 November 1979. L/4903. Available from https://www.wto.org/english/docs_e/legal_e/tokyo_enabling_e.pdf.

_____ (1994a). Understanding on the Interpretation of Article XXIV of the General Agreement on Tariffs and Trade 1994. Available from https://www.wto.org/english/docs_e/legal_e/10-24.pdf.

_____ (1994b). WTO Analytical Index: GATT. Available from https://www.wto.org/english/res_e/booksp_e/gatt_ai_e/gatt_ai_e.htm.

_____ (2003). Legal note on regional trade arrangements under the enabling clause. Note by the Secretariat. WT/COMTD/W/114. Available from http://www.wtocenter.org.tw/SmartKMS/fileviewer?id=4663.

_____ (2006). Transparency mechanism for regional trade agreements. Decision of 14 December 2006. WT/L/671. Available from https://www.wto.org/english/tratop_e/region_e/trans_mecha_e.htm.

_____ (2010). Systemic and specific issues arising out of the dual notification of the Gulf Cooperation Council customs union. Communication from China, Egypt and India. WT/COMTD/W/175. Available from https://docsonline.wto.org/dol2fe/Pages/SS/DirectDoc.aspx?filename=t%3A%2Fwt%2Fcomtd%2Fw175.doc&.

_____ (2012a). Trade policy review. Report by the Secretariat. The Kingdom of Saudi Arabia. WT/TPR/S/256. Available from https://www.wto.org/english/tratop_e/tpr_e/tp356_e.htm.

_____ (2012b). *World Trade Report 2012. Trade and Public Policies: A Closer Look at Non-tariff Measures in the 21st Century*. Geneva.

Younes, H. (2010). The contribution of trade to growth of the Arab countries. Paper presented at the Conference on Empirical Investigation in Trade & Investment. Tokyo, March.

Youngs, R. (2014). *Europe in the New Middle East: Opportunity or Exclusion?* Oxford: Oxford University Press.

Zartman, W. (1988). Opposition as a support of the State. In *Beyond Coercion: The Durability of the Arab State*, Adeed Dawisha and William Zartmann, eds. London: Croom Helm.

Zedillo, E., O. Cattaneo, and H. Wheeler, eds. (2015). *Africa at a Fork in the Road: Taking Off or Disappointment Once Again?* New Haven: Yale Center for the Study of Globalization. Available from http://www.ycsg.yale.edu/assets/downloads/africa.pdf.

Zoghby Research Services (2014). *Five Years After the Cairo Speech: How Arabs View President Obama and America*. Washington, D.C. Available from www.zogbyresearchservices.com/5-years-after-the-cairo-speech.

المراجع باللغة العربية

الاتحاد العربي للكهرباء (2013). النشرة الإحصائية، العدد الثاني والعشرون. http://www.auptde.org/Article_Files/2013.pdf.

المركز العربي للأبحاث ودراسة السياسات (2014). المؤشر العربي 2014. الدوحة: برنامج قياس الرأي العام العربي. http://www.dohainstitute.org/file/Get/36166627-39ba-445b-b902-996ecca4a6dc.

صندوق النقد العربي (2014). التقرير الاقتصادي العربي الموحد 2014. أبو ظبي. http://www.arabmonetaryfund.org/ar/jerep/2014.

منظمة العمل العربية (1965). الميثاق العربي للعمل ودستور منظمة العمل العربية. http://www.alolabor.org/final/ index.php?option=com_content&view=section&layout=blog&id=45&Itemid=156.

نادر فرجاني (2011). عتق أمة: من الهوان إلى النهضة في الوطن العربي. بيروت: دار الآداب.

خير الدين حسيب، وآخرون (1988). مستقبل الأمة العربية: التحديات... والخيارات. بيروت: مركز دراسات الوحدة العربية.

جامعة الدول العربية (2014) قرارات مجلس جامعة الدول العربية علي مستوى القمة الدورة العادية 25.

جامعة الدول العربية (1960). اتفاقية تنسيق السياسة البترولية.

Endnotes

Chapter 1

1 A notable exception is the report conducted by the Centre for Arab Unity Studies in the late 1980s. See Hassib and others, 1988.

2 UNDP, 2009b.

3 UNDP, 2012; ILO and UNDP, 2012; United Nations and League of Arab States, 2013; ESCWA, 2014c; ESCWA, 2014b; and ESCWA, 2013i.

4 ESCWA, 2014c.

5 UNDP, 2002; and ESCWA, 2014c.

6 ILO and UNDP, 2012.

7 ESCWA, 2014c.

8 Abu-Ismail and Sarangi, 2015.

9 ESCWA, 2014c.

10 ESCWA, 2014e.

11 Ibid.

12 NIC, 2012.

13 ESCWA, 2014b.

14 LDCs are included here because their development history is marred by rampant poverty, frequent internal conflicts and constant political instability.

15 Abu-Ismail and others, 2014.

16 Reviewed international forecasts include the following: United States National Intelligence Council, 2008; United States National Intelligence Council, 2012; European Union Institute for Security Studies, 2012; Gros and Alcidi, 2013; World Bank and Development Research Centre of the State Council, China, 2013; and United Nations Population Fund, 2014. Estimates and projections of several international organizations, including the Centre for European Studies, Food and Agriculture Organization of the United Nations, International Energy Agency, International Labour Organization, United Nations Conference on Trade and Development, United Nations Industrial Development Organization, World Bank, World Economic Forum, and World Trade Organization, were also examined.

17 This report draws upon the theories of such scholars as Fanon (1961; 1967), Cabral (1974), Said (1978; 1993), and Mitchell (1991).

18 Chang and Evans, 2005; Rodrik, 2004; and Amsden, 2001.

19 UNDP, 2009b.

20 Abu-Ismail and others, 2014.

21 A number of studies consider job-centred growth an effective poverty reduction strategy. For example, Squire (1993) recognizes that "economic growth that fosters the productive use of labour, the main asset owned by the poor, can generate rapid reductions in poverty". Extending this argument, Islam (2004) suggested that, conceptually, the links among output growth, employment and poverty can be analysed at macro- and micro-levels through the average productivity of the employed workforce and the nature of economic activities.

22 Sen, 1999.

23 Ibid.

24 Fritz and Menocal, 2007, p. 533.

25 ESCWA, 2014c.

26 Stiglitz, 2013; Piketty, 2014; Wilkinson and Pickett, 2009; Deaton, 2013; Sen, 1999.

27 Evans, 1995, p. 48.

28 Fritz and Menocal, 2007, p. 534.

29 Woo-Cumings, 1999, p. 1.

30 Ibid., p. 534.

31 ESCWA, 2014b.

32 UNODC, 2004.

33 Social protection is an element for realizing key human rights in article 22 of the Universal Declaration of Human Rights; article 9 of the International Covenant on Economic, Social and Cultural Rights; article 26 of the Convention on the Rights of the Child; and article 11 of the Convention on the Elimination of All Forms of Discrimination against Women.

34 ESCWA, 2012c.

35 The latest World Bank release revised the extreme poverty line from $1.25 a day purchasing power parity (PPP) in 2005 to $1.90 per day PPP in 2011 (World Bank, 2015b).

36 ESCWA, 2014b.

Chapter 2

37 The 1948 Arab-Israeli War; the 1956 Suez War; the 1967 Six-Day War; the 1973 October War; the 1978 Israeli invasion of southern Lebanon; the 1980-1988 Iran-Iraq War; the 1982 Israeli invasion of Lebanon; the 1983 Sudanese Civil war; the 1990 Gulf War; the 1993 and 1996 Israeli campaigns in Lebanon; the 2003 US-led invasion of Iraq; the 2006 Israeli war on Lebanon; the 2008, 2012 and 2014 Israeli wars on Gaza; and the 2011 civil wars in Iraq, Libya, Syrian Arab Republic, and Yemen.

38 Sharma and Gielen, 2014.

39 The United States has used its veto in matters related to Israel and Palestine/the Middle East in the United Nations Security Council 42 times. See http://research.un.org/en/docs/sc/quick.

40 NIC, 2008, p. 7.

41 Ibid, pp. 6-7.

42 Ibid, pp. 28-29.

43 Engdahl, 2012; IRSN, 2013.

44 CIA, n.d.a.; and CIA, n.d.b.

45 NIC, 2008, pp. 22-23.

46 Around 46 per cent of Iranians and 43 per cent of Turks are aged between 25 and 54. See CIA, n.d.a; CIA, n.d.b; and NIC, 2008, pp. 21-22.

47 Berman, 2015.

48 Ibid, pp. 24-25 and pp. 31-32.

49 After five decades of pretending otherwise, the Pentagon reluctantly confirmed that Israel does indeed possess nuclear bombs. Israeli stockpile is estimated by some accounts at some 100-120 warheads and possibly more, though Israel refuses to confirm or deny its existence under a policy of deliberate ambiguity (Greider, 2015).

50 Arab Center for Research and Policy Studies, 2014.

51 United Nations, 1947.

52 Alon and Benn, 2003.

53 Beaumont, 2014.

54 OHCHR, 1965.

55   CCPR/C/ISR/CO/4, 2014, para. 7; Jaraisy and Feldman, n. d.

56   Palestinian Central Bureau of Statistics, 2014b.

57   Palestinian Central Bureau of Statistics, 2014a.

58   CCPR/C/ISR/CO/4.

59   United Nations General Assembly, 2015.

60   United Nations, Committee on the Elimination of Racial Discrimination, 2012, para. 11. The International Convention on the Suppression and Punishment of the Crime of Apartheid (1973) defines "the crime of apartheid" as "policies and practices of racial segregation and discrimination as practiced in southern Africa" and "shall apply to the following inhuman acts committed for the purpose of establishing and maintaining domination by one racial group of persons over any other racial group of persons and systematically oppressing them"(article 2).

61   Adalah – The Legal Center for Arab Minority Rights in Israel, 2012.

62   United Nations General Assembly, 2015, paras. 6-21.

63   Ibid., para. 15.

64   United Nations, Committee on the Elimination of Racial Discrimination, 2012, paras. 11, 15 and 24-27.

65   United Nations, Human Rights Council, 2007, p. 3.

66   United Nations, Human Rights Council, 2014, para. 78.

67   United Nations, Department of Economic and Social Affairs, 2015, pp. 11-14.

68   Ibid.

69   United Nations, 1948b.

70   See, for example, a speech given by Israeli Prime Minister Netanyahu at the American Israel Public Affairs Committee (AIPAC) policy conference on 4 March 2014. Available from www.algemeiner.com/2014/03/04/full-transcript-prime-minister-netanyahu's-speech-at-2014-aipac-policy-conference/#.

71   ESCWA, 2014m.

72   Data from the Palestinian Central Bureau of Statistics. See also the Palestine-Israel Journal, available from http://www.pij.org/details.php?id=269, under Summary data/Settlements.

73   "Outpost" is the term used for settlements created without permission from the Israeli authorities, although many get official recognition at a later stage.

74   Peace Now, Settlement Watch reports, available from http://peacenow.org.il/eng/content/reports; and Israel's Central Bureau of Statistics, available from www1.cbs.gov.il/reader/cw_usr_view_Folder?ID=141.

75   United Nations, Department of Economic and Social Affairs, 2015, para. 20.

76   Horovitz, 2014.

77   Ravid, 2015.

78   Khalidi and Taghdisi-Rad, 2009; Farsakh, 2002; United Nations General Assembly, 2015.

79   International Crisis Group, 2010, pp. i-ii and 3.

80   Fjeldstad and Zagha, 2002, p. 4.

81   Arab World for Research and Development, 2010.

82   Taub, 2010.

83   NIC estimates from 2008 suggest that, by 2025, the number of Palestinians in the West Bank and Gaza will reach 6 million and the population of Israel 9 million, over a quarter of them Arabs. The total number of Arabs within the 1948 borders will thus reach 8.5 million, compared with fewer than 7 million Jewish Israelis.

84   UNHCR, 2015b; UNHCR, n.d.; and UNRWA, 2015.

85   ESCWA calculations based on data from UCDP, 2015. The classification employed does not necessarily take due regard of the fact that non-international armed conflicts remain distinguished from lesser forms of collective violence such as

civil unrest, riots, acts of terrorism or other sporadic acts of violence; even if a Government is forced to deploy armed units to restore law and order, such violence is considered not to constitute armed conflict (ICRC, 2012).

86   Sustainable Development Solutions Network and Global Association, 2015.

87   Al-Barghouti, 2008.

88   ESCWA, 2013j.

89   Ibid.

90   Ibid., pp. 18-20.

91   Reuters, 2015.

92   FARS News, 2015.

93   Freedom House, in *Freedom in the World 2015,* ranked Tunisia as the only "free" Arab country because of its progressive constitution, governance improvements … and the holding of free and fair parliamentary and presidential elections. Available from https://freedomhouse.org/report/freedom-world/freedom-world-2015#.VZzxffmeDRY.

Chapter 3

94   Risse, 2012.

95   Levi-Faur, 2011.

96   Max Weber's characterization of modern bureaucracy includes the following conditions: a clearly defined hierarchy of offices with defined spheres of competence; staff selected on the basis of technical qualifications; salary-based remuneration; careers developed in office; strict discipline; and control of public servants (Weber, 1978, pp. 220-221).

97   Tisdall, 2011.

98   See Beblawi, 1987; Brumberg, 2002; Huntington, 1996; King, 2003; Lewis, 1994; Lust-Okar, 2004; Malik and Awadallah, 2011; Moore, 2004; and Vatikiotis, 1987.

99   Acemoglu and others, 2008; Acemoglu and Robinson, 2006; Acemoglu and Robinson, 2012; Rigobon and Rodrik, 2005; Rodrik, 2007; Rodrik, Subramanian and Trebbi, 2004; and Sachs and others, 2004.

100 Arab countries rank across a wide spectrum, but generally low, with the exceptions of Jordan (57), Morocco (38), Lebanon (33), Egypt (13), Tunisia (11), Iraq (4), Saudi Arabia (1), and Qatar (0). For additional information, see http://internationalbudget.org/who-we-are/.

101 Acemoglu, Johnson and Robinson, 2001; Easterly and Levine, 2003; Hall and Jones, 1999; Rodrik, Subramanian and Trebbi, 2004; and Acemoglu and Robinson, 2012.

102 From sources such as the World Bank, International Country Risk Guide, Freedom House and Transparency International.

103 Capturing perceptions of corruption, implying that if gift giving or taking commissions is not illegal nor shunned upon and is transparent, then it is part of business practice and thus people do not consider it corruption.

104 Kunčič, 2014.

105 World Bank, 2015e.

106 Ibid.

107 Urdal, 2004; and Urdal, 2011.

108 Indrawati, 2013.

109 World Bank, n.d.c.

110 World Bank, 2012a.

111 "A Freedom of Information Systems/Right to Information/Access to Information framework aims to improve the efficiency of the government and increase the transparency of its functioning. Access to information can be protected

through a variety of legal mechanisms, from explicit constitutional safeguards to individual departmental orders". (World Bank, n.d.c).

112 "Most public officials are shielded from prosecution for duties performed in the capacity of the state. However, sweeping immunity laws prevent governments from holding corrupt actors to account and serve as obstacles to preventing further misconduct from taking place" (World Bank, n.d.c).

113 A/HRC/29/26/Add.3.

114 Al-Ali and Dafel, 2013; Ginsburg, 2013; and Olaya and Hussmann, 2013.

115 Measuring the perceived levels of public sector corruption in 175 countries/territories around the world with a score of 0 = worst perception of public sector corruption to 100 = best perception (Transparency International, 2014).

116 Cammett, 2014.

117 World Bank, n.d.a.

118 Nabli and Silva-Jáuregui, 2006; and Elbadawi, Makdisi and Milante, 2011.

119 Nabli and Ben Hammouda, forthcoming; El-Affendi, 2011; and Elbadawi, Makdisi and Milante, 2011.

120 USIP, 2010.

121 Drazen, 2000.

122 Acemoglu and others, 2008.

123 Barro, 1997; Rodrik, 1997; Rodrik, 1999; Rodrik and Wacziarg, 2005; Tavares and Wacziarg, 1996; and Masaki and Van de Walle, forthcoming.

124 Nabli and Ben Hammouda, forthcoming.

125 UNDP, 2010a.

126 Kunčič and Šušteršič, 2012.

127 Collier and Hoeffler, 2007.

128 Elbadawi and Soto, 2012.

129 Rijkers, Freund and Nucifora, 2014.

130 Ali and Elbadawi, 2012; and Hodler, 2013.

131 Blaydes, 2008; Gandhi and Lust-Okar, 2009; and Tessler, Jamal and Miguel, 2008.

132 Tessler, Jamal and Miguel, 2008.

133 Callahan, 2007.

134 Collier, 2010.

135 For more details on the discussion of the roles of citizens and administrators, how they are intertwined and how they reflect various public administration reform movements as well as differences in public opinion on the role of government, please refer to Callahan, 2007.

136 ESCWA, 2014c.

137 The Economist, 2009; and ESCWA, 2014c.

138 ESCWA, 2014c.

139 See Brady, Verba and Schlozman, 1995, p. 290 for a literature overview on the SES (socioeconomic status)-participation relationship.

140 According to the description of the measure of "voice and accountability".

141 According to the latest Arab MDGs report, the primary net enrollment rates have increased from 85 per cent in 1999 to 92 per cent in 2011; and the literacy rates of youth aged 15-24 years old have increased from 70 per cent in the 1990s to 89 per cent in 2010 (United Nations and League of Arab States, 2013).

142 The demographics of the Arab countries shows a distinct "youth bulge" (see http://www.cfr.org/egypt/demographics-arab-protests/p24096).

143 ILO, 2013.

144 "Another issue is the relevance of skills acquired for the labour market, as even a high level of education does not guarantee a job. Employers complain that youth are not well prepared and do not develop the needed skills. In Tunisia, the education system produces highly educated youth, with more than 57 per cent of new entrants to the labour market in 2010 holding a university degree. In an economy dominated by low-skill industries, however, few could find the jobs that university graduates expect". (United Nations and League of Arab States, 2013, p. 19).

145 Khatib, 2013.

146 ESCWA, 2013f.

147 Tisdall, 2011, p.1; and ESCWA, 2014c.

148 Mohammed bin Rashid Al Maktoum Foundation and UNDP, 2009, p. 64.

149 OHCHR, 2015b.

150 Committee on the Rights of the Child, 2013.

151 Gibney, Cornett and Wood, 2015.

152 Cingranelli, Richards and Chad Clay, 2014.

153 OHCHR, 2014; OHCHR, 2015a; and OHCHR, 2015c.

154 OHCHR, 2012.

155 A/HRC/WG.6/18/YEM/2.

156 Amnesty International, 2013; Qatar, National Human Rights Committee, 2013; Al-Najjar, 2002; ILO, 2004; and ILO, 2015.

157 ILO, 2004.

158 Human Rights Watch, 2015.

159 For results of a recent poll on women's rights in the Arab World, see http://www.trust.org/spotlight/poll-womens-rights-in-the-arab-world; and Kehoe, 2013 for the "fact box" compilation.

160 See http://www.un.org/womenwatch/daw/cedaw/reservations-country.htm.

161 UNFPA, 2013.

162 ESCWA, 2014a.

163 World Bank, 2008.

164 See https://www.kpk-rs.si/upload/datoteke/Supervizor%281%29.pdf.

165 Erdogan, 2014.

166 World Bank, n.d.a.

167 Galor and Michalopoulos, 2006.

168 From a House of Commons speech given on 11 November 1947.

169 ESCWA, 2015a.

170 UNDP, 2012.

Chapter 4

171 Nell, 1998.

172 See Ravallion and Datt, 1991; Kakwani, 1993; Ravallion and Chen, 1997; Bruno, Ravallion and Squire, 1998; Dagdeviran, Van der Hoeven and Weeks, 2001; Dollar and Kraay, 2002; Bourguignon, 2003; and Son and Kakwani, 2004.

173 UNIDO, 2013.

174 ESCWA, 2014c.

175 Sarangi and others, 2015.

176 Al-Darwish and others, 2015.

177 ESCWA, forthcoming b.

178 Ibid.

179 ESCWA, 2014i.

180 World Bank, n.d.b.

181 TEBAASPR, n.d.

182 ESCWA, 2015c.

183 See http://www.ilo.org/global/research/global-reports/global-employment-trends/2014/WCMS_234879/lang--en/index.htm.

184 Tzannatos, 2014.

185 UNDP, 2012.

186 Abu-Ismail, Abou Taleb and Ramadan, 2012.

187 World Bank, 2010.

188 UNDP, 2013.

189 Data are from an unpublished background paper prepared for ESCWA by FAO in 2015.

190 World Bank, FAO and IFAD, 2009.

191 ESCWA, 2007.

192 ESCWA, forthcoming a.

193 GIZ, BMZ and League of Arab States, 2012.

194 World Bank, Arab Water Council and Islamic Development Bank, 2011; and UNEP, 2011b.

195 ESCWA, 2015c.

196 Fattouh and El-Katiri, 2012.

197 الاتحاد العربي للكهرباء، 2013.

198 Ibid.

199 ESCWA, 2014f.

200 الاتحاد العربي للكهرباء، 2013.

201 UNEP, 2011a.

202 ESCWA, 2015b.

203 A structural transformation indicator, often GDP, is used as a dependent variable explained by the level of development (real GDP per capita as a proxy) and total population. The relationship is usually posited as non-linear in income and population (e.g., quadratic) and can be summarized as in Von Arnim and others (2011) as follows: the share of agriculture in GDP will decline over time and reach a minimum when real per capita income reaches about $12,150 (in 2005 constant prices); the share of industry in GDP will increase over time and reach a maximum when real per capita income reaches around $13,500 (in 2005 constant prices); the share of services in GDP will increase over time and reach a maximum when real per capita income reaches about $9,500 (in 2005 constant prices); and the share of manufacturing in GDP will increase over time without necessarily reaching a turning point in terms of real per capita income.

204 Ocampo, Rada and Taylor, 2009.

205 The model applied belongs to a class of global general equilibrium models called "Mirage". It depends on factors such as population, employment and productivity growth, and the accumulation of capital (see annex I for more technical details). Given that computable general equilibrium models always contain more variables than equations, some variables must be set outside the model, while the model estimates remain endogenous variables.

206 Rivera-Batiz, 2002.

207 The criteria used is the summation of the absolute changes of shares of all sectors, other than oil, gas and mining for non-oil producing countries (which is held constant), and agriculture in oil-producing countries (also held constant). Examining a moving average of a 10 year window yields the following structural transformation decades. For non-oil

producing countries: Korea 1971-1980; Turkey 1972-1981; and Viet Nam 2001-2010. For oil-producing countries: Malaysia 1972-1981; and Indonesia 1978-1987.

208 As implied by the computable general equilibrium model in 2025.

209 AWC, 2011.

210 World Bank, 2010.

211 FCCC/CP/2015/L.9/Rev.1.

212 UNDP, 2013.

213 Ibid.

214 ESCWA, 2014h.

215 Zubari, 2003.

216 Intensity in Egypt will fall from 625.5 tons of oil equivalent per $1million 2005 GDP in 2013 to 593.2 tons in 2020; in Kuwait from 345.9 tons to 344.4 tons; and in Qatar from 290.6 tons to 286.3 tons.

217 ESCWA, 2011b.

218 IEA, 2013.

219 Ibid.

220 World Bank, 2008.

221 Hemming, Kell and Mahfouz, 2002.

222 McKinley, 2003.

223 ESCWA, 2014c.

224 Sarangi, forthcoming.

225 Pedrosa-Gracia, 2013.

226 ESCWA, 2013c.

227 Rodrik, 2007.

228 Khan and Senhadji (2000) estimate that inflation becomes a drag on economic growth at 1-3 per cent for developed countries, and 11-12 per cent for developing ones. Employing newer econometric methods, Drukker, Gomis-Porqueras and Hernandez-Verme (2005) find two inflation thresholds in industrialized countries, one at 2.6 per cent and the other at 12.6 percent, and one threshold in non-industrialized economies of 19.2 per cent. Vaona and Schiavo (2007) use nonparametric methods on a combined sample to account for the non-linear relationship between inflation and growth, and find a threshold of 12 per cent. Last but not least, Kremer, Bick and Nautz (2013) use a dynamic panel model with threshold effects, and their findings support previous findings in the literature. Namely for developed industrialized economies the threshold they detect is consistent with the usual central bank targets of 2 per cent, while for non-industrialized economies, the estimated threshold is 17 per cent.

229 ESCWA calculations.

230 See http://ec.europa.eu/research/fp7/index_en.cfm; http://ec.europa.eu/research/bioeconomy/policy/coordination/jpi/index_en.htm; https://ec.europa.eu/jrc.

231 Some of the macroeconomic implications of these policies are addressed in United Nations, n.d.a.

232 Zedillo, Cattaneo and Wheeler, 2015.

233 Fattouh and Mallinson, 2013.

234 King and Levine, 1993.

235 Malecki, 1997.

236 Tzannatos, 2011.

237 ESCWA, 2012b.

238 El-Ashry, Saab and Zeitoon, 2010.

239 UNDP, 2009a.

240 ESCWA, 2009.

241 United Nations World Water Assessment Programme, 2015.

242 DLR, 2007.

243 ESCWA, forthcoming a.

244 World Bank, Arab Water Council and Islamic Development Bank, 2011.

245 Ibid.

246 Ibid.

247 Mirumachi, 2015.

248 ESCWA, forthcoming a.

249 Ibid.

250 League of Arab States, International Renewable Energy Agency and Regional Center for Renewable Energy and Energy Efficiency, 2014.

251 See http://www.desertec.org/concept.

252 Ibid.

253 ESCWA, 2014d.

254 Information available from http://www.unidir.org/publications/unidir-resources.

255 Al-Zubari, 2003.

256 ESCWA, 2014g.

Chapter 5

257 Sen, 2003.

258 UNDP, 2010b.

259 Sen, 1983.

260 Ibid.

261 Alkire and Deuenlin, n.d.

262 Ruggieri and others, 2003.

263 Ranis and Stewart, 2005.

264 Behrman, 1993; and Behrman, 1996.

265 Behrman, 1990a; Behrman, 1990b; and Strauss and Thomas, 1995.

266 Romer, 1990.

267 Ranis and Stewart, 2005.

268 National consultations have been convened by the United Nations in Algeria, Djibouti, Egypt, Iraq, Jordan, Lebanon, Morocco, the Sudan, and Yemen.

269 Abu-Ismail and others, 2014.

270 Sarangi and others, 2015.

271 Sen, 1985.

272 Alvaredo and Piketty, 2014.

273 United Nations and League of Arab States, 2013.

274 See http://www.webometrics.info/en/world.

275 Kuhn, 2011.

276 Sarangi and Abu-Ismail, 2015.

277 See Abu-Ismail and others, 2011b.

278 See Abu-Ismail and Sarangi, 2013.

279 United Nations and League of Arab States, 2013.

280 UNDP, 2010a.

281 United Nations and League of Arab States, 2013.

282 Sarangi and others, 2015.

283 Abu-Ismail and others, 2011b.

284 A critical analysis on setting an extreme poverty line is available in Deaton (2008) and Reddy (2009).

285 Ravallion, 1998.

286 The regional average is calculated by taking into account the populations of nine countries for which detailed household surveys are available. The populations of these nine countries accounted for 60 per cent of the total Arab population in 2011. The nine countries are Egypt, Iraq, Jordan, Lebanon, Oman, the Sudan, the Syrian Arab Republic, Tunisia, and Yemen (ESCWA, 2014c).

287 Credit Suisse, 2014.

288 World Bank, 2015c.

289 Hassine, 2014.

290 Deaton, 2003.

291 Sarangi and others, 2015.

292 World Bank, 2012b.

293 El-Jourchi, 2014.

294 The countries for which population undernourishment is calculated are: Algeria, Dibouti, Iraq, Mauritania, Morocco, Syrian Arab Republic, and Yemen. Countries that have reported less than 5 per cent undernourishment since 2000, such as Egypt, Jordan, Kuwait, Lebanon, Saudi Arabia, Tunisia, and the United Arab Emirates, are not included in the calculations. No data are available for Somalia and the Sudan. 2015 data for the Syrian Arab Republic are ESCWA estimates.

295 ESCWA estimates based on FAO, 2015; FAO, IFAD and WFP, 2014.

296 United Nations and League of Arab States, 2013.

297 ESCWA estimates based on FAO, 2015.

298 ESCWA, 2014c.

299 The figure is based on estimates for the Syrian Arab Republic until 2013 and for Yemen until 2011. The current could be worse in both countries, taking into account the impact of the ongoing conflict in the Syrian Arab Republic and the recent conflict in Yemen.

300 The MDG achievement index is based on 12 quantifiable MDG targets. The index measures the gap between the latest observed value and the expected value for the same year if the indicator was on the right path to meet the required target in 2015. It gives the percentage deviation of MDGs from the required targets for selected indicators and countries.

301 World Bank, 2015d.

302 ESCWA, 2012d, and more recent ESCWA estimates.

303 IMF, 2014b.

304 Sarangi and Abu-Ismail, 2015.

305 Assaad, 2014.

306 United Nations, Department of Economic and Social Affairs, n.d.a.

307 UN Women, 2011.

308 UNICEF, 2005.

309 In the Doha Declaration on Quality Education for All, adopted on 22 September 2010, Arab education ministers recognized the importance of monitoring the quality of education and decided to establish regular monitoring and evaluation mechanisms. The full text of the declaration is available from http://www.unesco.org/new/fileadmin/MULTIMEDIA/FIELD/Beirut/images/Education/Doha%20Declaration_Eng.pdf.

310 United Nations and League of Arab States, 2013.

311 UNESCO, 2012; and Diop, 2010.

312 Malik and Awadallah, 2011.

313 United Nations and League of Arab States, 2013.

314 The three pillars of a knowledge society are: broadening freedom of thought and expression (cognitive enablement); openness and effective communication with the evolution of knowledge and technology (co-native enablement); and a better response to the developmental needs of society (societal enablement). See Mohammed bin Rashid Al Maktoum Foundation and UNDP, 2009.

315 Mohammed bin Rashid Al Maktoum Foundation and UNDP, 2011.

316 ILO and UNDP, 2012.

317 ESCWA, 2014c.

318 Sarangi and Abu-Ismail, 2015.

319 ESCWA, 2013i.

320 Ibid.

321 Ibid.

322 United Nations, Department of Economic and Social Affairs, 2014.

323 ESCWA, 2012d.

324 The seven countries are Egypt, Iraq, Jordan, Morocco, Oman, Tunisia, and Yemen.

325 Abu-Ismail and Sarangi, 2015.

326 A/68/970.

327 Ibid.

328 ESCWA, 2013e.

329 World Bank, 2012b.

330 Ranis, Stewart and Ramirez, 2000.

331 United Nations, Economic and Social Council, 2014.

332 Ostry, Berg and Tsangarides, 2014.

333 Stockhammer, 2015; and Bhaduri and Marglin, 1990.

334 Onaran, 2015.

335 Sarangi, forthcoming.

336 United Nations and League of Arab States, 2013.

337 Ranis and Stewart, 2005.

338 ESCWA, 2014j.

339 United Nations, Department of Economic and Social Affairs, 2014.

340 See Mauro, 1996; and Gupta, Davoodi and Tiongson, 2000.

341 Fukuda-Parr and others, 2003.

342 Sarangi and others 2015.

343 United Nations, 2013.

344 ESCWA, 2013c.

345 Sarangi and others, 2015.

346 See Abu-Ismail and others, 2014.

347 Abu-Ismail and others, 2015.

348 ESCWA, 2014j.

349 See ILO, 2012b.

350 The Global Dryland Alliance, a Qatari initiative launched in 2010, is a good example in this regard. It is aimed at addressing the challenges posed by climate change and its impact on food security. Available from http://globaldrylandalliance.com.

351 See Wahbi, 2012; and http://www.fao.org/fileadmin/templates/cfs/Docs0910/CFS36Docs/CFS36_Session_Presentations/CFS36_Agenda_Item_V_AOAD.pdf.

352 Hossain, Nyamu Musembi and Hughes, 2010.

353 ESCWA, 2011a.

354 For the purpose of costing, the basic social protection floor excludes universal access to certain areas, such as education and health care.

355 The selected countries include Algeria, Egypt, Lebanon, Morocco, Saudi Arabia, the Syrian Arab Republic, Tunisia, and Yemen.

356 ESCWA, 2012a. Using an alternative estimate, it would have been 2.84 per cent of GDP in Egypt (Rabi, 2012).

357 ILO, 2008.

358 ESCWA estimates based on ESCWA, 2012c. It should be noted that estimates are preliminary and the actual expenditure may not follow the constant ratio of GDP over the years.

359 Fattouh and El-Katiri, 2012.

360 ESCWA, 2014k.

361 UNDP, 2002.

Chapter 6

362 World Bank, 2005, p. 36.

363 Mansfield and Pevehouse, 2000.

364 World Bank, 2005.

365 Ibid.

366 Busse and others, 2007.

367 IMF, 2005b.

368 Hall and Chuck-A-Sang, 2012.

369 Dicaprio and Gallagher, 2006.

370 UNIDO, 2013.

371 Dion, 2004.

372 Schulz, Söderbaum and Öjendal, 2001.

373 Al-Atrash and Yousef, 2000.

374 Péridy and Ghoneim, 2008.

375 ESCWA, forthcoming b.

376 Hoekman and Sakkat, 2010.

377 ESCWA, 2013b.

378 Bulgaria, National Statistics Institute, n.d.

379 Sea traffic plays a dominant role in the external foreign trade of the European Union. Its share of total extra-EU trade (in tons) amounted to 71.7 per cent in 2004. Following at a great distance were pipelines with 14 per cent and road transport

with 5.1 per cent, while 4.5 per cent fell to rail transport. The share of air transport, at 0.5 per cent, was very low. Rotterdam employs more than 70,000 personnel, handles 400 million tons per annum with 34,000 outbound vessels and 133,000 inbound vessels per annum (Grossmann and others, 2007).

380 Ghoneim and others, 2012.

381 Ibid.

382 Reed, 2013.

383 World Bank, 2007.

384 Galal and Hoekman, 2003.

385 Stiglitz, 1998.

386 Omran, 2001.

387 Youngs, 2014.

388 WTO, 2012b.

389 See https://www.wto.org/english/tratop_e/region_e/scope_rta_e.htm.

390 Youngs, 2014.

391 World Bank, 2012b.

392 ITC, 2012.

393 Ghoneim and others, 2012.

394 UNIDO, 2013; and Cattaneo and others, 2013.

395 Brenton, 2011.

396 Donner Abreu, 2013.

397 Trade Preferences for apparel and the role of rules of origin – the case of Africa: Brenton and Özden (2009) argue that strict rules of origin are "often supported by the argument that they are necessary to encourage substantial value-added activities in developing countries and as a mechanism for encouraging the development of integrated production structures within individual developing countries, or within regional groups of countries through cumulation mechanisms, to maximize the impact on employment and to ensure that it is not just low value-added activities that are undertaken in the developing countries there is no evidence that strict rules of origin over the past 30 years have done anything to stimulate the development of integrated production structures in developing countries".

398 Abdmoulah and Laabas, 2010.

399 Van Marrewijk, 2008.

400 Estevadeordal and Suominen, 2008.

401 ICTSD and WEF, 2013.

402 See http://ec.europa.eu/enlargement/neighbourhood/consultation/consultation.pdf.

403 Lawrence, 2006.

404 Sachs, 2015.

405 Roy and Zarrouk, 2002.

406 Melatos and Woodland, 2009.

407 See https://www.wto.org/english/docs_e/legal_e/legal_e.htm#services.

408 Dadush and Falcao, 2009.

409 See http://www.wipo.int/wipolex/en/other_treaties/details.jsp?treaty_id=417.

410 United Arab Emirates, Department of Economic Development, n.d.

411 WTO, 2012a.

412 Behr, 2010.

413 Financial Times, 2013.

414 Machowski, 2011.

415 VanGrasstek, 2013.

416 Weiss, 2013.

417 VanGrasstek, 2013.

418 Ahmad, 2014.

419 ICTSD, 2004.

420 Murray Kemp and Henry Wan (1976) showed that if customs unions are required to set their compensating external tariffs, i.e., if the member countries must adjust their tariffs to leave their trade with non-members constant, then for any such customs union there are intra-union income transfers such that no member loses.

421 Bruder, 2015.

422 Meeus, n.d.

423 Financial Times, 2014.

424 Mohammed bin Rashid Al Maktoum Foundation and UNDP, 2009.

425 Krueger, 1993.

426 This means: complete elimination of intra-Arab ad valorem and specific tariff and non-tariff protection for industrial commodities; liberalizing supportive services and their four modes of supply for trade logistics/transport/construction/financial services; pooling of private capital and public investments (for instance, improving non-banking solutions and through the enhanced access to venture capital); and provide for labour mobility packages in medium and high-tech manufacturing as well as skill upgrading through specialized Pan-Arab funded programmes for technical education and vocational training in advanced manufacturing technologies.

427 Replicating the European Observatory, which is a single access point for statistical information, analysis and mapping of clusters and cluster policy in Europe. It aims at promoting the development of more world-class clusters in Europe, notably with a view to fostering competitiveness and entrepreneurship in emerging industries and facilitating SMEs' access to clusters and internationalization activities through clusters.

428 Examples of such cases include the 1975 Sweden footwear case, the 1982 European Economic Community-Falkland case and the 1991 European Economic Community-Yugoslavia case.

429 ESCWA, 2013b.

430 Nunn and Trefler, 2006.

431 The large number of applied tariff lines currently set at duty-free levels in the Arab region, coupled with the proximities with trade-weighted average tariffs, reflects a bias towards raising the effective rate of protection for current manufacturing patterns and industry, rather than encourage structural change and diversification.

432 Abu Dhabi Fund for Development (ADFD); Kuwait Fund for Arab Economic Development (KFAED); Saudi Fund for Development (SFD); Arab Fund for Economic and Social Development; Islamic Development Bank; OPEC Fund for International Development; Arab Bank for Economic Development in Africa; Arab Gulf Programme for United Nations Development Organizations (AGFUND); Arab Monetary Fund; Islamic Corporation for the Insurance of Investment and Export Credit (ICIEC); Arab Authority for Agricultural Investment and Development (AAAID); Arab Investment Company; Arab Petroleum Investments Corporation (APICORP); Arab Trade Financing Program (ATFP); Gulf Investment Corporation; Inter-Arab Investment Guarantee Corporation (IAIGC); Abu Dhabi Investment Company (ADIC); Kuwait Finance House; Kuwait Investment Company (KIC); Kuwait International Investment Company (KIIC); Union of Arab Banks comprising more than (330) Arab banking and financial institutions.

433 ESCWA, 2015e.

434 صندوق النقد العربي، 2014.

435 ESCWA 2014k, p. 73.

436   ESCWA, 2014i.

437   ESCWA, forthcoming b.

438   ESCWA, n.d.